# TITANS RISING:
## THE BUSINESS OF WRITING SCIENCE FICTION, FANTASY, AND HORROR IN THE 21ST CENTURY

William Alan Webb & Chris Kennedy

Quillcraft Press
Coinjock, NC

Chris Kennedy/Quillcraft Press
1097 Waterlily Rd.
Coinjock, NC 27923
https://chriskennedypublishing.com/

Publisher's Note: This is a work of fiction. Names, characters, places, and incidents are a product of the author's imagination. Locales and public names are sometimes used for atmospheric purposes. Any resemblance to actual people, living or dead, or to businesses, companies, events, institutions, or locales is completely coincidental.

Cover Design by Shezaad Sudar.

Ordering Information:
Quantity sales. Special discounts are available on quantity purchases by corporations, associations, and others. For details, contact the "Special Sales Department" at the address above.

Titans Rising/William Alan Webb & Chris Kennedy -- 1st ed.
ISBN: 978-1648553325

*With many thanks to Christopher Mazuk for his help with certain aspects of the research for this book.*

# Contents

\* \* \* \* \*

# Chapter One:
# Introduction

This is not a book about the craft of writing. There are many of those already on the market; the editors both have such works available through Quillcraft Press. Instead, "Titans Rising" is about something which mystifies writers more than the proper use of the Oxford comma, namely, the *Business* of Writing.

Napoleon Hill authored what has become perhaps the most famous business book in the past century with the publication of "Think and Grow Rich" in 1937. In that work, Hill is said to have espoused no philosophy of his own, but rather those of the great entrepreneurs of his day, with the focus on how they became America's wealthiest businessmen, regardless of their individual industry or business platform. That book was an expansion of Hill's earlier work "The Laws of Success," which might be even more applicable to the writer of today than "Think and Grow Rich."

Hill said that he studied the richest men of his day and distilled their experiences into 14 principles which governed their success. Why does this matter to 21st century writers? At its heart Hill's work is about self-discipline and individual work ethic, which are the foundation for any successful business, including a writing career, and it was the ongoing relevance of "Think and Grow Rich" that inspired the writing of "Titans Rising," and for the same purpose—

to allow those who are re-creating the publishing industry to share what they've learned for the benefit of all.

It should be pointed out that some critics dispute the value of Napoleon Hill's works, as is inevitable with any book that draws hard conclusions and relies on self-motivation and self-discipline to achieve success using the concepts that are espoused. As of this writing, two percent of those who have rated Dale Carnegie's seminal work "How to Win Friends and Influence People" on Amazon rated it using one star. Does that invalidate the value of Carnegie's work? Hardly.

Yet, while such criticisms should not be ignored, they are critical to judging the work's value. In Hill's case, the objective reader has to decide if "Think and Grow Rich" stands up to the often vitriolic rants directed at what is, at its heart, an unrepentant glorification of the American Way of Business. If the reader rejects the criticisms, then the book's ongoing value is thereby proven to them. Should the judgment be that the criticisms have merit, then Hill's philosophies are disabused for that individual. "Titans Rising" is the glorification of such entrepreneurship as applied to a writing career, so you may judge for yourself whether to keep reading or not, depending on your own views.

If you judge sales as a definitive measure of continued relevance, then "Think and Grow Rich" remains among the first books that a prospective business owner should read. In 2007, *Business Week* magazine listed "Think and Grow Rich" as the 6th best-selling business paperback on its bestseller list, and on August 12, 2020, the Kindle version was the #1 Bestseller in the Amazon book category of Microeconomics. Likewise, a new edition released on November 22, 2021, the day of this writing, ranks as Amazon's #1 ebook in the category of Financial Engineering. On both dates, the book's overall ranking placed it in the top 99.98 percent of all books on Amazon. If that does not define "relevance," then the term has no meaning.

This book is a Treasure Map leading to success as an author. If that seems like a bold claim, it is not. A map shows you where to turn, how far to go (hopefully), and what to avoid. It actually does none of those things for you, however. Just like a real Treasure Map, *you* have to do the work. You have to walk the distance, figure out the clues, and avoid the pitfalls the map does not explain. Having a map does not reduce the fatigue, sweat, and sacrifice necessary to find the treasure, but if you follow the directions, it might reduce them.

The concept for "Titans Rising" is ambitious in the extreme, namely, to be the "Think and Grow Rich" for 21st century writers. "Titans Rising" is intended to be a unique book to help the modern writer achieve success. At its heart it is a survey to gather, categorize, and interpret lessons learned by a new breed of publishing greats, the innovators who are leading the market rather than following it. Writers at any stage of their careers should study the lessons contained herein, keeping in mind the adage that "if someone has what you want, do what they do."

This book has multiple entry points. It's a history book as well as a book about the writing business, and the lessons herein are applicable to a much broader, non-publishing-industry business audience. The beginning section is a brief, high-level overview of the history of science fiction, fantasy, and horror. If a broader approach was taken to such a task, then doing it justice would be a herculean work of epic proportion. Therefore, the authors have chosen to concentrate on a few specific writers in the various periods of this short history, and to use them as representations for the publishing industry in their periods.

Like "Think and Grow Rich," this book is meant to be timely and timeless. The stories related here are those of the new titans of publishing, the disruptors, people whose lessons will be studied in business textbooks for years to come by those who recognize that being a successful writer only *begins* with the quality of their prose. Their words and experiences will remain relevant for decades to come, just as Napoleon Hill discovered with the subjects he studied and wrote about.

If you read Webb's previous book "Have Keyboard, Will Travel," or Kennedy's "Indie Publishing for Profit," then you know both men are relentlessly honest about sharing their research, conclusions, and experiences. The co-editors of this book both do everything within their power to help less experienced writers who deserve a break, and, if they give an opinion, they map out the circumstances that led them to arrive at their conclusion. That way, you might examine the same evidence through your own eyes.

Now that concept is being expanded to encompass more of the movers and shakers who are redefining both writing and publishing. The mere fact of the Titans herein being invited to participate in this ground-breaking work proves the worth of their words. As a reader who is interested in the world of writing and publishing, or a writer doing your due diligence, you do not have to agree with the people profiled in this book, but you ignore their advice at your own peril.

Lastly, if the authors might be forgiven a moment's indulgence, we find it surprising that as of this writing in November of 2021, nobody outside of a tight circle of successful authors has really paid much attention to the rise of the Independent Publishing powerhouses that are in this book, and their relationship to more traditional publishers. It's fascinating to watch, if you realize what you are seeing. The business model these publishers are using to gain dominance in their genres is precisely the opposite of traditional publishers, and if that's not being a business disruptor, then what is?

These are amazing people who came to their writing and/or publishing careers from all walks of life and all levels of previous success, and who share one common trait: instead of seeing the existing publishing model as how things had to be, they saw the gaping maw of opportunity, leapt into the monster's mouth, and slew the beast from the inside. A traditionally published author who attended the recent 20Booksto50k® Writing Conference in Las Vegas expressed amazement at the sheer number of successful authors on hand and also the legion of aspirants. Despite tremendous success in the world of traditionally published science fiction and fantasy, the author in question had no idea that the Indie/small press world existed on such a scale.

Given all of that, how far back might we fairly trace the publishing industry to understand how we arrived at this point? Context is everything when judging the effects of evolution or revolution. If claims that the people profiled in this book are changing how books are produced and sold, that they are the disruptors of the 21st century, those changes will make no sense unless it is first established *what* they are disrupting.

# Chapter Two:
## A Brief and Candid Survey of Science Fiction, Fantasy, and Horror (SFFH)

*Maros-Pangkep arst, South Sulawesi, Indonesia*
*41,900 BC*

Looking back, we can imagine the scene.[1] Sweating despite the chill of the cave, the artist stepped back to examine his work on the cave wall. The pigs and small buffalo depicted there, animals he'd hunted many times, came to life in the vividness of his art. He'd drawn such things before, but not often and never in such detail. Life was short and hard. Chores for the tribe took up most of his time, and painting on the walls not only earned scoffs from the others, but sometimes anger. Outside, a raging storm rendered hunting impossible, and for once he'd had a moment of leisure.

As he studied his creation, the artist was particularly happy with how the beings that archeologists would one day call "Therianthropes" had turned out. He'd modeled them on his fellow hunters, eight in total, but wasn't satisfied with simply depicting his fellow humans as they were. Long before anyone coined the term "creative

---

[1] Ferriera, Becky, *Mythical Beings May Be Earliest Imaginative Cave Art by Humans*,
(New York Times: November 12, 2019),
https://www.nytimes.com/2019/12/11/science/cave-art-indonesia.html.
Accessed August 12, 2020.

license," the unnamed artist gave them extra features. "'This scene may not be a depiction of an actual hunting scene but could be about animistic beliefs and the relationship between people and animals, or even a shamanic ritual,' said Sue O'Connor, an Archeologist at Australian National University."[2]

And while O'Connor's speculation is not universally accepted, that really isn't the point. The nameless artist may have died more than 44 millennia in the past, but there is a very real possibility that his creation is the earliest known work of fantasy. What if, instead of portraying life as it was, he portrayed life as he imagined it? If that is true, if the creatures he drew were indeed a hybrid of humans and animals, and they do not differ in any substantial way from the countless fantasy books written or illustrated since then that do the same thing.

Accepting that theory leads to the conclusion that fantasy as a genre has been around since at least 44,000 years ago and likely much, much longer, perhaps since the first moment that our human ancestors became self-aware. Nor, if you think about it, is that Indonesian cave painting substantially different from clacking away on a keyboard or scratching on a drawing pad. It was the method available to the artist during his lifetime and differs little from every pictographic language, drawing, painting, sketch, or graphic novel that has since been created. Is it impossible to think that the artist convinced someone from a nearby tribe to visit his cave to view his creation? Or that he or she used it as part of a courtship ritual? A pre-historic version of "would you like to come to my home and see my etchings," perhaps? If human nature is truly unchanging, then why

---

[2] Ferriera, *Mythical Beings*, Accessed August 12, 2020.

couldn't those be true, and why couldn't we still love reading tales of fantasy and science fiction 440 centuries later?

O'Connor is only one example of many opinions that trace the beginnings of speculative fiction far back in the timeline of humanity. "Science fiction is a literature with a heritage reaching back into ancient times, to a pre-scientific world inhabited by peoples whose myths, legends, and superstitions became a way of thinking about and explaining the wonders of the universe. The seeds of science fiction were planted thousands of years ago, as the human species dreamed of the great unknown."[3]

Aside from simply reinforcing O'Connor's views on what the cave paintings represent, the above quote also inadvertently makes an additional point that is a recurring theme of this book, namely, there has always existed a subtle, and often not-so-subtle, intellectual elitism toward views considered unworthy of anything more than dismissive contempt. In the above quote, beliefs once strongly held by human beings as truth are waved off as "myths, legends, and superstitions" because they lived in a "pre-scientific world," an opinion stated as if its truth is self-evident.

Maybe so, but that smacks of snobbery and academic condescension of the worst sort, implying that people of the past could not possibly have had knowledge of, or experienced anything, that remains opaque to modern scholarship. For example, what if aliens really *did* visit Earth thousands of years ago and the cultures they encountered recorded their visit in the only ways they knew how? Skeptics might challenge there is no empirical proof of such a visit, to which the aliens might laugh and respond, "Of course not, with

---

[3] Tymn, Marshal B., *Science Fiction: a Brief History and Review of Criticism*, (American Studies International, Volume XXIII, No. 1, April, 1985), p. 1.

our advanced technology, why would we leave bread crumbs for your primitive science to find?" If that is considered a ridiculous straw man argument, remember that in 2019, the US Navy admitted UFOs (renamed Unnamed Aerial Phenomena in an effort to redefine the discussion away from alien craft) are real. That doesn't mean that short, gray men in round ships powered by anti-gravity propulsion systems will land at halftime of the next Super Bowl, but it doesn't mean they won't, either, and if the US Navy's UFO investigation program is ongoing, it is not unreasonable to ask why. Even if its purpose is to investigate the possibility of foreign technology that is unknown to us, that does not invalidate the question.

The Titans who share their thoughts in this work are the cream of the SFFH crop. They are the ones who are remaking the rules, while ignoring the erstwhile restraints placed on them by the gate-keepers who held down so many before. Some are themselves gate-keepers, as all businesses must have, yet as Titans they bring a young and vibrant spirit of disruptive innovation never before seen in the world of science fiction, fantasy, and horror. It is they who are creating the future.

The same argument has been made against small press and self-published authors for decades, and with the same back-handed wave of dismissal. If the book was any good, wouldn't *they*, the sifters of what is and isn't quality for the science fiction, fantasy, and horror genres, have published them? Were not those gatekeepers in their positions because of a superior sense of what the reading public *should* pay money to read? And if they did not anoint the books of small presses or self-published authors as worthy, must it not therefore follow that those books were unworthy? In other words, mustn't they have been trash? In the years before the advent of ebooks, which fueled the explosive growth of small press publishers, the word "trash" was more or less synonymous with "self-published" in the circles of traditional publishing.

For the SFFH writers who sought publication before digital books, this was the battlefield on which they fought. Or, rather, the battlefield on which they fought to gain an agent. The giant publishers held all the cards, and, without an agent, you had no hope of landing a publishing deal, even one that was confiscatory in nature, a siphon off whatever money you earned. Looking back now, we recognize such pioneering publishing houses as Gnome Press, Fantasy Press, and Shasta Publishing, among others, as visionaries. At the time, however, the 1940s-1950s, they were labors of love that operated on shoe-string budgets. Even the best Gnome Press copies extant in 2022 have darkened pages because of the cheap paper used, and, lest that seem an outlier, the same is found with first editions of Terry Brook's "The Sword of Shannara," published in 1975. It is only very recently that SFFH in general, and small presses and Indies in particular, have had an equal chance at the marketplace.

Then came the moment that sent gatekeepers into paroxysms of fear and rage, the moment when digital books became a reality. Savvy publishers didn't tremble in terror, they adapted and therefore prospered. For the Indies, forward-thinking traditional publishers, and hybrid authors,[4] it was a turning point that changed everything.

---

[4] Hybrid authors publish with a combination of traditional publishers and small press publishers, and they self-publish.

Suddenly, everyone was on the same level as the narrow-minded elitists, and people such as the Titans included in this book waved goodbye to the publishing dinosaurs while roaring past on the way to success. You would think that those mired in the publishing world of 1980 would have adapted by now... but you would be wrong.

Counted among the Titans are traditional publishers who understand the modern marketplace, small press publishers who are carving out empires, some of the worlds' most well-known and heralded authors, hybrid authors, and Indies. The road to being a successful writer has never been broader or more studded with potholes. Freedom brings with it a whole new set of challenges; navigating through those challenges is what this book is all about.

Moving forward in time from our unknown genius cave-painter, the influences of modern fantasy and science fiction continue to be identifiable in the historical record. When the first known Pharaoh, Narmer, united Upper and Lower Egypt circa 3,300 BC,[5] several assumptions might safely be made about that event. First, since the Pharaoh was the religious leader of Egypt, it seems inconceivable that Egypt's complex religion of gods, goddesses, rituals, and incantations, were not foremost in Narmer's mind at all times. They had to be, since he was the semi-divine connection between Egypt's Pantheon of deities and its people, the one who maintained Ma'at, order

---

[5] Sources differ on the Pharaoh's exact name and the date of Egypt's unification. The ones used here reflect reliable estimates based on current research.

on Earth, against Isfet, or chaos. Furthermore, it seems reasonable to say that the Pharaoh believed his religion to be true and accurate, at least in public. It was and continued to be the main source of the Pharaoh's authority to rule.

The second assumption would appear to be even more obvious, namely, that Egypt's pantheon of deities did not develop overnight. Prior to the written Egyptian records, their system of beliefs must have been evolving and becoming codified for hundreds or thousands of years, passed from person to person in the oral tradition until a system of writing became complex and reliable enough to record them. Once again, while such a theory might be debated, it stretches incredulity to think that one day Narmer ordered his priests (or scribes, or would-be priests, or anybody else) to sit down and whip up a religion out of thin air. Since presumably everyone reading this is a writer, imagine world-building on such a scale, and doing so without even pen and paper to write it down, having instead to use crude pens and papyrus, which, in itself, was a complex and time-consuming process. No, what is far more likely is that existing beliefs became incorporated into something new, to combine in Pharaoh the powers of Head of State and a liaison to the gods for the Egyptian people on Earth.

Summing up, then, Egyptians more than five thousand years ago believed that Narmer was the intermediary between the world of the living and the world of the gods, and the Egyptian religious practices must surely have developed over a long period of time, hundreds, if not thousands, of years.

So what do the arcane religious practices of a long-dead empire have to do with the 21st century world of science fiction, fantasy, and horror publishing? That is the first moment in time when a case can be made for the beginning of the SFFH publishing industry. Not because we have empirical evidence that Egyptian religion, or *any* religion, is true or untrue; that misses the point. Rather, those ancient beliefs are the first known grist for the mill of contemporary story-tellers. The cave paintings of Maros-Pangkep may have inspired future artists, and it's not impossible there are more cave paintings by imitators that haven't been found yet. Who knows? Perhaps someone reading about them will be inspired to write a fantasy novel about them? But what we do know is that the track record for Ancient Egypt as a mine of ideas for genre writers can't be argued, and their influence on ancient writers is equally undeniable.

Some may say that other ancient cultures provided such fodder before the Egyptians, and that seems a fair point. Certainly ancient civilizations in the Levant, the islands and lands surrounding the Ionian Sea, China, India, and South America may have claim to even earlier fodder for 21st century creators, yet, even if that turns out to be true, it seems a distinction without a difference. Everything above as it relates to the Egyptians would be equally true of other societies and religions. There is even new and mounting evidence of ancient civilizations that fit the narrative for Atlantis, with ruins to match the theories. For those who doubt that Atlantis existed and Homer wrote fantasy, you may yet be proven wrong.

And, after all that, of showing history as an inspiration for countless stories of science fiction, fantasy, and horror... so what, you might fairly ask? Story ideas can come from everywhere, but if you make a list of inspirations for SFFH tales, ancient mythologies would undoubtedly rank very high on that list, with Egyptian mythology and history at or near the top, and either Greek or Roman history close behind. The number of the novels featuring Egyptian religious practices, including magic (known to them as "heka") is probably unknowable, but suffice to say it's a lot, and if you add movies to the mix, and any movie novelizations that accompany them, the count rises exponentially. More to the point, they have been ongoing for centuries.

Texts dating to Pre-Dynastic Egypt are well known. The Egyptians did not consider them fiction, but when the first scribes huddled in a dusty mud-brick home to write down the genealogy of the Egyptians gods, using oil lamps to illuminate the writing surface, could they ever have imagined that 5,000 years later modern humans would make an action movie titled *Gods of Egypt*? (Assuming they could wrap their brains around the concept of a movie.) Or that their ritual method of preserving the bodies of the dead for use in the afterlife would spawn a dizzying array of mummy movies, books, video games and even pictorial cards for use in games?

Would they have understood the world's fascination when, in 1922, Howard Carter entered the grave of a Pharaoh who lived 2,000 years after Narmer, not simply desecrating the tomb but plundering it for his own gain and the gain of his patron? (On second thought, *that* they would have understood, since grave robbers were a well-oiled machine of plunder during Pharaonic days.) Today, we think nothing of despoiling the graves of ancient cultures, as we writers use the accoutrements of their dead as ideas for novels, but what if it was grave robbers digging up George Washington's corpse in real life? What if they displayed it for the masses, as we do with mummies, perhaps charging extra to touch the clothes in which Washington was buried? And yet today we can watch Josh Gates, on his popular show *Expedition Unknown*, be invited to the opening of a sarcophagus live on television, accompanied by renowned Egyptologist Dr. Zahi

Hawass. Ideas come from everywhere, and it's all grist for the writer's mill.

Approval or disapproval of these practices isn't the point. What *is* the point is that what most people consider to be modern genres is just the opposite, as old as Mankind itself. Egyptology has long been a popular topic for movies and novels, with Indiana Jones in movies and Elizabeth Peters' Amelia Peabody series of books being only two of the most obvious examples, and that is unlikely to change anytime soon. Indeed, the Amelia Peabody series of novels is based on "A Thousand Miles up the Nile" by Amelia Edwards, the 1880s memoir of a wealthy English tourist prowling among the ruins of Ancient Egypt. Even Egyptian tombs inspire tales and stories, as evidenced by books claiming everything from the Great Pyramid being an alien power conduit, to novels centered on what happened to the now-missing capstone.

From Narmer's time, the list of what we find fascinating about the SFFH field only grows, and there is ample evidence that ancient writers agreed. One could persuasively argue that Homer wrote fantasy before anyone conceived of the idea, or that the Romans knowingly accepted fantasy as the basis for their own origin story in the tale of Romulus and Remus; existing evidence about how the Romans viewed the tale of their city's founding is clear that all knew it was the marriage of two conflicting stories, with a heaping helping of "aren't we awesome?" thrown in for good measure. But they didn't care how much of it was fantasy because it was a great story, and today only academicians worry about whether Rome had seven kings or seventy. It certainly hasn't mattered to writers or artists, since the legend has influenced countless creators over the intervening years.

And while the printing press was still many centuries in the future, in ancient times those works *were* disseminated for money, mostly in oral fashion but with physical copies generally being available for those who could afford them. By any measure, this constituted a primitive publishing industry. People made their living making up stories and entertaining an audience with them, which seems an excellent definition for what writers still do up to this day, and presumably will forever.

During Roman times, the 2nd century A.D. writer Lucian penned "True History," in which he traveled to the Moon and found the inhabitants in a war with the People of the Sun. Change the Moon to Titus 749 in the Regium System, and the People of the Sun to the people of the closest other planet, and you've got the plot summary for an SF writer's next book.

As the ages passed, and the Roman Empire died, written books became less needed as the reading population dropped to all but a select few. In Europe, this mostly meant monks. But the need for myths and legends became stronger than ever, thus keeping alive the story telling tradition.

Many tales from the Dark Ages are bedrock influences on modern SFFH storytelling, including, but by no means limited to, King Arthur, "Beowulf," "The Thousand and One Nights," and the Japanese classic "The Tale of the Bamboo Cutter," all of which are still mined to this day as prime source material, and if all of those don't fall under the SFFH umbrella, then nothing does. Nor does it stretch the imagination to think the author of "Beowulf" would feel right at home discussing dragons and magic in the hotel bar at LibertyCon.

It is self-evident, then, that if traditional sagas such as "Beowulf" are not fantasy stories, then such a genre does not exist. No less an icon than JRR Tolkien wrote a translation of "Beowulf," and while his rendering of Old English into the modern version has been criticized, there is no question the late 10th or early 11th century poem, or earlier if you ascribe to that branch of research, greatly influenced Tolkien's vision of Middle Earth. And if you've never thought about the similarities between Leprechauns and Hobbits, now's your chance. Tolkien only mined the best resources.

Regarding King Arthur, is it really necessary to even try and enumerate how much the Knights of the Round Table and their famous king have impacted modern fantasy? Wizards like Merlin and Morgan le Fay, Excalibur the magic sword, the Lady of the Lake... but for how modern writers adapted the classic Arthurian legends, if you have not read Roger Zelazny's classic short story "The Last Defender of Camelot," then you have missed out on a wonderful variation on the mythos.

"The Thousand and One Nights" might be the most influential SFFH book from the Dark Ages, and perhaps the entire history of fantasy. Consider the enduring pervasiveness of the story of Aladdin and the Lamp, with creators using it for everything from the *I Dream of Jeanie* television program, the Disney movie *Aladdin*, and the title for David Bowie's classic album *Aladdin Sane*. Nor does this brief sampling even begin to factor in the narrative tales and mythologies from Africa, Asia, North and South America, all of which might be richer even than those of Europe and the Middle East.

When considering fantasy's kissing cousin, Brian Aldiss argued that Mary Shelley's "Frankenstein," published in 1818, is the first science fiction novel, which is hard (but not impossible) to argue with. Others go back much further, to aforementioned Assyrian author Lucian's 2nd century AD book "A True Story," which featured travel to other worlds, interplanetary warfare, and extra-terrestrials. Or a case could be made for the story of Archimedes destroying a Roman fleet that had sailed to Sicily to capture Syracuse by setting it afire using polished mirrors. Without debating whether this actually happened or not, or was even possible, the tale manipulates science in pursuit of a good story. If it's true, then it's history. If the story is not true, then it's certainly science fiction. Whichever you choose to accept, those examples or a different work entirely, science fiction has been around for a long time, and, regardless of where you start the count, after "Frankenstein" the publishing of SFFH slowly began to pick up steam.

Meanwhile, tales of horror seem so endemic to the human condition that trying to find an early example is moot, because surely stories of terror being told around a cook fire pre-dates the earlier example of our unknown artist painting on the cave walls beside the animals he'd eaten for dinner. So if we add only the most famous of horror writers to the list of 19th century authors who could be included on a list of those writing in the collective genres of SFFH, the list would still be long and, in some cases perhaps, surprising. Edgar Allan Poe, Mark Twain, H.G. Wells, Charles Dickens, Jules Verne, Sir Arthur Conan Doyle, Guy de Maupassant, Jack London, W.E.B. Du Bois, and Enrique Gaspar y Rimbau,[6] among many others,

---

[6] In *El anacronópete* (1887) Rimbau introduced the first literary time machine.

should all be recognizable names to those who love, study, and/or write in the SFFH genre.

But despite the near reverence that the works of those authors may elicit from modern readers, in their own time many had uneven reputations. For example, Poe had only moderate success until "The Raven" made him a household name, and, despite his fame, money problems haunted him until he died. It was only with the publication of a scurrilous biography after his death, written by a mortal enemy in revenge against the dead man, that sales of Poe's books skyrocketed and likely enshrined his place in literary history.

If we include Dickens in this grouping, which admittedly is a stretch for some people, but is included here because "A Christmas Carol" is one of the world's best known ghost stories, then we can credit him for using the magazine format of serial fiction which still exists today. Just as several volumes of Michael Moorcock's "Elric" series first saw publication in the pages of *Fantastic* magazine, so did Dicken's "The Pickwick Letters" first wind up in the hands of readers in a serial format of 19 issues, something which had never been done before.

Nailing down hard statistics on the monetary success of writers in the 21st century is virtually impossible. What *are* possible, are generalizations that tell the bigger truth. For example, multiple studies and anecdotal evidence agree that, when measured as a percentage, about twice as many self-published authors make over $10,000 a year than traditionally published ones. Better, or worse, depending on your point of view, the disparities become greater as income increases.

In the higher brackets, the numbers are more depressing. If it inspires you to note that 2,500 authors make $50,000—arguably a middle class salary—you might remember that only 220 Big Four authors and around 100 small to medium press authors now earn this amount from Amazon sales. $100,000? There are 1,340 of those, and only 115 from Big Publishing, at least among authors who debuted within the last five years.[7]

With modern data mining, the nature of the beast makes such precise comparisons possible, although one should view such statistics as having a reasonable margin for error. But worrying about whether or not the self-versus-traditional ratio used above is precisely correct misses the point; earning a living as a writer no longer depends on the whims and biases of middleman gatekeepers like literary agents.

And this is another emerging reality. In the 21st century writing environment, the power in the agent-writer relationship is returning where it belongs, with the creator. Why should an author making six figures a year sign with a traditional publisher, who needs the writer more than the writer needs *them*? That will become the successful agent's job, to broker such deals to the benefit of all, not to forward large numbers of manuscripts in hopes that a traditional publisher will buy one. Sometimes lightning strikes and the book heads to auction, where it sells for six or seven figures.

That's nice when it happens, but, as the paragraph quoted above about earnings makes clear, it's also rare. The odds of winning the

---

[7] Sturgeon, Jonathan, *How Much Money Are Authors Making?*, Flavorwire, June 6, 2016, https://www.flavorwire.com/579201/how-much-money-are-authors-making. Accessed September 13, 2021.

lottery are only slightly worse. For the writers left behind in such relationships with Big 4 traditional publishers, they will have wasted invaluable time, usually years, hoping for fame and fortune that never comes. Indie authors, whether traditionally published by a small press, self-published, or a hybrid of the two, have and will have a very different experience. The learning curve is higher, it's true, but the pay scale is also greater.

Another limitation for writers over the centuries has been the number of people who knew how to read. Literacy rates in Britain and the USA during the 19th century were higher than is sometimes thought. The exact percentages are debatable because of unreliable or non-existent records, but the precise details matter less than the greater truth that most people could read.

Regarding the literacy situation in Britain, "R. K. Webb, a specialist historian of literacy, offers the following conclusions about conditions in Britain in the late 1830s: 'In so far as one dare generalize about a national average in an extraordinarily varied situation, the figure would seem to run between two-thirds and three-quarters of the working classes as literate… there was, moreover, an appreciable rate of growth in literacy.'"[8]

---

[8] West, Edwin, *The Spread of Education before Compulsion: Britain and America in the Nineteenth Century*, (https://fee.org/articles/the-spread-of-education-before-compulsion-britain-and-america-in-the-nineteenth-century/). Accessed 13 August, 2020.

The same source also deals with American literacy. "Between 1800 and 1840 literacy in the North rose from 75 percent to between 91 and 97 percent. In the South, the rate grew from about 55 percent to 81 percent."[9] Without burdening the discussion with Canadian statistics, it seems safe to assume those at least equaled American rates.

Whether the percentages quoted above are accurate or off by a few percentage points is irrelevant to this discussion. The larger truth is that the vast majority of people in the English speaking world knew how to read,[10] thereby removing one obstacle to the growth of the SFFH genres. Yet once people knew *how* to read in large numbers, thus solving one of the biggest roadblocks to selling books, authors then had to concentrate on convincing them about *what* to read, a task which bedevils writers to this very day.

Those who write genre fiction, and SFFH in particular, have had (and often do have) the added disadvantage of being faced with the elitist snobbery often found in gatekeepers and writing teachers. Although not as severe or openly contemptuous as in past times, this attitude still exists. At its core, it casts such work as unworthy of the attention of readers with critical skills, because genre writers' first and foremost concern is to entertain their readers. One of this book's editors faced such elitism firsthand, having been told during his time as a Creative Writing Major that, "If you hand me a fantasy story, it's an automatic F." How and when such an attitude developed is harder to pin down, but certainly the early workers in SFFH

---

[9] West, *Spread of Education*, Accessed August 13, 2020.

[10] For American statistics, it must be acknowledged that these did not apply to black people, where in many states it was illegal to teach a black person how to read or write. The effects of those policies are still being felt today.

ran into these self-appointed keepers of culture on a regular basis. Fortunately, the close-mindedness that spawned such attitudes has been temporarily banished into the shadows, where it belongs. One of the Titans featured herein, Kevin J. Anderson, coordinates a Master's Degree program at Western Colorado with a concentration in publishing, while Orson Scott Card offers several writing courses and is on the faculty of Southern Virginia University for Creative Writing. Times have indeed changed.

But that is now. From at least the mid-19th century on, *serious* readers were expected to read nonfiction, preferably history. Anything with sales potential, dismissively written off with a sniff and a wave as "commercial," left no doubt that such people considered genre fiction as beneath them. This led to the creation of a category called "literary fiction," with the unavoidable inference that genre fiction must therefore be "non-literary fiction."

Such smug self-righteousness ruled much of the traditional publishing world in the 19th and 20th centuries, and, in some cases, still does today. Just because much has changed doesn't mean that *everything* has changed. This shouldn't be interpreted as meaning *all* traditional publishers feel that way, or even most. One such, Baen Books, is at the forefront of the emerging publishing world, and indeed is one of the chief inspirations for this book. Yet they remain the exception that proves the rule.

As one reads the profiles of the people in this book and considers the amount of money left on the table by today's traditional publishing imprints, it quickly becomes obvious that even with the overall world of SFFH writers, elitism toward those who write for entertainment rather than social or political motives are disdained as being unworthy of notice. While this is nothing new, and is both hardly surprising and likely inevitable, this attitude is wholly irrelevant to Indie, small press, and authors published by traditional publishers such as Baen. Those authors recognize that what matters in the marketplace are good stories and good books, and they hope to earn a reasonable living from creating such works.

Even in today's world, the famous rhetorical question "would you rather be right or rich" is answered by many in world Big 4 SFFH publishers with "right." Orson Welles said of Hollywood that "they regard the artist as their enemy." Being specific to writers, New York Times Bestselling author Michael Levin didn't pull any punches in his article *Why Book Publishers Hate Authors;* "publishing houses despise authors and are doing everything they can to make their lives miserable."[11] Levin paints with a broad brush, and the writer of 2022 is cautioned to understand that publishers like Baen are exceptions, yet where many traditional publishers are concerned, his points are hard to refute.

Without spending too much more time dwelling on this point, elitists feel *they* are the arbiters of what is and isn't quality, as summed up in the following quote: "One particular convention revealed an undercurrent of this industry… in a nutshell, this faction believes that movie and TV SF/F/H dumbs down the genre, appealing only

---

[11] (https://www.huffpost.com/entry/why-book-publishers-hate-_b_2122317). Accessed September 13, 2021.

to the lowest common denominator of fan."[12] Although referring here to inclusion of visual media for convention purposes, it is the last five words that are operative, "lowest common denominator of fan." Such stratification of fans into highest and lowest levels of fandom could only be made by self-appointed guardians of what is and isn't quality material; no other objective interpretation is possible. Certainly those profiled in this book don't engage in such condescending pomposity, because, if they did, they wouldn't have had the success to qualify them for inclusion here.

This is not a new issue, though. Ray Bradbury once called Edgar Rice Burroughs "the most influential writer in the whole history of the world."[13] And in 1939, Golsan noted, "the *Saturday Evening Post* declared Burroughs 'the greatest living writer'… by that year Burroughs had earned more than ten million dollars for his work, sold twenty-five million copies of the Tarzan series alone, and seen his fiction translated into fifty-six languages."[14] Yet, despite such remarkable praise by one of America's then-most important magazines and from a man generally considered as one of the greatest writers ever to work in SFFH, Burroughs has received virtually no critical attention since his death in 1950. Moreover, for a period of up to two decades, some of his books were not even available until finally being reprinted in the early 1960s.

[12] Morris, Tee, *The Scifi Superiority Complex: Elitism in SF/F/H*, (http://strangehorizons.com/non-fiction/articles/the-scifi-superiority-complex-elitism-in-sffh/). Accessed August 13, 2020.
[13] Weller, Sam (February 4, 2019), *"Ray Bradbury, The Art of Fiction No. 203"*, (https://www.theparisreview.org/interviews/6012/the-art-of-fiction-no-203-ray-bradbury). Accessed August 14, 2020.
[14] Golsan, Richard J., *Perversion and Pulp: Reading Edgar Rice Burroughs and Figuring America in "Les Bienveillantes,"* (Yale French Studies No. 121, Literature and History: Around "Suite Française" and "Les Bienveillantes," 2012), p. 211.

So why have the works of such an iconic writer, and his place in 20th century American literature, been so totally ignored? Certainly few writers even 70 years after Burroughs' death can *envision* such numbers of books sold, much less imagine actually selling them, and ten million in 1939 dollars equals about 187 million dollars in 2020. But the elitism that still exists in some corners toward SFFH often discounts monetary arguments as being beside the point, or as proof that confirms their own biases. Within that particular discourse can be found one of the key legacies between those profiled in this book and the writers who came before them such as Edgar Rice Burroughs; namely, that writing is both a career and a business, and one cannot succeed without the other. Regardless of a writer's perception of their own value, if the market doesn't buy their work, they don't eat, and writers who can't feed themselves don't last long.

The attitude toward Burroughs and writers like him is best summed up in a throw-away line from an episode of the extremely popular BBC Television series *Downton Abbey*, when one of the characters refers to an event as being so far beyond belief that it sounds like something from an H. Rider Haggard novel.[15] Despite Haggard's immense popularity in late 19th, and early 20th century England and America, his books were and are routinely dismissed by contemptuous literati, whose own writings are generally unknown and unlamented.

"Academic literary critics have... dismissed Haggard as a... 'tiresome success' who 'mechanically manufactured imitations;' the important thing about ideas to him 'was not whether they were true,

---

[15] Haggard remains an influential author in the 21st Century. His best-known novel is *King Solomon's Mines*, which is generally accepted as the first Lost World novel, and uses a plot device that is now a staple of SFFH across all genres and sub-genres.

but whether they were marketable.'"[16] And if the idea of writing for profit isn't enough to bring out the worst intellectual snobbishness, "the fact that a great number of these books are still in print is no doubt an interesting sociological fact."[17]

How dare people read because they enjoy something! Unlike his contemporary, H.G. Wells, whose fiction was of a decidedly more political bent, Haggard wrote to entertain readers during the period in which he lived. It is true that no less an SFFH icon than C.S. Lewis found Haggard's work as "insufferably shallow,"[18] but no one should be surprised that Wells detested it, given their fundamental political differences. On the plus side, Sigmund Freud attributed a breakthrough in his work to the depth of Haggard's writing; Henry Miller found the hidden meanings in Haggard's work fascinating; Graham Greene praised him for the depth of his investigation into human nature, and Margaret Atwood agreed. In short, those who wrote Haggard's works off as merely fodder for the masses missed the whole point.

The same can be said of Burroughs' writings and indeed most writers of any age throughout human history. And while Haggard's views on race and imperialism have been usurped today by a far greater understanding and desire for diversity of thoughts and ideas, and people retroactively condemn his fiction, or that of Burroughs or even Robert E. Howard, it is to repress history rather than learn from it. One might as well condemn someone for reading Julius Caesar's "Gallic Wars," because in it he openly admitted to enslaving one

[16] Etherington, Norman A., *Rider Haggard, Imperialism and the Layered Personality*, (Victorian Studies
Vol. 22, No. 1 (Autumn, 1978), p. 72.
[17] Etherington, *Rider Haggard*, p. 72.
[18] Etherington, *Riger Haggard*, p. 72.

million Gauls and killing one million more, all for glory and the expansion of Roman power. Caesar stole everything that wasn't nailed down, and today you can still find fresh flowers on his grave in the Forum Romanum. The lingering success of both Haggard and Burroughs, and many, many others that space doesn't permit to be examined here, should therefore be *studied* by critics and academia, not dismissed by them.

But, more than most, during their respective lifetimes, Burroughs, Haggard, and their readers would never have seen more from elitist critics than an upturned nose, perhaps accompanied by a sniff of derision, and in some corners this same attitude still exists in the 21st century toward all of Haggard's literary progeny, namely, writers and readers who share a love of exciting and engaging books. In the mindsets of critics like the ones quoted above, if you enjoy books like Haggard's, then you must obviously be of a lower intellectual class. The difference today is that the people in this book no longer have to care what the gatekeepers and their sycophantic critical allies think about their work.

Into such a climate have countless thousands of SFFH writers plunged in search of publication. Some have found fame and fortune, while the vast majority has not. Since publishers were and are businesses, it could be assumed they keep a vigilant watch for new authors to cultivate and feature, but that has always only been as true as the gatekeepers deciding on which manuscripts would move forward. The power of one or two people to make decisions affecting a host of readers gave them godlike powers over their publishing house.

If we stick with the example of Burroughs, after having moderate success selling adventure stories to the pulp magazines of the early 20th century, he sold his first novel to a company who was far better known as a book distributor rather than as a publisher, A.C. McClurg & Co. Today, we might call them a small press. The books were reasonably well made and the covers by J. Allen St. John first rate, yet they were small in size and the paper quality wasn't particularly good.

"Tarzan of the Apes" was a massive and immediate success. Calling the novel a cultural phenomena would not be overstating the case. Being a savvy businessman, Burroughs published ten books with McClurg before doing something that many of those profiled in this book have also done: he self-published his own books from that point forward, until 1939. His reason was the same as for writers who leave traditional publishing today, namely, he made a lot more money.

Even so, the 1914 Top 10 bestseller list from *Publishers Weekly* has zero SFFH titles on it, although romances are well represented.[19] For 1915, Zane Grey made the list for a western, which he did quite often both before and after, but again, the rest were variants on social activist novels, the odd occasional historical novel, or variances on a romance. H.G. Wells made the list in 1916, but with "Mr. Stripling Sees It Through," about wartime experiences in the First World War, not for an SFFH book. With the passage of time, more and more adventure, western, and historical fiction titles became bestsellers, but only by stretching the definition of SFFH can we include Mika Waltari's "The Egyptian" as the very first fantasy book to do so, and

---

[19] 108 years later, Romance remains the most popular genre in America.

that wasn't until 1949.[20] If we do *not* include "The Egyptian," then the first undisputed SFFH novel on the *Publishers Weekly* list would not arrive until 1957, with the publication of Nevil Shute's "On the Beach," which by anyone's parameters must qualify as a post-Apocalyptic novel.

How is such a thing even possible? The 43 years spanned in the above cited figures include Burroughs' entire career, which as we have seen from 1939, 11 years before his death, already included 25 million books sold, for an average of more than one million books per year. Granted, he was prolific, but are we to assume that not one of his books sold enough to crack the top 10? Or, rather, are we to believe that the deck was stacked against him because of how the list was developed, very much as it still is today?

There are marketing companies that, for a walloping fee, will buy copies, spread out to appear more like individual purchases in hopes of triggering the reporting mechanisms that gets a title on the New York Times list.[21]

Put simply, the game is rigged, and always has been.

Until 2007, paths to publication had not changed much in thousands of years. The technology had, yes, but not the general process. In ancient times, a low percentage of people could read or write, and

---

[20] Waltari's book hit the list again in 1954 after it was made into a movie.
[21] Sherman, Erik, *Here's How People Fake Being Best-Selling Authors*, Inc.com, undated, (https://www.inc.com/erik-sherman/heres-how-people-fake-being-best-selling-authors.html). Accessed September 13, 2021.

anything more than a slab of wood or wax tablet to write on was expensive. Creating papyrus, amate,[22] and parchment was a laborious process until the Chinese developed paper sometime around 0 A.D. Because the method for producing manuscripts was so limited and labor intensive, authors in that world who were not independently wealthy usually sought a patron or patrons to fund their work. In return, they might entertain guests at the patron's social functions and generally associate with their benefactor in an early but similar form of crowd-funding, such as is represented by modern companies like Patreon, Kickstarter, Indiegogo, and Podia.

Just as with Indie authors today, ancient writers had to do everything for themselves. They had to seek out patrons, buy their own supplies, correct their own work, produce material, and generally try to be the Mark Twain of Athens, Rome, or Beijing. Later, once mass-production of books made it possible for people other than wealthy nobles to afford them, the subscription model came into being as an outgrowth of this patronage system. For successful authors, this could be a financial windfall.

Just as Edgar Rice Burroughs had knowledge of those who came before him, we have an even longer history to use as our guide, and he likely relied upon the then-best-known example of an Indie author to show him the most profitable path to moving forward with his career: Mark Twain.

In the late 19th century there were only two realistic choices for publishing whole books,[23] which remained the status quo until 2007. First was the traditional route, which remains substantially un-

---

[22] A fibrous proto-paper made from tree bark in what is now Mexico.
[23] This doesn't include serialized books, which would eventually have to take one of the two paths to market mentioned here.

changed in 2020, and the second was by subscription, which we call self-published, or one form of Indie. And if "one form of Indie" sounds like an amorphous term, that's because it is; the *raison d'etre* for this book is the current rapid evolution that affects even the terminology of the industry.

The publishing world of 1885 bears a striking resemblance to that of 2006, and for the same reason: the gatekeepers had all the power. Self-published (subscription) authors could not sell their books in traditional bookstores, just as was true in the pre-digital age. There were exceptions, of course, but they were few and far between. Therefore, 19th century Indies often resorted to selling their books using "canvassers," door-to-door salesmen, which, although different in form, is essentially what authors do in 2020 by running Amazon, Instagram, or Facebook ads.

The impetus for this was identical to the publishing world of 2020. Either subscription authors couldn't get past the gatekeepers, or they were successful traditionally published authors driven by poor pay rates to try something different. A perfect example is the 1879 publication of Mark Twain's "A Tramp Abroad," which brought in $218,000 in gross revenue for his publisher, but of which the author only received $32,000.[24] Because of this inequity, Twain formed his own publishing company, much as many featured in this book have. When he published the memoirs of former Union general and President of the United States Ulysses S. Grant, a personal friend, Twain wrote Grant's widow the largest royalty check in the history of American publishing until that time.

---

[24] Friedman, Walter A., *"Selling US Grant's Memoirs, The Art of the Canvasser," Birth of Salesman, The Transformation of Selling in America*, (Cambridge: Harvard University Press, 2004), p. 67.

There is no question that, over the years, elitist snobbery has limited the path to publication for innumerable authors who *should* have been published, but it should also be kept in mind that, without judging that most indefinable and elusive term relating to art, namely "quality," the overwhelming majority of Indie books are not financial successes. (For that matter, the same is true of traditionally published books, which leads to the question of who gate-keeps the gatekeepers?) The people profiled here are spectacular exceptions to this, and while all publishers *must* and do have gatekeepers, the differences in the two are both substantial and a main focus of this work.

Starting in 1860, one of the most important offshoots of traditional publishing for SFFH arose with the first of the dime novels, which ultimately spawned not only pulp magazines but also paperbacks. Dime novels were cheaply printed and bound books of about 100 pages, with bright covers and formulaic plots. Limited creative license was allowed because the point was to make money, and, if that sounds crass, it shouldn't; writers and publishers who ignore the realities of business are bound to fail, which not only deprives them, their employees, and any stockholders of income, but also might leave their readers in the lurch. More to the point, and for those who found (and still find) no value in such literature, one of SFFH's most iconic influencers wrote extensively for dime novels under a pseudonym; Jack London.

But London was only one of many famous writers who saw the typical royalties from such a book, $200-300 each, as tempting incentive to crank out cheap fiction. Among many others who wrote dime novels were Horatio Alger, Louisa May Alcott, Henry Wadsworth Longfellow, Robert Louis Stevenson, Alfred Lord Tennyson, and Upton Sinclair. Legend has it that Colonel Prentiss Ingraham, who took the real life Buffalo Bill Cody and turned him into something of a western superhero while writing more than 600 novels in his lifetime, once churned out 40,000(!) words in one day to fulfill a contract… without using a typewriter. This type of production may or may not be apocryphal, but such literalness is irrelevant. A massive production of prose does *not* prohibit that work from being of a high and entertaining quality, as the life and career of Robert E. Howard make crystal clear.

Howard wrote almost exclusively for pulp magazines. Those were the direct successors to dime novels, and, as might be expected, elitists hated them just as much. Even today, a cursory internet search turns up snobbish comments describing them as containing trash and low-quality literature. Considering only a few of the now-legendary authors who wrote for the pulps, Howard being the Father of Modern Sword and Sorcery, and H.P. Lovecraft having created an entire sub-genre of horror, such casual elitism shows that literary snobbishness is alive and well in 2021.

Pulp magazines used the cheapest wood pulp paper available to keep down production costs. In fairly short order, the paper turned brown and became brittle, which didn't matter to readers who enjoyed them. What mattered was the prose, not the *form* of the prose, and pulps can be seen as the direct predecessor to the digital book in that regard. Beginning in 1896, the explosive growth of pulps mirrored that of dime novels in the 1860s, fueled by a climbing literacy rate. It's impossible to overstate their importance to the SFFH publishing reality of today.

Pulps could either be a collection of shorter works or full length novels, often changing from one to the other from issue to issue. They typically offered great value, with lengths sometimes reaching

150,000 words.[25] By 1910, reliable figures indicate that "The Argosy" had a circulation of 500,000 per issue, and sales in the 1920s and 1930s reached one million copies per issue for some titles. To put that into perspective, the United States population in the mid-1930s, when pulps hit their peak of popularity, was 127 million people, of whom approximately 30 percent were under the age of 18.[26]

This was a critically important transition in the evolution of modern SFFH. The first pulp was "The Argosy," founded in 1896 by Frank A. Munsey. His rationale in publishing them was not only simple, but it can now be recognized as the spiritual foundation of those profiled in this book. "The story is more important than the book it is printed on."[27] Or *not* printed on, as with digital books.

This quote flies in the face of elitism, where plot was and is secondary to characterization and prose, instead of a well-balanced blend. Put another way, in the pulps, as in some traditional and most Indie SFFH of the 21st century, the reader wants nothing more than a well-told and entertaining story. Elitism comes into play by defining what that means, with intellectual snobbishness so ingrained that even elitists who argue that elitism is a bad thing can't completely disavow their own condescension.

Nor are elitists confined to the genre of literary fiction, which by its very name *sounds* elitist. Imposing the opinion of what is or isn't quality literature falls entirely on the views of readers, whether the

---

[25] The Pulp Magazine Project, (https://www.pulpmags.org/contexts/graphs/pulp-circulations.html). Accessed August 18. 2020.

[26] (https://www.census.gov/newsroom/cspan/1940census/CSPAN_1940slides.pdf,). Accessed August 15, 2020.

[27] Haining, Peter, *The Fantastic Pulps: Twenty-One Tales of Fantasy, Horror, Mystery and Science Fiction from Famous Pulp Magazines of Yesteryear*, (New York: Vintage Books, 1976), p. 13.

book is a western, literary fiction, or SFFH. None is intrinsically good or bad; millions of readers have enjoyed the works of William Faulkner, while millions more find multi-page sentences indulgent and tedious. All of them are right, because what matters is reader enjoyment and satisfaction; at least, that's the belief of the revolutionaries in this book.

In an article written for *Salon.com,* author Laura Miller puts it this way about the opposite readership poles:

[Maybe genre readers] "were told to put away the comics or teased for de-stressing with a romance novel on coffee break. Or, conversely, they might dream of being included in some brainy (and possibly entirely imaginary) community of letters while at the same time worrying that they won't make the grade. There are those whose fantasies of leading a 'literary' life largely involve having their own superior discrimination and erudition admired by other superior minds."[28]

She goes on to say,

"Intellectual insecurity is, alas, a pervasive problem in the literary world. You can find it among fans of easy-to-read commercial fiction who insist (on very little evidence) that the higher-brow stuff is uniformly fraudulent and dull, and you can find it among those mandarin bibliophiles who dismiss whole genres (on equally thin evidence) out of hand."[29]

---

[28] Miller, Laura, *Is the Literary World Elitist?* (https://www.salon.com/2014/02/07/is_the_literary_world_elitist/). Accessed August 2020.
[29] Miller, *Is the Literary World Elitist?* Accessed August 18, 2020.

For an example of pretentious condescension, even among those who are "reaching down" to try and seem reasonable toward genre fiction in the modern world, you wind up with quotes like this one in 2014, "in essence, the best genre fiction contains great writing, with the goal of telling a captivating story to *escape from reality*. Literary fiction is comprised of the heart and soul of a writer's being, and is experienced as an *emotional journey* through the symphony of words, leading to a stronger grasp of the universe and of ourselves."[30]

There's no mistaking the meaning here; a few SFFH writers might actually use high-quality prose, but they don't put their hearts and souls into their work as do literary fiction writers, they don't take their readers on an emotional journey and they don't have a vision of the greater universe. To cut through the gauzy haze of snobbishness, some genre writers might tell captivating stories, but they are stories of no substance.

If such blatant elitism existed in 2014, imagine what it must have been like for writers trying to sell stories and novels in 1920, 1930, or even 2006. "Tarzan of the Apes" has outlived those who sneered when McClurg published a book that had already been serialized in "The Argosy," but one can visualize a critic sniffing that while it might be a captivating story, the author put no heart and soul into it, it didn't pull the reader into the story emotionally, and certainly revealed nothing new about the greater universe.

We have already seen the bestseller lists for this period from *Publisher's Weekly*, and it's not a stretch to see the total lack of SFFH titles as definitive proof of elitism within the traditional publishing ranks of that time. Yet, given the chance, the market will always fill a

[30] Petite, Steven, *Literary Fiction v. Genre Fiction*, (https://www.huffpost.com/entry/literary-fiction-vs-genre-fiction_b_4859609). Accessed August 18, 2020.

vacuum, and SFFH writers found a haven in the pulps. It could be argued that, by making so many early SFFH works affordable via the pulps, the very elitism that forced SFFH into what traditional publishing viewed as a secondary market unworthy of its attention, led genre fiction in general, and SFFH in particular, into being a popular and lucrative writing market in 2021. In other words, the elitists themselves are to thank for the growth of genre fiction.

Pulp writers got paid per word, the same as contributors to modern SFFH magazines such as *Analog* and *Fantasy and Science Fiction Magazine*. Some writers wrote stories for the pulps as a supplement to their work for other magazines and/or books, but, for many others, it was their sole source of writing-related income. This led many of them to write stories in multiple genres at the same time. The list of legendary SFFH writers who got their start in pulps is long, and any in-depth investigation is beyond the scope of this book. However, it would be useful to at least mention the more influential of them, and perhaps a few who should be re-discovered.

Robert E. Howard is most famous for Conan of Cimmeria and might fairly be called the father of the modern sub-genre of sword & sorcery, yet the staggering quantity of his literary output in a career of only twelve years spanned the genres of not only fantasy, but science fiction, horror, westerns, boxing, adventure, and even crime. The most cursory investigation of his accomplishments must generate admiration, if not awe, yet he elicits little serious literary investigation.

"Some readers and critics will continue to pass by Robert E. Howard with their noses high in the air. Some will continue to view Howard as, at best, a minor writer... We may never see Howard enshrined in the Library of America. But if Howard never makes it, that will reflect the lopsided judgment of the great series' publishers rather than any objective criteria."[31]

Whether or not the people profiled in this book have read or been influenced by Howard, there can be no doubt that the marketplace in which they work reflects his legacy. Howard's place in the history of pulps is often combined with that of H.P. Lovecraft, Howard's contemporary writer and pen pal, and a man whose Cthulu horror universe is not only still actively read today, but generates new stories from such writers as one of the co-authors of this book.[32] As influential as Howard was in fantasy, Lovecraft was in horror. Yet aside from Howard, Lovecraft, H.G. Wells and Burroughs, the pulps gave a platform to the likes of Fritz Leiber, Edward Elmer "E.E. Doc" Smith, Sax Rohmer, Talbot Mundy, August Derleth, Clark Ashton Smith, and hundreds of others.

The heyday of the pulps provided the foundation of the SFFH publishing industry we see today, from graphic novels and comics, to streaming TV shows, movies and books. But just as happened with dime novels evolving into pulps, so did pulps evolve into compact magazines, and it began in January of 1930 with the first issue of *Astounding Stories of Super-Science.*

---

[31] Washburn, Michael, *Robert E. Howard, Literary Artist or Pulp Hack?* (https://bookandfilmglobe.com/creators/robert-e-howard-literary-artist-or-pulp-hack/). Accessed August 18. 2020.

[32] As this is written, Lovecraft has come under fire for supposedly being a white supremacist, on the heels of a movie titled *Lovecraft Country*. If there is or isn't any truth to such accusations is beyond the scope of this work, but simply making them proves Lovecraft's relevance more than 80 years after his death.

If a science fiction convention is ever looking for an arcane but lively topic for a panel discussion, debating which magazine-style publication had the greatest influence on SFFH would be a good one. There have been some truly wonderful periodicals over the decades, but when all is said and done there can really only be three choices to consider; *Unknown, Weird Tales,* and *Astounding. Weird Tales* most famously published Howard, August Derleth, Clark Ashton Smith, and Lovecraft, while lesser known (today) authors such as Seabury Quinn also stamped their indelible mark on the 21st century SFFH world. The magazine began as a pulp in 1923, and, though ceasing publication on several occasions and briefly changing its name, as of this writing, *Weird Tales* is still publishing new issues.

In Quinn's time, his detective, Jules de Grandin, was immensely popular. Grandin was a private eye who specialized in cases dealing with the supernatural and paranormal, a direct ancestor of such enormously popular characters as Harry Dresden. Jim Butcher may or may not have read Quinn's work, yet it's hard to imagine that the influences haven't permeated the genre to such a degree that Butcher's creation was untouched by them in one way or another. So if we credit Howard with being the Father of Sword & Sorcery, and Lovecraft with creating the horror sub-genre of the Cthulu Mythos, then recognizing Quinn as the Grandfather of Fictional Paranormal Investigators must be seen as only fair.

Another important writer who carved out a successful career writing for the pulps, but who is all but forgotten today, was H. Bedford-Jones. Over the course of a 40-year professional writing career Bedford-Jones wrote more than 25 *million* words and often shared a cover with Edgar Rice Burroughs, and, while most of his work falls into adventure or pirate fiction, it would not be too much of a stretch to include it under the SFFH umbrella.

The second contender for most influential magazine would be *Unknown*, which fails only because of its short existence, 1939-1943. Yet the fact that it belongs in the conversation at all is remarkable. Its history is inextricably linked to *Astounding!* Since, for its entire run, *Unknown* was also edited by the legendary John W. Campbell. Under Campbell's guidance, *Unknown* brought fantasy into the modern era.

Before *Unknown,* fantasy was either an ill-defined offshoot of science fiction, such as Burroughs' John Carter of Mars and Carson's Napier of Venus series which, while not featuring magic of any type, certainly blended elements of what we now consider fantasy into science fiction settings. Viewed from more than 100 years distance, it would be fair to consider most of Burroughs' work as more fantasy than science fiction anyway. As a tangent to this train of thought, another question for our fictional convention panel about the most influential publications would be to ask which magazine John W. Campbell might have placed Burroughs had the stories been submitted to him, or whether Campbell would have published them at all.

During the 19th century, novels with fantastic elements began evolving into what can be seen from a 21st century perspective as out-and-out fantasy. "Alice's Adventures in Wonderland," published in 1865 and its sequel, "Through the Looking Glass," 1871, are fantasy novels by any standard, but George MacDonald's 1872 publication of "The Princess and the Goblin" is generally reckoned as the beginning of the modern fantasy genre. Both C.S. Lewis and J.R.R. Tolkien found MacDonald's work profoundly influential.

Other early modern fantasy books by William Morris, author of "The Well at the World's End," E.R. Eddison's "The Worm Ouroboros," and "The Wizard of Oz" by L. Frank Baum, are representative of the changing nature of fantasy literature. Newer authors began having a foundation to build upon and draw on for inspirations. MacDonald, for example, heavily influenced Tolkien. Every Orc, Goblin, Hobgoblin, and Uruk-hai that runs amok in "The Lord of the Rings," can be traced directly back to "The Princess and the Goblin." By extension, the widespread use of those creatures, which have become convenient cannon fodder for evil fantasy armies, also owe their existence to MacDonald, whether the author has read the earlier work or not. Even writers who intentionally avoid patterning their creations after Tolkien reflect another form of influence, albeit one of omission rather than commission.

During the early decades of the 20th century, despite an increasing appeal to older readers through longer and more complex novels, stories with fantasy elements were still far more acceptable in children's literature than in "grownup" fiction. The similarity with the early years of digital fiction is therefore remarkable. Just as Big 4 traditional publishers and the long tail of agents, editors, marketers, distributors, and booksellers who depended on them for income, told anyone who would listen that self-published books were by definition inferior products, so were fantasy novels viewed as being works unsuitable for serious readers.

Marketing for both Lewis' "The Lion, the Witch and the Wardrobe" and Tolkien's "The Hobbit" originally pitched them as being for children, which was not inaccurate as far as it went. Tolkien famously wrote "The Hobbit" for his children, along with lesser-known works such as "The Father Christmas Letters." To this day the Narnia Septuplet is on middle school reading lists. But the bigger truth happened when those children grew up and not only wanted more such books to read, but they also wanted more mature books. Many of those who grew up reading Tolkien and Lewis bought their own children (or grandchildren) "Harry Potter and the Sorcerer's Stone."

Things began to change when the aforementioned pulps came on the scene, with an older audience tapping into those fantasy stories. The popular evolution of the SFFH genre began in the late 19th and early 20th century and continued with the growing popularity of pulps, accelerating toward critical mass in the 1930s. The two primary audiences for fantasy, children[33] and adult fantasy, exhibited a natural attraction, thus beginning an evolution which continues to the present day. A 13-year-old who read a Conan story in *Weird Tales*, or "The Hobbit" in book form, or even a Lovecraft tale, might develop a taste for the genre that demanded material suitable for older audiences.

The Golden Age of Science Fiction is generally dated from 1938 or 1939, through 1946, although that is by no means a universal opinion. Robert Silverberg, for example, disagrees without reservation.

"Historians of science fiction often speak of the years 1939–1942 as 'the golden age.' But it was more like a false dawn. The real golden age arrived a decade later, and—what is not always true of golden ages—we knew what it was while it was happening. That earlier

---

[33] What we now might call Middle Grade and YA, Young Adult.

golden age was centered entirely in a single magazine, John W. Campbell's *Astounding Science Fiction*, and the war aborted it in mid-stride."[34]

Labels and semantics aside, 1937 seems to be the year when modern SFFH turned down the road that has led to the modern marketplace. Although its impact in the United States was not as immediate as in Britain, 1937 saw publication of "The Hobbit,"[35] and John W. Campbell joined the editorial team at *Astounding*. Despite the award that was established to honor his legacy having its name changed in 2019, the influence of John W. Campbell stands unrivaled over the 21st century marketplace. Regardless of the validity of 21st century criticisms concerning his politics, just as Tolkien is the Father of Modern Heroic Fantasy, and George MacDonald is its Grandfather, so does science fiction trace its modern underpinnings to the ascension of Campbell as editor of *Astounding*.

If we include *Unknown*, which was Campbell's brainchild and for which he was the only editor, then, among others that he discovered, encouraged, or helped shape the craftsmanship of, were such legends as Robert A. Heinlein, Jack Williamson, Isaac Asimov, Hal Clement, Fritz Leiber, L. Sprague de Camp, L. Ron Hubbard (who disliked science fiction until Campbell showed him the money), Frederik Pohl, Lester del Rey, and A.E. van Vogt. This list is only representative; the actual number of now near-mythical writers who worked

---

[34] Silverberg, Robert, *Science Fiction in the Fifties: The Golden Age*, (https://web.archive.org/web/20120825082507/http://www.loa.org/scienc efiction/why_silverberg.jsp). Accessed August 31, 2020.

[35] Although it didn't have the revolutionary long-term impact of "The Hobbit,"Tolkien also published "Farmer Giles of Ham" in that year.

under Campbell's editorial hand would require a book all by itself. Many of what we now consider classics of SFFH arose from Campbell feeding ideas to the writers he worked with, such as Asimov's "Robot" series and van Vogt's best known story, "Slan."

Unlike his predecessors and competitors, Campbell insisted on a scientific approach to the fiction he bought for *Asounding!* Quality of prose remained important, but now, for the first time, accuracy and plausibility came into play, and, if Campbell had to pick one over the other, he always sided with the latter. This backing of science fiction with *science* was an evolutionary maturation that broadened readership into areas hitherto unreached, including engineers, scientists, and academics in the sciences. The young people who'd grown up reading pulps had become adults who often gravitated to the sciences for their careers, and Campbell found in them a ready audience.

The pivotal year for SFFH came in 1939 with a confluence of events whose ramifications still ripple through the industry to this day and set the stage for the Titans in this book. For direct influence on the genre it is simply incomparable to anything else in the pre-digital era. It was the first full year of Campbell's tenure as sole editor of *Astounding*, and he bought the first story by the man whose influence still dominates science fiction to this day: Robert A. Heinlein. To paraphrase the grand master's reaction, "Why didn't somebody tell me about this before?" Although Heinlein's "Starship Troopers" had a few precursors in the sub-genre of military science fiction, it was the publication of that novel, along with H. Beam Piper's "Uller Uprising," and Gordon R. Dickson's "Dorsai," that defined what is now one of SFFH's best selling categories. Many of the Titans in this book owe their success in part or in full to Heinlein, Piper, and Dickson.

On September 1, 1939, Germany invaded Poland to initiate the Second World War in Europe. More than any other single event, that horrific cataclysm drove science fiction forward on the heels of advancing technology. Given the large number of science fiction writers with either advanced scientific degrees or military experience, it was inevitable they would become part of the giant machine fighting against Fascism in Europe and Japanese Expansionism in Asia and the Pacific. As a former naval officer, Heinlein worked for the Navy as an aeronautical engineer, while Isaac Asimov worked at the Philadelphia Naval Yard as a chemist. Not only were Campbell and his stable of writers involved in the war effort, but the war also swept up the visionary Arthur C. Clarke, too, who imagined satellites circling the Earth and bouncing radio signals to enhance their range. They are only a few of the countless writers of SFFH who used their brains and their craft to fight the Axis.

The genocidal brutality of the war affected all prose that came after, to one degree or another, but that crucible of human depravity also drove technological advances that began as science fiction in 1939 and had become reality by 1945. Atomic fission is only the most obvious example of the rapid development of weapons intended to kill.

When the war started, England's armed forces still had biplanes as front-line aircraft, yet by war's end the Gloster Meteor jet fighter had entered service and fought its first dogfight. Japan developed the rocket-powered Yokosuka MXY-7 *Ohka* suicide aircraft, which, in a dive, flirted with the speed of sound at more than 600 mph. And the German *wunderwaffe*[36] program gave the world the deadly V2 rocket, which became the forerunner to America's early missile program, among other advanced weaponry such as the world's first smart bombs, the radio-controlled Fritz X, and Henschel HS-293. The latter missile sank the Italian battleship *Roma* with one hit, and the British troop transport HMT *Rohna*, killing more than 1,000 men. Only after the war did SFFH writers have time to digest and incorporate the war into their fiction, the effects of which still produce new material in the 21st century, such as Amazon's TV series developed from Philip K. Dick's classic alternate history novel "The Man in the High Castle."

Yet the two events of 1939 that most define the modern SFFH marketplace, as it affects writers, occurred in New York the first week of July with the first Worldcon and its protest spinoff attended by Frederik Pohl, Donald Wollheim, and a few others, who have since been dubbed the "Futurians." The spinoff was created when Worldcon (allegedly) banned certain writers for political reasons.[37] Forrest J. Ackerman and his girlfriend Myrtle Douglas showed up in

---

[36] Wonder weapons.

[37] In his autobiography Pohl disputed this, claiming it was less political and more personal dislike, and this would seem to have some credibility. For example, at this point Heinlein was further to the Left politically than he would be later in life, as his novel "For Us the Living," written during this period, flirts with Socialist Utopianism.

homemade costumes that were the direct forerunners to modern cosplay.

These two gatherings, the smaller of which was less convention and more get-together, define the SFFH landscape of 1939 and beyond for three key reasons. First, in the pre-COVID-19 world, the biggest marketing advantage that writers of SFFH had was access to hundreds of conventions every year, in every state and nearly every country. And even with the restrictions that will forever symbolize the years 2020 and 2021, virtual cons still drew respectable numbers of fans. Most of all, authors were able to connect directly with people who might read their books. In no other genre does the symbiotic need for finding one's "tribe" exist as it does in the world of SFFH.

Attendees at cons provide authors with a built-in audience that is eager to meet its heroes in person, to purchase genre-related books and treasures, and generally to discuss SFFH in all its forms. It would be safe to say that both authors of this book have been there and done that, and on both sides of the dealer room table. Yet cons also illustrate the divide between Big 4 traditional publishers and the Titans herein.

Ask at a general interest SFFH convention whether the attendees are familiar with a popular small-press or Indie author's work, and most will answer that question in the negative. Yet in many cases, the unknown author is out-earning the Big 4 traditional author by an order of magnitude. This has led to the further evolution of cons. Under the big umbrella of SFFH, where authors and artists often work in more than one medium, the 21st century convention scene finds general interest SFFH cons existing alongside comicons, media cons, and all manner of hybrids, from general SFFH cons with an emphasis on a specialized track, such as writing, to specialized conferences such as Superstars Writing Seminar and 20Booksto50k®, where networking and learning the business of writing is the goal.

Some newer cons, such as FantaSci, arose from a coming together of far-sighted traditional authors and publishers. Others like LibertyCon are long-running affairs with limited attendance, because everyone prefers it that way. And new iterations are on the way. In October of 2021, Chris Kennedy Publishing hosted FactoryCon, bringing together scores of authors and fans for a relaxed weekend of fishing, grilling, and talking all things SFFH on the North Carolina coast.

This state of affairs, where the booksellers remain in perfect lockstep with the Big 4 traditional publishing industry, could be leading to their downfall. If readers of Indie SFFH can generate tens of millions of dollars in royalties for writers not associated with Big 4 traditional publishing, how much money are the Indie booksellers leaving on the table by ignoring small press and Indie authors? Only at their peril do they continue to sell the same books, from the same distributors, as powerhouses like Amazon, Costco, Sam's Club, Walmart, and other discounters. Worse, most chain and Indie bookstores have to sell the books at list price, while the discounting giants offer discounts up to 40% and more.

Traditional booksellers are in actuality book consignment brokers. Through conventional book distributors such as Ingram, books that don't sell are sent back for full credit, which further burdens the supply chain with labor, storage, and transportation costs, not to mention handling the books once they have arrived back at the publisher. Some are destroyed and some are marked so they cannot be sold as new and become "remainders." Those are resold in bulk and reshipped all over again to the same stores that sent them back in the first place. They are then sold for $5.95-$8.95 as "Former Bestsellers."

Most of the great bookstores of the past are in the cemetery of failed businesses now, and, as brick and mortar bookstores follow the dictates of Big 4 traditional publishing, it seems sure that more will follow... unless they do something different. Hastings Entertainment tried adding used books and media to attract repeat customers, but used materials took up valuable shelf space without the proximate return on investment necessary to justify it, and what had once been a half-billion-dollar business with 126 stores went bankrupt in 2016.

But not all retail bookstores are blind to the possibilities. Some have recognized that promoting small press and Indie authors can be a welcome boost to their bottom line. Since bookstores only pay for the books they actually sell, the most common arrangements for small press and Indie authors are sales through a distributor who caters to their market, such as Ingram-Spark, or a separate consignment agreement. Under such an arrangement, which is most commonly used for book signings, the author provides the books, the store sells them, and pays the author for sales after the event has ended. Unsold books go home with the author. Typically the store keeps 40%.

So what does all of this have to do with SFFH, other than as being a brief word about today's marketplace? Without getting ahead of the narrative, Baen Books is developing a new model that might lead to financial success for others too, if they're paying attention. This holds especially true for brick and mortar bookstores. What remains to be seen is how many are smart enough to follow suit. A further discussion of this will follow when discussing the lessons of the Titans.

For now, this gets us back to the original point that 21st century Big 4 traditional publishers, despite (or perhaps because of) their greater capitalization, are far more rigid in their approach to the market and in what they publish than are small presses and Indies. In its own way, this was just as true in 1939 as in 2021, because, regardless of the reason for the Futurians being ousted from the first Worldcon, a sharp division of the SFFH genre into two camps dates from this period.

Big 4 traditional publishers of 2021 follow the corporate imperative of doing things the way they have always been done, to protect capital. Innovation is not their hallmark. As we saw with the Michael Levin quote, authors are often seen as a necessary evil, as would be expected from an industry dominated by corporate conglomerates. Big 4 traditional publishing will always do what is safe, like all established corporations, not only because they have a fiduciary duty to their shareholders, but also because innovation carries with it great personal career risk for the executive who proposes or backs change. This often leads to the squandering of opportunities, such as will be looked at later when discussing the development of the Nook e-reader.

Nor is there anything intrinsically wrong with corporate caution, aside from it being sluggish and inflexible. Yet in a field like publishing, where essentially nothing had changed for hundreds of years, being able to rapidly adapt had never before been necessary. Assuming competent management, in the pre-digital world, sluggish and inflexible worked well enough to keep churning out profits forever, and, regardless of smokescreens about other responsibilities and concerns, that was and is the only reason for the giant Big 4 traditional publishers, or any other business, to exist.

Repetition of success evolved over time into monolithic intransigence. With hubris of the highest order, by the early 2000s, the industry seemed to believe that readers would buy whatever they printed, and with some justification. There wasn't much else for readers to buy, after all.

One nation emerged from the cataclysm of World War Two as an economic powerhouse: the United States of America. Four years of rationed food, fuel, and the luxuries of life, including new cars, appliances, and stylish clothes, left the American public with a huge appetite for the fruits of victory. The same pent-up desire affected the other Allied nations too, but only the USA came out of the conflict with its industry and infrastructure intact and operating at full capacity. Money saved during the war burned a hole in American pockets.

The other nations all teetered on the brink of bankruptcy, having poured their wealth into the American Arsenal of Democracy in exchange for the weapons of war and spent decades recovering from the war's physical damage. For example, two years after the war, in Britain it was a criminal offense to heat your home without government permission, while, at the same moment, Americans headed into 15 years of unparalleled economic growth.

Millions of veterans returned stateside with pockets full of cash, the GI Bill to pay for college, and the rigors of wartime behind them, wanting nothing more than to get married, build a family, and enjoy life. Along with houses, cars, and babies, they craved entertainment. Books now had to compete not only with movies for the public's discretionary income, but also with the new medium of television. Yet, as always, traditional publishing mostly ignored SFFH.

Except this time, there were exceptions. By this point, most fans considered Robert A. Heinlein as one of, if not the single greatest, SFFH writer in the world, and Charles Scribner's Sons published Heinlein's second novel and the first to see print, "Rocket Ship Galileo," in 1947. Yet even the top writer in the field got little respect from such a respected traditional publisher.

It was the first of eight so-called "Juvenille" novels, which were heavily edited to avoid them being considered appropriate material for adults. Although willing to publish these now-iconic SFFH classics as children's books, Scribner's was not willing to put their reputation on the line by allowing Heinlein access to their older audience. One can visualize the gatekeepers holding their noses while cashing the checks earned on the sale of his books. By the mid and late 50s, however, the smell of money began to overpower the imagined stench the elitists had always attached to the SFFH genres.

If this could happen to the most popular and influential author of his time, then what chance did writers not named Heinlein have of earning a traditional publishing contract, particularly female authors like Leigh Brackett or Andre Norton? Early SFFH publishers such as Buffalo Book Company brought very little to the table for an author beyond publishing a book, but like all free markets given enough time to mature, SFFH authors could not be held down forever. Irritated at the shoddy operations of Buffalo Book Company, Lloyd Arthur Eschbach founded Fantasy Press in 1946 to give SFFH authors the quality of published book they deserved. Fantasy Press editions used high quality paper, were well bound in full cloth, and had beautiful interior drawings and jackets. In an update to the tried-and-true subscription model of pre-release sales, Eschbach produced special signed editions for those who bought the books early. That value-added-for-early-payment model is a direct forerunner of today's Kickstarter and Patreon campaigns used by Indie authors.

Shasta Publishing and Gnome Press soon followed, as SFFH fans wanted to see their favorite authors given the respect their works deserved. As it did until very recently, this respect translated as being the prestige of a hardback book, because even as the SFFH market exploded with new authors and stories in the late 1940's and into the 1950's, most of those stories came to the market in magazines or as paperbacks. The success of those imprints contained the seeds of their own downfall, however, as along with a few other less well known publishers, they attracted the attention of better capitalized traditional publishers who wanted in on the profits. Even so, Scribners refused to publish a Heinlein novel that crossed too far into the adult lane and let him walk. The publisher G.P. Putnam's Sons wasn't so short-sighted, and Heinlein finally broke into the adult fiction novel market in 1959, when Putnam released one of the most influential SFFH novels ever written, "Starship Troopers."

Isaac Asimov famously said that "the dropping of the atom bomb in 1945 made science fiction respectable."[38] The genre's new-found status didn't take hold right away, but, like the fission explosion to which Asimov's quote referred, once begun, it continued to build exponentially. Nevertheless, by the time Scribners decided they no longer wanted to associate with Heinlein, the explosion was too well underway to reverse. The more it grew, and the greater the potential revenues became, the more SFFH attracted larger and larger publishers. Thus began the homogenization of the SFFH publishing world that only ended in 2007, a period during which already powerful gatekeepers became the sole arbiters of what was and wasn't published in SFFH, and major corporations gobbled up independent imprints like bluefin tuna attacking a bait-ball of anchovies.

Throughout the immediate postwar period, though, new authors, magazines, imprints, movies, and even TV shows brought SFFH to

---

[38] Asimov, Isaac, *Nightfall and other Stories*, (New York: Doubleday, 1969), p 93.

the American public in ways and in quantities never seen before. Even prior to the Second World War, the appetite for SFFH was great. Orson Welles' Halloween 1938 dramatic broadcast of "War of the Worlds" engendered panic in those who didn't listen to the disclaimers, thereby proving the power of electronic media when combined with SFFH. The growing popularity of the field led to scores of movies which fired the imaginations of fans across the world. Heinlein worked on the script for 1950's *Destination Moon*, which won an Academy Award for Special Effects. Then 1951's *The Day the Earth Stood Still* gave the world the immortal phrase "Gort, Klaatu barada nikto," and *Invasion of the Body Snatchers* from 1956 remains an underappreciated classic. The decade culminated in perhaps the most beautiful SFFH movie ever filmed, *Forbidden Planet*, which is generally credited as the first time that science fiction was given the same serious treatment as other major films. Now more than 60 years old, *Forbidden Planet* remains a pinnacle of the art.

With the increasing demand, authors and publishers looked for ways to carve out market share. As one example of this, in 1953, Doubleday, then the largest publisher in America, created the Science Fiction Book Club to make hardbacks available to the general reader at a lower price than previously possible. This initiative eventually grew into a ubiquitous ad campaign that promised 4, 6, or 8 books for a penny, if you agreed to buy one book a month for a year. The club developed its own imprint, Nelson Doubleday, which it used from 1970-1989, when it became GuildAmerica. In turn, that imprint gave way to The Science Fiction Book Club, SFBC, in 1998. Some of the early works included specially commissioned covers by top artists, notably Frank Frazetta's covers for the Edgar Rice Burroughs Mars books.

So many people, having so much fun, was bound to attract the attention of those who are driven to make sure that people have fun the *right* way. In her crusade to prohibit alcohol and tobacco, Carrie Nation described her life's mission as, "...destroyer of the works of the Devil by the direct order of God."[39] The companion growth of comic books during the 1950s led to censorship efforts such as Frederic Wertham's attempt to link comics to juvenile delinquency in 1954's "Seduction of the Innocent." The uproar caused by that treatise led to the creation of the Comics Code Authority, ostensibly to protect America's children from the latent danger of sex, drugs, and adult fare in comics. Overlap into the world of SFFH wasn't a far leap, since magazines and paperbacks often rivaled comics in the lurid nature of their covers. Drawing a line from the relatively graphic, horror-based stories in EC Comics to SFFH authors such as Robert Bloch and Richard Matheson was not difficult. Nor, under the umbrella of censoring comics, could scenes such as Conan's frequent cleaving of his enemies' skulls to the teeth, though written in the 1930s, be far from the next potential target.

By the 1960s, the original wave of authors that began in the 1930s was hitting their stride. Decades of working through a crucible of difficulties, from low royalty rates and the attendant economic hardships, to disrespect from critics and much of the media, left Heinlein, Asimov, Pohl, Leigh Brackett, and their contemporaries producing mature works that not only reflected ever more imagina-

---

[39] (https://www.azquotes.com/author/24362-Carrie_Nation). Accessed September 14, 2021.

tive concepts, but also the skills to make those books interesting to an audience beyond the hard core of SFFH readers.

The 1950s and 1960s were also the decades when the "children" of the early writers came of age in large numbers, many of whom also became writers, creating a pantheon that far outstrips the limits of this book to do them justice. Writers such as Arthur C. Clarke, Robert Silverberg, Larry Niven, Jerry Pournelle, and Roger Zelazny, to name only a few of many, many now-legendary authors, rose to prominence during this time. Anne McCaffrey became the first woman to win both a Hugo Award (in 1968), and Nebula Award (in 1969.)

The causes for the escalating popularity of SFFH were several. In science fiction, however far-fetched the technologies presented might have seemed, they were still technologies, and consumers were becoming conditioned to a dizzying cycle of new technologies in their everyday lives. H-bombs, jets flying faster than the speed of sound, affordable televisions (with color!), automation, and countless other innovations inundated the buying public on a continuous basis, gradually raising the bar of what was possible in the minds of the potential SFFH audience. Interstellar flight wasn't possible by any known technology, but there were theories about how it might be possible that did not stretch willing suspension of disbelief to the breaking point.

Wormholes *could* exist, since scientific theory said it was possible, couldn't they? There *might* be things beyond a black hole's event horizon, mightn't there? And who was to say that a computer couldn't take over the world, since the idea of a thinking machine was new and revolutionary? Implausible science was acceptable, par-

ticularly when so many writers using those devices came from physics and engineering backgrounds, and they could trace some line of
logic back to a source grounded in a veneer of known science. Regardless of how thin that veneer might have been, as long as it was
internally consistent and the story was good, SFFH audiences were
open to accepting the premise.

Fantasy, on the other hand, did not have nearly the mass-market
appeal of science fiction during this period, which is reflected by the
relative handful of authors who made an impact of the genre, and
none more so than C.S. Lewis and J.R.R. Tolkien. A few others,
Richard Matheson, Fritz Leiber, T.H. White, and, on occasion, Ray
Bradbury, contributed stellar works here and there, but, until the mid
1960s, fantasy remained a secondary genre. Because of the reasons
listed above, the buying public, particularly in America, found the
concept of UFOs, aliens, ray guns, and space travel far more engaging than wizards, elves, talking animals, and monsters.

Then, with fantasy slipping ever more into the background in relation to science fiction, the most improbable literary process to ever
hit the SFFH community occurred. On college campuses across the
United States, rejection of the stringent societal morals of post-war
America reached the state of a mass movement in the mid-60s. And
like all such movements, it had unintended consequences, one of
which was the adoption of Frodo Baggins as representing the coun-
ter-culture lifestyle of love and simple living. "The Lord of the
Rings" had been in print for more than a decade by that point,[40] and

---

[40] It is worth noting that after first pulling the manuscript away from his
British publisher, Allen and Unwin, over a dispute about *The Silmarillion*,

sales were desultory in America until 1965, when the authorized paperback edition hit the market. The colorful, semi-psychedelic cover illustrations by Barbara Remington—which when all three books were put side by side made up one giant image—struck a chord with university students and inspired a mass-cult adulation of Middle Earth. With Amazon having now, in 2021, sunk more than $1 billion into a Middle Earth television series based on the Second Age of Tolkien's world, a period about which he wrote no fiction but only essays and fragments, it seems safe to say that "The Lord of the Rings" became the most influential fantasy novel of them all for 21st century writers.

With Tolkien's work exploding in the marketplace from the late 1960s and through the 1970s, publishers scrambled to supply a market suddenly obsessed with all things fantasy. With L. Sprague de Camp directing the Robert E. Howard literary estate,[41] Lancer Books bought the rights to Conan, and commissioned stunning covers from Frank Frazetta for a series of cheaply bound paperbacks that brought those forgotten stories back to a public who devoured them. Tolkien's dear friend, C.S. Lewis, nearly matched the popularity of Middle Earth with his Narnia books. Older titles, some long out of print, found new life, such as E.R. Eddison's "The Worm Ouroboros" and "The Zimiamvian Trilogy" and Mervyn Peake's "Gormenghast Trilogy," each with covers that strongly resembled Remington's work on

---

Tolkien had to more or less beg them to publish any part of it they might be willing to publish.

[41] Opinions about whether having de Camp at the helm was a good or a bad thing remain divided, mostly because of his editing of Howard's original stories, and the inclusion of non-Howard books in the Conan series that rarely lived up to the high standard set by Howard.

"The Lord of the Rings." [Editor's note: Because of her Tolkien covers, Remington was hired to do the same thing for Eddison's work.]

Suddenly, fantasy was hot. Fritz Leiber's iconic Fafhrd and the Grey Mouser found new life; original stories followed older ones in a series of paperbacks that sold well and are still in print. Michael Moorcock could not write stories about Elric of Melniboné fast enough, and, when he killed off the albino protagonist, reader demand for new material continued so high that The Eternal Champion was born. Karl Edward Wagner trod the line between horror and fantasy in a string of underappreciated stories about Kane, with Frank Frazetta covers that have now become part of the American landscape. Roger Zelazny redefined fantasy in ways that had not before been imagined, with books such as "Lord of Light" and "Nine Princes in Amber."

But the heart of this genre revolution remained Tolkien, who, after 1955, never published another major work of fiction during his lifetime. Filling that void with new material led to such blatant but commercially successful derivations as Terry Brooks' "The Sword of Shannara" series. Anne McCaffrey's "Pern" series was labeled fantasy because it featured dragons, although the author insisted it was actually science fiction. Authors who heretofore had been shunned or ignored for producing fantasy, now found themselves welcomed and even sought out. Even Heinlein got into the act. Although having written fantasy short stories before, "Glory Road" is a fantasy novel par excellence.

Simultaneous with this explosion of interest in fantasy, a science fiction equivalent might have been Heinlein's "Stranger in a Strange

Land."[42] Students prowled college campuses "grokking" each other well into the 1970s, and the more people looked at them in confusion when they said things like, "I grok you man," the more they grokked. The explosion of emotions that rocked the United States throughout the 60s and 70s found free expression in SFFH, where writers created worlds of adventure, rage, hope, and equality. Indeed, nowhere did the complex issues and emotions of the early 1970s find a more fertile ground for expression than in SFFH. Jerry Pournelle and Larry Niven's classic 1974 novel of contact with aliens, "The Mote in God's Eye," was set in the world of the CoDominium, where the conflicting ideologies of the United States and the USSR tried to coexist for the good of all the peoples of Earth. That the CoDominium failed would come as no surprise to a world still traumatized by the Vietnam War, and mired in the Cold War.

If the 1980s were a societal hangover from the 1970s, filled with glitz, glamour, and a "let's forget all that bad stuff ever happened" kind of vibe, it was reflected in the world of SFFH. Life became bigger and so did the genre, in numbers and in worldviews. The Old Guard was mostly still around—Heinlein, Asimov, Pohl, Clarke, Zelazny, and Poul Anderson, to name a few—but newer authors were becoming more and more prominent, from Greg Bear and Lois McMaster Bujold, to C.J. Cherryh, Gregory Benford, Dean Koontz, and Kevin J. Anderson.[43]

---

[42] It is reasonable to quibble whether "Stranger in a Strange Land" is science fiction or fantasy, but for purposes of this book, it is nearly always referred to as science fiction.

[43] Although Kevin J. Anderson's first novel wasn't published until 1988, it was nominated for a Bram Stoker Award.

William Gibson's 1984 classic "Neuromancer" began the cyberpunk movement, with its DNA spawning a wide array of mutations, from modern artificial intelligence tropes, to movies such as *The Matrix* and even LitRPG stories.[44] A year later, Orson Scott Card shocked the world with "Ender's Game," which not only questioned the price for making war, but also foreshadowed today's world of digital influencers. Following on the success of Niven and Pournelle's "Lucifer's Hammer," David Brin took the post-apocalypse genre a step farther with "The Postman" in 1985, and, in turn, that most certainly influenced Emily St. John Mandel's super-seller "Station 11."

The growing numbers of titles and authors reflected decades of young people who grew up reading SFFH and were inspired to write their own stories. Ask any author who was a child reading SFFH during the 1940s and 1950s whether Heinlein's juveniles had an effect on their imaginations, and the answer will be a near universal "yes." Those same readers would, one way or another, have also found Andre Norton, Raymond F. Jones, Donald Wollheim, and a host of others. But, in the 1980s and 1990s, they had become the new wave of trend-setters. The post-Second World War wonder and awe of the 1950s had matured to more nuanced views, which, in some cases, were jaded or angry.

As the 20th century gave way to the 21st, the ever-accelerating pace of technological innovation made possible by advancements in computer technology brought with it an integration of machines into everyday life that by itself would have been science fiction a mere

---

[44] And from a retrospective point of view, it does not seem coincidental that book was released in 1984.

two decades earlier. SFFH authors led the way in theorizing those changes and anticipating their effects on life.

Throughout the 1990s and early 2000s, the world of SFFH publishing kept chugging along on a tried-and-true road to success. But unbeknownst to the world at large, behind closed doors, a disruptive innovation that would forever change the publishing landscape was being created. In 1971, Michael S. Hart launched Project Gutenberg and digitized the US Constitution, thus creating the first electronic book. Building on that concept, in 1985, Voyager Company began publishing books on CD-Rom, and, in 1993, Digital Book, Inc. published 50 books on floppy discs.

Fast forward to 1998, and four important events happened:

1) the first dedicated ebook readers were launched: Rocket E-book and Softbook,

2) the first ISBN issued to an ebook was obtained,

3) US Libraries began providing free ebooks to the public through their web sites and associated services, and

4) Google was founded by Larry Page and Sergey Brin.[45]

The evolution of digital publishing continued. Stephen King's novella "Riding the Bullet" appeared in digital form only in 2000. Showing unusual flexibility, Random House and HarperCollins began publishing digital books. In 2004, Sony once again led a wave of technological innovation by introducing the first e-reader to incorpo-

[45] (https://govbooktalk.gpo.gov/2014/03/10/the-history-of-e-books-from-1930s-readies-to-todays-gpo-e-book-services/). Accessed September 14, 2021.

rate electronic paper, the Librie, follow by the Sony Reader two years later. As should be obvious, during this period a disruptively innovative marketer could have re-written history. A cooperative agreement between the well-financed traditional publishers and Sony might have first created and then captured the digital market. Done well, it could have left new competitors with an uphill battle. If it had incorporated what we have now come to call small press publishers and Indie writers.

Instead, in 2007, Amazon introduced the Kindle, irrevocably changing how readers acquire books. In isolation, though, the Kindle was simply another e-reader. What changed the world happened in May, 2009, when Amazon first allowed self-published books onto their platform. Overnight, all categories of gatekeepers vanished as the arbiters of what was published. Critics and most traditional publishers decried the new wave of Indies as unworthy, not without some justification. Even in 2021, traces of that elitist mentality remain, regardless of people like the Titans, but now it comes across for what it is: bitterness and rank condescension of the worst sort.

As with many innovations, the products took time to mature, but mature they did. The small press and Indie markets now have the same coterie of professionals as the Big 4 traditional publishers: full-time editors, either freelance or on staff, first-rate cover artists, affordable software dedicated to various aspects of the publishing process, formatters, advertisers, and a host of niche specialists and training courses. Perhaps the only area where small press, hybrid, or Indie authors lag behind is in business management, including marketing and audience-building, duties heretofore handled by traditional publishers in exchange for the vast bulk of a book's royalties. Yet even that gap is closing for those who attend writing conferences such as 20Booksto50k® and Superstars Writing Seminar.

Examples of why such business-oriented conferences matter are legion: the networking possibilities (such get-togethers tend to become a creative orgy producing a host of offspring), in-depth discussions of contracts, best advertising practices, and how-to-maximize your social media presence, to mention only a few topics. The time it takes to become a Jack-of-all-Trades is huge, but so is the potential payoff. One other thing you learn about is the need to have a clearly defined contract.

One such highly publicized case is that of Alan Dean Foster and the Disney Corporation, which opened a can of worms that has affected multiple authors across different writer organizations. The contracts in question involved paying royalties after the original companies that signed publishing agreements were sold to Disney. Like most legal disputes, determining fault is far too complicated for parties not involved in the legal machinations, but the abiding lesson should be clear; ignorance of contract law is no excuse. As Kevin O'Leary of *Shark Tank* fame often declares, "business is war."[46] Authors who think that *any* large corporation involved in publishing their books have the author's best interest at heart are fooling themselves. Their best protection is a good contract.

[46] (https://www.brainyquote.com/quotes/kevin_oleary_424984), Accessed September 14, 2021.

# Chapter Three:
## Barnes & Noble's Betamax Moment

*"Technology does not abide by common sense. Our goal is to break down ideas people have come to accept as common sense."*

- Nobutoshi Kihara, Sony engineer, 1964

The rest of Kevin O'Leary's quote from the previous section is the perfect lead-in for this part of our history of SFFH publishing.

"I go out there, I want to kill the competitors. I want to make their lives miserable. I want to steal their market share. I want them to fear me and I want everyone on my team thinking we're going to win."

For one brief moment in time Barnes & Noble had a last chance to avert disaster in the digital battlefield, and they blew it. To set the stage, a brief look at the market as it existed in the year of the Kindle's debut, 2007, would be helpful. Amazon reported total sales that year of $14.84 billion, with virtually zero net profits. Their influence on the book industry, prior to the introduction of the Kindle, was limited to being an online bookselling platform, which was not then, nor is it now, something exclusive to Amazon. The company was very good at what they did, it's true, but that was simply outcompeting the competition. Amazon had nothing proprietary behind

75

their success, aside from immense financial backing which allowed the company to lose lots and lots of money until it became profitable.

But the traditional publishing industry made and continues to make the same mistakes as Sony did with the Betamax. The Librie and Sony Reader beat the Kindle to the market, yet both are now gone from the marketplace. Both Sony and the traditional publishers disruptively innovated the marketplace, but with no clear vision of what to do next. Barnes & Noble followed the same pattern. Namely, all of them doubled-down on a stubborn insistence to impose their views of what consumers should consume, with themselves as the arbiters, compounded by a poor understanding of the market and an appeal to government to force people into accepting their *diktat* of what was good for the masses. Sony did it with the Betamax and now the traditional publishing industry is doing it via anti-trust lawsuits against Amazon. Authors of SFFH should pay close attention to the results and ramifications.

The opaqueness of Amazon's platform makes it hard for writers to take their side, but in whatever way Amazon might exploit small press and Indie writers who depend on their site to making a living, the fact remains they do provide that opportunity. But the greatest advantage of being a writer outside of the traditional publishers is flexibility, and the writer who is not aware of alternatives is squandering that advantage.

Whether the US Congress will follow the lead of the Japanese Diet and refuse to intercede, remains to be seen. Nor can the results for any current (or future) anti-trust suits be anticipated. Certainly for Indie authors who sign up for Kindle Direct Publishing and Kindle Select, putting all of their royalty eggs into one basket is an uncomfortable way to make a living, even in the best of times. Yet subscription models such as Kindle Unlimited are hard to give up, and while

Kobo Plus is a wonderful alternative, building an audience outside of Amazon requires a rock-solid business plan.

In its Shareholder report for 2007, Barnes & Noble reported gross sales (including its B. Dalton Bookseller chain) of $5.4 billion and a healthy 10.4% increase in online sales, despite competition from Amazon.[47] There were other chains too, such as Books-A-Million and Borders, but it was Barnes & Noble that made the innovative decision to directly challenge Sony and Amazon on the digital book battlefield. And then it all fell apart. How did such a massive, forward-thinking company nosedive into approaching oblivion? The same way all companies fail, by listening to the wrong people.

In 1971, after years of cooperating to develop a home video system for the Japanese consumer, Sony and JVC completed the project with the development of U-Matic, the forerunner to both of the systems that would soon stage a fight to the death for dominance of the video market, Betamax and Video Home System, aka VHS. Given the plusses and minuses of both systems, it is no surprise Sony and JVC's period of cooperation came to an end.

Most critics at the time agreed that Betamax had by far the better picture. Colors were brighter, images sharper, everything about it made the viewing experience more enjoyable... except for two things: Betamax could not record long enough, and it cost more than VHS.

---

[47] *Barnes & Noble 2007 Annual Report*,
(https://www.annualreports.com/HostedData/AnnualReportArchive/b/NYSE_BKS_2007.pdf). Accessed August 24, 2020.

Rather than let consumers choose which format they preferred, Sony and Sanyo, the co-developers of Betamax, decided to try and force the Japanese market to accept Betamax as the only allowable format, through pressure on the government to pass such a regulation. That was in response to an initiative by the overseeing government agency, the Ministry of International Trade and Industry, to allow the market to decide. Sony/Sanyo saw Betamax as the better machine, assumed that consumers would prefer quality over quantity, and did not want anyone else to dilute their pricing structures through competition.

As it relates to the publishing world, the reader need think no further than Sony circa 1975 as Sony in 2004, first to market with an e-reader, only to end up the big loser in the digital books war. In this analogy, Kindle could be VHS, and Barnes & Noble the descendant of Betamax.

When Sony was attempting to force Betamax down the throat of the Japanese consumer as the only government-approved format, Matsushita, parent company of Panasonic and majority stockholder in JVC, took a different approach. VHS had twice the recording length of Betamax, albeit at the price of inferior picture clarity. In addition, VHS had much faster rewind and fast-forward times, and a simpler loading mechanism, which meant fewer mechanical repairs. As the largest electronics company in Japan, Matsushita wielded far more clout than Sony did. They fought the effort to cut VHS out of the market by enlisting other powerhouse firms, such as Hitachi and Sharp, who received licenses to manufacture VHS in return for their support.

Under such an avalanche of powerful competition, Sony never had a chance. It lost the fight, and both formats first hit the Japanese market and then the American. Rather than try to win the video wars in the court of public opinion, Sony tried to force people to buy their product. The manufacturers of VHS flooded the market with cheap machines, which soon became disposable, and, at one point, some banks gave away VHS recorders free to those who opened new checking accounts. Sony, meanwhile, stubbornly struggled along, trying to sell expensive machines to people who did not understand why they should buy them. By 1980, the battle was largely over, and Sony had been erased from the market.

Barnes & Noble's Betamax moment came sometime in the days after the first Kindle hit the market, but before Amazon allowed self-published authors access to the Kindle platform. For one moment in time, Barnes & Noble had the chance to become the leader in digital books. But that would have required radical thinking—disruptive innovation of the highest magnitude—by allowing *all* books equal access to Nook. Instead, the company tied its future to ebooks produced by traditional publishers only, and, in 2021, Nook is no longer a significant force in the marketplace.

The series of events leading up to that critical moment in 2009 began years before. For example, the December, 2003, issue of *Wired* magazine published an article about Amazon's growing database of digital books. At that point, however, the books were like those of Random House and HarperCollins, pages scanned into computers from printed material. In other words, pages in physical books were literally copied, and, if that seems crude less than 20 years later, it is a reminder of how fast the publishing world is evolving, thus making this book all the more relevant.

But here's the kicker: Jeff Bezos, founder of Amazon, had reached out to traditional publishers to enlist their help in building the archive, the stated intent of which was selling more books for everybody. Amazon is and always has been a disruptor company, and, if there is one thing that traditional publishers loathe, it is major change.

When the Nook showed up in 2009, five years had already elapsed since the introduction of Sony's Librie. A three-way partnership between Sony, traditional publishers, and the major bookstore chains might have prevented Amazon's domination of the nascent e-reader market. When that did not materialize, to Barnes & Noble's credit, the company did not simply cede the ebook market to Amazon, but developed the Nook. By the time Nook hit the market, though, the two-year head start that Kindle had was substantial and would have taken a huge effort to counter, although Nook could still have captured a significant share of the market. The critical point was allowing all books on the platform, and the Nook appeared simultaneously with Amazon opening up the Kindle platform. As of this writing in late 2021, rumors of Nook's impending demise had yet to be countered by the company's CEO, James Daunt.

As the previously mentioned revenue figures show, in 2007, Barnes & Noble was still one-third as large as the entire company of Amazon. By itself, then, Barnes & Noble remained the big kid on the block in book sales. In 2008, the list of booksellers in America included Barnes & Noble, a much larger version of Books-A-Million, Border's Books, Crown Books, Hastings, and others, not including regional chains and independent booksellers. Taken as a whole, they represented a massive counterweight to the not-yet-monolithic Amazon.

What those chains had in common was their dependence on traditional publishers for products. They were all selling exactly the same books, in exactly the same way, produced by exactly the same publishers. Until Kindle Direct Publishing showed up, the bookstores had no choice. But, after May of 2009, they *chose* to have no choice. As print-on-demand books came online, the overwhelming majority of those booksellers *chose* to ignore and denigrate them.

In 2021, virtually nothing has changed in that regard, except the appeals to Congress to save them from their own business decisions.

This should not be seen as an endorsement of Amazon. Amazon is in business for Amazon. There is nothing altruistic in how the company operates vis-à-vis authors, and it would be a failure to understand their business practices to think there was. That is not to say that corporations must be capricious business partners—far from it—but regardless of an author's personal opinion about the marketplace as it currently exists, the business-oriented writer works within the rules as they exist.

Amazon gives small press publishers and Indie authors a place to sell their books because it is good for Amazon. That is how it should be. It also means that small press publishers and Indie authors must keep up with the trends of publishing so they may become or remain successful. That is also as it should be, regardless of the nature of the business.

This should not be perceived as an attack on traditional publishing. Business leaders are charged with doing what they think best for their company. The intention of this book is to give background to the marketplace of 2022 and context to the views of the Titans. The individual decision on how to approach one's literary career is disserved by side-stepping uncomfortable issues and the lessons they teach.

Any thoughts that elitism in the publishing industry is on the wane vanished when, on August 20, 2020, the American Booksellers Association, the Author's Guild, and the American Association of Publishers wrote the United States Congress a letter complaining that

Amazon had used their own poor business practices against them and had become too powerful. In essence, the one-time all-powerful triumvirate of the American publishing industry wanted Congress to step in and roll back marketplace conditions to 2005, before online selling and the digital book made them superfluous.

Specifically, they wanted Congress to, "Prohibit Amazon from leveraging data from the operation of its online platform to compete with and disadvantage the suppliers doing business there," it said. "The data that Amazon collects from across its platform not only gives Amazon leverage over its book suppliers, it also gives Amazon an insurmountable lead over any would-be distribution rivals—a lead so daunting that, at this point, absent government intervention, there is no possibility of meaningful competition from anyone, whether they be publishers, booksellers, or emerging platforms."[48]

Put another way, "they did what we were too blind to do and now we want you to punish them for it."

Before this discussion gets too far along, it must be pointed out that Amazon is at best an opaque business partner for small press publishers and Indie authors. For those who enroll in KDP Select, and that is a large majority of SFFH Indie authors, the best analogy for the arrangement might be a comparison to gold mining. When an author enrolls in the Kindle Unlimited Program, they do not know what they will be paid until three weeks *after* the month is over. So, for example, if a gold miner digs up an ounce of gold in February when the price is $1,600 per ounce, in the third week of March they might find the price has dropped to $1,300, or risen to $1,900. That makes creating a business plan for advertising budget iffy for small

[48] Gault, Matthew, *Book Publishers Warn Congress Amazon is too Powerful*, (https://www.vice.com/en_us/article/wxqkx5/book-publishers-warn-congress-amazon-is-too-powerful), Accessed August 24, 2020.

press publishers and Indie authors, who can only rely on historical figures for revenue projections.

To understand what this means, you must first understand the meaning of a Kindle Edition Normalized Page (KENP). Without making it unduly difficult, think of a page as every time someone taps the right side of their Kindle to advance another page. That's an oversimplification, but works for our purposes here. In June of 2020, the KENP rate was $0.0045. So, roughly every two times someone advanced the page on their Kindle, the author got paid a penny. That may sound trivial, but it's not when you think in terms of multiples of 100,000 KENP, where that rate would earn $450 for that month. Obviously it follows that 1,000,000 KENP earns $4,500, which if done consistently is a full-time income almost anywhere in the world.

Now what happens when, in July of 2020, the KENP rate falls to $0.0042, which is a 6.7 percent drop? Income goes down by 6.7 percent, of course, and, by any standard, that is a significant decrease. Worse, you cannot factor such lowered revenue into your business plan ahead of time and perhaps make adjustments in advertising, pricing, marketing avenues, etc. to compensate. All you can do is take it and grumble, so if a new company comes along to perhaps give Amazon some competition, or make things better for small press publishers and Indie authors, very few people are going to complain, and many will actively cheer them on.

Yet those whose cause may momentarily be championed now are the same ones who small press publishers and Indie writers have vilified since the dawn of artistic expression. Returning to the bad old days of yesteryear also means reviving a time when authors were starved of royalties and forced to sign contracts with such odious terms as non-compete clauses, effectively making them indentured servants of the traditional publisher to whom they sold their soul.

Those clauses are still routinely included in traditional contracts to-day.

If Amazon were simply market exposure for writers who otherwise could not have been published, the elitists in traditional publishing might have written off the situation as Amazon publishing their rejects. However, traditional publishers and their attendant industries have to ask Congress for help, instead of competing in the marketplace, because Amazon dared to *innovate* and pays fair royalty rates on digital books.

As of this writing, digital books across most platforms that are priced between $.01 and $2.98 earn a 35 percent royalty, while those priced from $2.99 and $9.99 get a whopping 70 percent payout. Therefore, if a small press publisher or Indie author sells a book for $4.99, they earn a $3.50 royalty. Above the $9.99 price point, the rate drops back down to 35 percent. In the case of an ebook that sells for $4.99, small press publishers typically pay between a 40 and 60 percent royalty, since they share with traditional publishers the absorption of all costs for editing, covers, formatting, uploading, and scheduling that Indie authors must do for themselves. Indie authors would keep the whole $3.50. There are complaints that Amazon siphons off some of the author's rightful royalties in dubious "delivery fees," however, since that is the nature of the playing field, it should be viewed as an annoying business expense.

Contrast that to traditional publishing, which as one New York Times Bestselling author who wished to remain anonymous put it to one of the editors, "25% is the best they'll do across the board." It is also true that traditional publishers in the field of SFFH often, if not in most cases, price their digital books *above* $9.99. For those that do so, there is really only one possible reason as to why they would follow such an incomprehensible marketing strategy, aside from a complete lack of comprehension for basic math.

The foremost reason is that traditional publishers have never wanted to sell ebooks, and they still do not want to do so now. Given that it was traditional publishers who were the first to market digital books, if this fact seems incomprehensible, that is because it *is* incomprehensible. The reasons why they prefer the labor-intensive, higher-risk, and capital-gobbling supply chain model is anyone's guess, since the various answers given over the years fly in the face of the very reason for this book, namely, new and innovative business practices that are evolving in the publishing industry. And this seems to be a good place for a reminder that not *all* traditional publishers are so willfully and stubbornly blind.

But those that are blind have now run to Congress for protection from their own mistakes, not to give them time to retool and catch up, but instead to force those failed practices on an Indie publishing industry that rejected them in the first place and neither wants or needs them now.

So when did all this happen? When did the rich, powerful, and dominant traditional publishers squander their advantages? Can we tie this down to a single moment in time? We can; Barnes & Noble's Betamax moment. That was the moment when everything changed. It is by no means all the fault of Barnes & Noble. The demise of Borders cannot be blamed on their competitor, or that of Hastings, or any other company. Rather, 2009 was when the traditional publishers made the conscious decision to turn over the distribution of ebooks to Amazon.

Pointless as it may now seem to imagine what might have been, such theoretical musings do serve a purpose. For instance, what if the leaders in publishing had learned the lessons to be gleaned from Sony's Betamax moment? What if, instead of trying to suppress Indie publishing by ignoring it, Barnes & Noble had chosen to embrace it as Amazon had, perhaps with even higher royalty rates to attract Indie writers? Would they have been abandoned by traditional publishers? No, because they were America's largest bookstore chain, and the publishers needed *them*, not the other way around.

Amazon's secret weapon for success in ebooks resides in every single Indie/small press/hybrid author reading this book. It is *you*. The value of the advertising from thousands of such writers each building their business by driving customers to Amazon's platform is incalculable. Based on their marketing decisions, Barnes & Noble never understood that. Yes, they allowed non-traditional authors onto the platform, but they never made it a priority the way Amazon did. Instead, they offered digital versions of traditional print books, a product that even the publishers themselves only half-heartedly supported.

For future study, however, let us imagine what if, just as Matsushita had done, Barnes & Noble had signed agreements with *other* booksellers to give them a share of Nook in return for their support? For those who say that would not have worked, the Betamax example says otherwise. JVC, Panasonic, GE, Zenith, Magnavox, and dozens of other VHS brands argue otherwise. All of them sold the exact same technology, at more or less a comparable price, with the only significant differences being their marketing. Once two large booksellers joined forces, say Barnes & Noble and Borders, the pressure for others to join would only have increased, and that might, in turn, have forced the grudging cooperation of traditional publishers. Amazon could have had serious competition from the start. Had they then reached out to Indie/small press/hybrid authors, Amazon might not now be the dominant force in the ebook market. It was the conscious choice of those associations who are now appealing to Congress for help, no doubt with the full support of traditional publishers, *not* to be disruptors… or even innovators.

And yet at least one traditional SFFH publisher *is* evolving with the times, as will be seen later in this book. Baen Books, under the leadership of Toni Weisskopf, goes to great lengths to engage their audience both online and in person. Where Baen's publishing schedule may not be able to publish all of their authors' books, those works are published by several other publishers of high quality books, like Eric Flint's Ring of Fire Press and Chris Kennedy Publishing.

Nor are all bookstores rolling over and waiting for traditional publishers to rub their belly. In 2019, Books-A-Million, a chain that up until this point had been even more hostile to Indies than even Barnes & Noble, tried its own innovative approach, albeit one that seems doomed to fail.

Instead of trying to make money by attracting and selling Indie books, such as Amazon and Kobo do, Books-A-Million decided to jump into the miasma of producing Indie books for a fee, with the lure to writers of putting them on their bookstore shelves. One of the editors of this book, William Alan Webb, has personally tried to get his small press titles into Books-A-Million, with, at one point, a nine-store book tour arranged. The individual store managers were excited and thought sales would be excellent. Books-A-Million Corporate, however, quashed the effort because their centralized method of procuring inventory prohibited such initiatives. Instead, the author who is not traditionally published had (and still has) to follow a Byzantine procedure that makes introduction of such inventory nearly impossible.

The process was, and is, archaic, involving physical copies of a book being mailed to Books-A-Million's own distributor, which they own outright, followed by weeks of waiting for an answer, and a list of requirements that fall outside of the normal book parameters for any other distribution channel. For example, the price must clearly be printed on the book, despite this not being mandatory for traditionally published books like those from university presses, which frequently list no price. Rejections are final and cannot be appealed.

In 2015, the chain stepped into the murky waters of being a publishing service for authors. For nearly four years they tried to be both publisher and distributor. For a hefty four-figure fee, Books-A-Million promised to "edit" your manuscript and provide a cover, print it (probably using Print-on-Demand technology), and then allow it to be stocked on their shelves. That assumed that the individual store managers might want it, which was by no means guaranteed. That all abruptly ended in March of 2019, when BAM discontinued the service.

One thing that can be said for the attempt is that it showed out-of-the-box thinking to generate a new revenue stream. In the past, traditional publishers have done the same thing by opening bookstores to carry the content they created, but *only after it had been created*. That is, the bookstores generated revenue through the sale of books, and while it was true that those books had been created by the bookstore owner, the endgame was sellable books.

But Books-A-Million took what could have been a good concept—developing a stable of writers who sold a lot of books and collecting both royalties and profits on those books through various networks of distribution, including their own stores—and corrupted it into something with no hope of long-term success. Put succinctly, the process of publishing a book will *always* consume resources, with revenue generation coming from sales. For legitimate companies to try and monetize the process of publishing will *always* be doomed from the start. Sure, you might collect money from inexperienced (and desperate) authors who don't know better, but once they have paid out thousands of dollars to have their book edited, formatted, and a cover created,[49] what are the odds they will ever earn back that investment?

Even if the publisher involved is on the up-and-up, which is often not the case with pay-for-play publishers, the chances of the author breaking even are long indeed. So why would the author pay the same company more money to publish a second book? If we consider it a given that the vast majority of writers would learn after the first mistake, they would not. Therefore, a pay-for-play publisher must keep filling their sales funnel with new authors. That implies advertising, which further increases the cost of doing business.

In today's world of information overload, would the number of authors who sign up for such a service really matter? Let us consider BAM again, since the service they offered came from a known company. It can serve as an example for any future such enterprises.

Books-A-Million's online sales in 2020 totaled $43.5 million,[50] a respectable total but paltry compared to Amazon. Overall sales figures in brick and mortar stores are more difficult to pin down. But what if, instead of monetizing their publication process back in 2015, they had mimicked Amazon and created their own imprints, publishing authors at no charge but keeping a percentage of the royalties, and then helped authors market their books through free teaching seminars? Could such a thing have provided a significant revenue boost? Could it still, for them or others?

Because Books-A-Million has such a small national market share, and no international, it would surely be hard to attract writers who

---

[49] This does not begin to address the well known issues of those edits and covers being second or third rate, thereby producing a sub-standard product.

[50] (https://ecommercedb.com/en/store/booksamillion.com). Accessed August 24, 2020.

could sell enough books to make the program work, but what if they formed an alliance with other bookstore chains and independents?

It is not too late for brick and mortar stores to tap into the lucrative Indie publishing industry; indeed, doing so could be a lifesaver for those stores. Some are partnering with Kobo or other Amazon competitors to supplement income, yet they still resist promoting the Indie/small press/hybrid authors who sell on the digital platform. This may not be universally true, but it certainly describes many independent bookstores.

Granted, it would be much harder for them to compete with Amazon now than it was in 2009, but it could still be done. As of late 2021, however, hopes are pinned on Congress to dismantle Amazon through legislation and antitrust violations. This is not the time or place to argue the merits of such action, but awareness of the multiple lawsuits that Amazon is currently defending should be known to all writers so they can make well-informed business decisions. Knee-jerk reactions for one side or the other on this issue should be tempered against the reality that whatever the outcome, for authors it will have both positive and negative effects.

So what might innovation look like in 2022 and beyond? In 2018, word came out that Walmart and Kobo had teamed up to distribute not only digital books in their stores, but also Kobo's e-reader, the Rakuten. Indie authors rejoiced at the possibility of another viable channel of distribution for their books, one with enough clout to challenge Amazon and perhaps increase royalties, while also remaining skeptical of what might come from such a partnership. As things turned out, as of this writing their skepticism was well placed.

With Amazon, a $9.99 a month subscription fee buys you access to as many books enrolled in Kindle Unlimited as you can read, while the author gets paid according to the KENP schedule already discussed. Kobo has their own version of this called Kobo Plus, which was late to the party but has contributed to a shift of writers away from exclusivity with Amazon. At least one Titan made the conscious decision to "go wide," Lydia Sherrer, and you will read her story later in this book. Other digital distributors also have subscription models like Kindle Unlimited. So far, the number of writers who have gone wide is comparatively small, but it only takes one tiny breach to break a dam, and there *are* breaches.

Kobo is an excellent platform with many Indie authors who choose to publish wide instead of only with Amazon, but the failure to entice Indie authors to leave Amazon and join the new enterprise might best be compared to swimming with a concrete block tied to your foot. It's not Kobo's fault; there simply are not many choices. All of their potential partners are playing catch up. But they *are* in the game, and some authors are doing very well with them. And, once you have cut the cord with Amazon, there is nothing to keep you from distributing to all the alternate sources, from Nook and Kobo to Apple.

As mentioned, Kobo has now reached out to independent bookstores, so the store can enter the digital marketplace, and Indie authors and/or publishers can only hope this proves to boost Kobo's market share. Unlike those trying to squelch competition among the distribution platforms, Indie authors should welcome it. Yet, for all the hope and fanfare associated with the potentially game-changing partnerships, four years later, the attempt seems to have fizzled, not for any lack of trying on Kobo's part. Rather, from the outside looking in, it is the ponderous Walmart, and the remaining independent bookstores which, if they market digital books at all, do so as an afterthought. As with Indie print books, just the word "Indie" is enough to make some people look away.[51] So, even as the Indie author may cheer on Kobo, many see their only alternative as staying exclusive to Amazon.

But some authors *are* doing quite well by marketing through Amazon alternatives such as Kobo, ibooks, et al, and the Indie world is watching. Because, what Walmart and the traditional publishing industry have always failed to understand, and still don't, is the aggregate effect of so many thousands of Indie authors directing their friends, families, and readers to a particular platform. Some SFFH authors in traditional publishing still sell tens of thousands of books virtually overnight, such as happens when Jim Butcher releases a Harry Dresden novel or Brandon Sanderson a new Mistborn title. But they are the exceptions that prove the rule, because, at the end of the day, Amazon's relation to traditional publishing transcends Barnes & Nobles' in three very important ways, all of which threaten traditional publishing's position as the ultimate gatekeepers.

First Amazon is now a direct competitor with specialized imprints for each genre that produce physical books, in the same way as traditional publishers. Thomas & Mercer is the imprint for Mysteries and Thrillers, Skyscape for Children and Young Adult fiction and so forth. In the SFFH world, the Amazon imprint is 47North. From the standpoint of the traditional publishers, this is bad enough, but, overall, it isn't much different from having a new competitor in the lineup.

Second, Amazon has now taken on Barnes & Noble in a *tête-à-tête* death match, by opening a chain of brick and mortar bookstores. However, in a potentially significant side effect, 87 kiosk stores Am-

---

[51] To once again reiterate, this is not *all* Independent bookstores. What is ironic, though, is the idea of Independent bookstores siding with big publishers against Independent writers. You would think the contradiction is obvious, but it is not.

azon had opened to showcase their electronic devices failed in the marketplace.[52] Whether Amazonbooks, the name of the chain, proves successful in the long-term is not yet known, but even if it too fails, Amazon innovated by only featuring books with four and five star ratings. Whether that is good or bad in the eyes of Indie authors likely varies. Regardless, Amazon can afford failures to find innovation, while traditional vendors like Barnes & Noble cannot.

The publishing world evolves at such a frantic pace it is nearly impossible to keep up; it is, however, still useful to look back and wonder what might have been. Post-mortems of failed business strategies offer the same insights as failed military campaigns, so it is well within reason to wonder what the bookstores could have done to avoid their fate. Once that is done, we can then see if those lessons might be used to future advantage. As we have seen, that answer is both simple and impossible: independent bookstores would have had to stop blindly following the imperatives of the traditional publishers and change with the marketplace. In particular, they would have had to embrace Independent Authors and digital books, both of which are anathema to traditional publishers and, by extension, bookstores such as Barnes & Noble.[53]

Traditional publishers began the third decade of the 21st century by keeping their digital books priced high while producing fewer and fewer titles, and politicizing their catalogs to offend and exclude a huge part of the market. COVID-19 undoubtedly had an effect on both the traditional publishers and the bookstores, but exactly what

---

[52] Schneider, Avie, *Amazon's Latest Retail Shift Means Closing 87 Kiosks*, (NPR.org: March 7, 2019), https://www.npr.org/2019/03/07/701044877/amazons-latest-retail-shift-means-closing-87-pop-up-kiosks. Accessed September 7, 2021.

[53] Various services report that in 2020, digital book sales comprised 12% of revenue for the Big 4 publishers.

the long-term ramifications might be remains to be seen. Will they embrace change?

Sometimes looking back is the way to look forward. For example, what if Barnes & Noble, Borders, and Books-A-Million had partnered with smaller chains and Independent stores to offer more digital content at lower prices? What if they had told the traditional publishers they needed more and less expensive digital content, and if the traditional publishers could not produce it, the consortium of sellers would fight Amazon by offering incentives to Indie authors on the Nook platform? In other words, what if they had used their collective economic power to take on Amazon directly?

The questions are not moot, because Betamax moments still happen. Not very often, and you have to be alert enough to see them for what they are, but they are not unique to Sony. They are going to happen again, too, because they are an inevitable part of the business cycle. They have happened repeatedly over the past few years to many of the people profiled in this book, and it is a good bet they're going to happen again very soon... as in, right now. We are living through just such a flash in time; it's the *raison d'etre* for this book.

If we speak of the recording industry as being inclusive of all avenues of distribution, as we do with the publishing industry, then some parallels and lessons might be drawn.

"... today's most influential music companies... are increasingly eating into one another's core businesses in a bid to grow their prosperity. At the center of this trend are those music-streaming services 'doing a Netflix,' i.e., investing money into independent artists to create their own content outside the traditional record-company structure."[54]

That, in a nutshell, is today's divide between traditional publishers, and Indies, small presses, and hybrids. Using an historical analogy, the Indies of today, be they small presses or self-published authors, might be described as England's Royal Navy in 1588, while the traditional publishing houses are the Spanish Armada. The traditional publishers are bigger and individually far more powerful, but they require a ponderous logistics chain, including warehouses, shippers, bookstores, and a large office staff, not to mention sales people and marketers. Given a stationary target they can obliterate it. Pivoting quickly, however, is not their forte—nor is even pivoting slowly. Much like the enormous Spanish warships, they are not built to pivot at all, but to make slow turns over a long period of time.

Like the English ships, the Indies move fast and turn faster. Decisions are made in minutes, not months and years. When the market changes, they are better able to adapt. The Indie supply chain is far shorter than for those supporting traditional publishers. Moreover, the measure of success for an Indie/small press/hybrid author is far lower than a Traditionally Published author, because the revenue is not being siphoned off to support the ponderous traditional publisher supply chain, and therefore a much greater percentage goes in the author's pocket.

And that was *before* COVID-19. The pandemic caused massive misery on a global scale. However, from the standpoint of the Indie/small press/hybrid author, it gave an unprecedented boost to sales. No business pivot was needed for them, while disruptions in

---

[54] Ingham, Tim, *Every Music Company is Morphing into the Same Thing*, (Rolling Stone, 2020, as reproduced at https://getpocket.com/explore/item/every-music-company-is-morphing-into-the-same-thing?utm_source=pocket-newtab). Accessed September 19, 2020.

the supply chain have had effects for traditional publishers that will linger far into 2022 and beyond.

The ongoing COVID-19 pandemic has been exacerbating existing problems in the global supply chain for nearly two years now. Add to that pressure a global labor shortage, a paper shortage, the consolidation of the American printing industry, and an increased demand for books from bored stay-at-homers across the US, and you're faced with what Baehr says is a "perfect storm" of factors to create what some observers are calling a book shortage.[55]

Indie/small press/hybrid authors might be forgiven if they were unaware of any book shortage, since that is not a problem for authors whose business model relies mostly on digital books for generating revenue. For traditional publishers, though, it is a much different story.

On October 1, 2020, Houghton Mifflin Harcourt fired 525 employees after more than 150 employees took early retirement in September. In all, their workforce dropped by over 20%, from about 3,300 to 2,600. They have implemented other cost-cutting measures, most related to the increased popularity of ebooks and a new "digital first" approach.[56] This approach is geared toward students in K-12 and teachers, but it is hardly a stretch to see this as introduction to an overall movement toward digital across all genres. Yet, given traditional publishing's historical reticence to pivot, a healthy dose of skepticism seems in order.

If we grant that writers write and produce enough material to sell, it allows the discussion to then narrow the focus to how we have

---

[55] Grady, Constance, *The Great Book Shortage of 2021, explained*, Vox.com: October 6, 2021, (https://www.vox.com/culture/22687960/book-shortage-paper-ink-printing-labor-explained). Accessed November 22, 2021.

[56] *Publishing News,* (Locus November 14, 2020). Accessed November 15, 2020.

arrived at the industry realities of the 21st century. Throughout the history of publishing, writers have faced four major problems in developing their careers: the cost of their works; income from their works; path to publication; and letting the reading public know their works exist, which we now call "marketing."

The coming of digital books changed everything regarding the cost of books, which for most of history had been expensive luxuries. Producing books before the 15th century was a long and labor-intensive process which involved hand-copying manuscripts. The complicated effort this involved is beyond the scope of this history, except to say that if literacy in those years was severely limited, the number of those capable of *producing* books was even more restricted. And, even with the invention of the printing press, creating books remained an expensive and laborious effort.

More to the point, books were expensive, and authors were not well paid for their efforts. However, it is worth noting that when we speak of traditional publishing, such a term only truly begins to apply with the invention of the printing press. Prior to that, the process of creating books was so time consuming and labor intensive as to be quantitatively rare. We could also lump those works into the broad category of self-published, since a patron usually commissioned the work, paid the scribe, and covered the costs. Whether that patron was Augustus Caesar saving "The Aeneid" against Horace's deathbed wishes, or him paying Horace to write an epistle, it yet remains that one would have to consider those as self-published, since the author produced and sold them.

Traditional publishers in the Middle Ages took on enormous monetary risks in producing books, which is why fiction was not something they immediately gravitated toward. From 1377 in Korea, and 1452 in Europe,[57] publishers using printing presses with movea-

---

[57] And as early as the 7th Century Tang Dynasty in China.

ble type relied on religious, historical, and natural history texts to recoup their investments. Fiction came later and was a tremendous gamble, with the authors earning little money because the risk and overhead of book production was so high. For *some* of those working in the world of traditional publishing in the 20th and 21st centuries, little has changed. In a complaint more often used against the network marketing industry, critics argue that, in traditional publishing, only the people at the top make real money.

Most writers who break into traditional publishing are done in two books. Maybe three if they are lucky. And, when I say most, I would give a conservative guess of 95%, but it is more than likely closer to 99%. A lot of writers are chewed up and spit out to get that one writer who sticks past three books. But, even then, a ten or twenty book writer is often tossed aside if anything goes south along the way.[58]

As a percentage of the whole, very few writers have ever before been able to make a living from their efforts, especially those writing in SFFH. Most had to supplement their income doing other things or by finding a patron.

If anyone doubted that Amazon had taken direct aim at traditional bookstores, that changed in 2018 when the company introduced Amazon 4-Star Stores. The concept was to have a store full of curated items that all rate at least 4 stars or above on the Amazon

---

[58] Smith, Dean Wesley, *Why am I so Against Traditional Publishing?*, May 31, 2020, (https://www.deanwesleysmith.com/why-am-i-so-against-traditional-publishing/). Accessed 29 August, 2021.

and Goodreads platforms.[59] While this is good news for small press publishers and Indie/hybrid authors, the important word in the discussion is "curated." There are still gatekeepers who determine the availability of books in the stores.

Even in 2022, though, many independent bookstores stubbornly cling to outdated ideas. Brick and mortar bookstores could broaden their stock by selecting and supporting Independent Authors. Some do, and likely have a better chance of survival than those who choose to sell books at full retail against discounter giants like Costco, Sam's Club, and Amazon. Most do not. To them, an "Amazon" author is anathema, despite traditional publisher authors also being "Amazon" authors. It is the same elitism that got them into this mess in the first place.

In late 2020, this headline ran in the *Wall Street Journal*, "Barnes & Noble's New Boss Tries to Save the Chain—and Traditional Bookselling."[60] The accompanying article underscores the state of the publishing industry in 2022 and beyond.

"A year ago, James Daunt had little control over the book selection at the Barnes & Noble store he manages in Idaho Falls, Idaho.

[59] Amazon bought Goodreads in 2013.

[60] Trachenberg, Jeffrey, *Barnes & Noble's New Boss Tries to Save the Chain – and Traditional Bookselling*, December 5, 2021, (https://www.wsj.com/articles/barnes-nobles-new-boss-tries-to-save-the-chainand-traditional-bookselling-11607144485). Accessed October 4, 2021.

Executives in New York decided which titles to carry. The retailer's 600-plus stores were expected to follow that blueprint... He was forced to buy books for which there was no local demand. In Mr. Daunt's view, the very survival of bookstores is on the line."

In a nutshell, that defines the current state of publishing. Traditional publishers and bookstores are fighting not simply Amazon, but the market itself, as represented by the rise of small presses and Indie/hybrid authors. It is not stated in the article, but perhaps Daunt has recognized that everything old is new again, and that traditional publishers are likely to mimic part of Amazon's business model, by becoming the supplier for both content and product. The more books they sell directly from their own distribution channels, whether some form of brick and mortar bookstore or via the internet, the more money they make. With margins shrinking due to increasing costs for fuel, labor, warehousing, COVID, advertising, etc, and with staffs already reduced, new revenue streams have to be found somewhere.

Many say direct-to-reader sales are only going to increase from traditional publishers. In a blog entry titled *The New Holy Grail of Traditional Publishers: Direct-to-Reader Relationships*, highly respected industry commentator Jane Friedman had this to say about what is coming:

"Why, in this new digital age, should publishers stick with old practices that effectively cut them off from any access to, and contact with, the individuals who are the ultimate consumers and readers of their books? Why should they allow one retailer [Amazon] to monopolize information about book buyers, turn this information into a proprietary asset, and then use this asset as a means to strengthen their own position in the field, sometimes at the expense of the very publishers who supply them with books?"[61]

Why indeed? Moreover, it is not only the traditional publishers who are coming to this realization, but Indie/small press/hybrid authors, too. One of the fundamental decisions that a small press publisher and Indie/hybrid author has to make in 2022, is whether to list their digital books exclusively with Amazon so they can access the Kindle Unlimited potential for revenue, or to go "wide," listing their books with other distributors such as Kobo, Nook, Apple Books, or Google Play Books. There are plusses and minuses to both strategies, but forward-thinking traditional publishers, such as the company that is run by one of the Titans herein, Baen Books, have spent much time and effort to establish a personal relationship with their readership. Most have not. For successful small press publishers, such as Chris Kennedy Publishing, Shadow Alley Press, Mountaindale Press, or Craig Martelle, Inc, efforts to connect with readers are a fundamental part of the work.

Most traditional publishers are not heading in the direction of subscription sales, however. In 2019, Monojoy Bhattacharjee, in an article titled *Publishers Still Rely on Traditional Revenue Streams, Research Shows*, reported on the results of a wide-ranging survey of more than 100 publishers. While reporting that many publishers saw subscription models as being a bright revenue source moving forward, most were not heading in that direction.[62]

---

[61] Friedman, Jane, *The New Holy Grail of Traditional Publishers: Direct-to-Reader Relationships*, Jane Friedman: May 7, 2021 (https://www.janefriedman.com/holy-grail-grail-of-trade-publishers-direct-to-reader-relationships/). Accessed October 4, 2021.

[62] Bhattacharjee, Monojoy, *Publishers Still Rely on Traditional Revenue Streams, Research Shows*, What's New in Publishing, 2019, (https://whatsnewinpublishing.com/publishers-still-rely-on-traditional-revenue-streams-research-shows/). Accessed October 4, 2021.

To Barnes & Noble's credit, in February of 2021 they *did* launch an initiative with potential, by announcing they would pay a flat 70 percent royalty on all ebooks sold on their platform. Digital distributor Playbooks did the same thing in 2020. Formerly, Barnes & Noble had a tiered structure like Amazon, with royalties based on price, although Barnes & Noble didn't charge delivery fees like Amazon. Yet, despite the company's talk of re-entering the fight for ebook market share in a big way, in November, 2021, Nook remains a non-factor in the marketplace, with few authors even aware of Barnes & Noble's latest efforts.

For all of the hoopla, Daunt's effort to rapidly turn Barnes & Noble from the path it has followed for decades so far appears to be only a tweaking of former policies. Granting stock ordering autonomy to store managers will be welcome news to non-traditional publishers and writers, if the managers are allowed to purchase their titles. But, as of late 2021, Daunt is not publicly diverting Barnes & Noble from its marriage to traditional publishing. For all the disruptively innovative rhetoric, the goal seems closer to "stay the course." If predictions about increased direct marketing from traditional publishers are correct, that leaves sellers like Barnes & Noble high and dry for product on which they can make enough profit to stay in business.

This should not be judged as an attack on Barnes & Noble or any other bookstore. To be clear, *all* small press publishers and Indie/hybrid authors should cheer for Barnes & Noble to grow strong again and for a new wave of independent bookstores to rise. Such an occurence could only help *all* writers. The more potential markets for books, the better.

Forecasts of digital market share vary from a low of 3.4% compounded through 2025, to a staggering 15.7% year over year through 2027. A good middle ground report projects that "according to the research report "E-Book Market - Forecast and Analysis Report 2021-2025," the market is expected to have a YOY growth rate of 6.04% in 2021 and is expected to grow at a compound annual growth rate of 7% between 2020 and 2025." That amounts to $6.94 billion.[63] In percentage terms, that is a 33% increase. Whichever prediction turns out to be true, the amount of money at stake is enormous.

So where is the publishing industry heading in 2022 and beyond? And how should Indie, small press, and hybrid authors plan to navigate what are sure to sometimes be rough waters? By following one of the fundamental Laws of Business: when someone has what you want, do what they do. Which brings us to The Titans.

---

[63] Technavio, *E-Book Market size to increase by USD 6.93 Bn | Technavio's Research Insights Highlights Benefits & Reader Engagement of E-books as Key Driver*, November 10, 2021, (https://www.prnewswire.com/news-releases/e-book-market-size-to-increase-by-usd-6-93-bn--technavios-research-insights-highlights-benefits--reader-engagement-of-e-books-as-key-driver-301420115.html) (Accessed 22 November, 2021).

# Chapter Four:
# The Titans

Regardless of Amazon designing its platform to give all authors equal access, the online Kindle store would not have come to dominate without writers supplying it with books that people wanted to read. It is those writers who are changing the publishing industry, not Amazon, Kobo, or anybody else. They are the stars, the ones leading the way, the Titans of our age.

Introducing a lineup of such luminaries as the Titans is daunting. Each one has not only created a successful author brand but has done so in his or her own unique way. These are people whose success demands attention. Time is finite, and the lessons and advice they used their time to dispense so freely are something for which we should all be eternally grateful. Here they are, in their own words.

# Chapter Five:
# Joe Solari

If we're going to talk of "Titans Rising," then let's embrace Greek mythology with all its tragedy. Envy, betrayal, disruption, and destruction abound in these stories of creation. The story goes that after Chronos, the youngest of the titans, destroyed his father, Uranus, a golden age ensued. It was prophesied that his children would overthrow Cronos, so he ate them. His youngest, Zeus, escaped this fate and hid away, planning how to release his brothers and sisters from his father's stomach. Zeus became the ruler of Olympia after he rescued his siblings and, together, they banished their father, the king of the titans.

Each generation looks upon its predecessor as an obstacle to their rule, while, at the same time, those in power fight to uphold the status quo.

Why do we relate to these stories?

Because they understand the envy of success and the desire to make the entire system better for all, today's upstart authors see a better future and have little attachment to the past. They are influenced by pop culture and pulp fiction, and ignited by the spark of entrepreneurship. They look to earn a living from writing and see an even brighter future, where they create the content they wish had been there for them.

Today's usurpers have overthrown the traditional concepts of publishing by evading the gatekeepers and going out into the wilderness to find their people. While traditional publishing sees genre fiction shrinking, they've discovered how significant the opportunities are in the wild. Here, fresh stories are created and alternative methods of storytelling are explored.

Make no mistake, this coup was not against traditional publishing. Instead, it is against the convention that what is available in the marketplace was what readers wanted or all there is.

The future of publishing will be different. Where and how you sell books won't be the same as today. What that world will look like doesn't matter. We don't need the Oracle of Delphi to predict the future. Those predictions always come with some terrible twist typically caused by us resisting the change that fate has in store for us. Instead, today's writers should understand and hold faithful to the immutable truths of content creation in this golden age of content creation.

### Know Your Why and Embrace It!

Maybe you just want to write a book for the fun of it—something to tick off your bucket list and have a copy of on your shelf. You can do that. If your dream is to make a living from your writing, understand that a big part of your why will be writing the books people want to buy. It takes courage to earn a living from your vocation. If you are compelled to do so, understand that it's easier for you to write to the market than the market to conform to what you want; it's not impossible, but it's the less-traveled path.

### The Reader is the Sole Source of Income; Everything else is Friction

As markets change, new mediums become available and the economics change; never lose sight of the symbiotic relationship between the reader and writer. Without a story, the reader has no entertainment, and without a reader willing to pay, the author has no business. The most destructive element to the status quo in the golden age is disintermediation. That's the fancy term for getting rid of the middlemen. They will protect the status quo because they have the most to lose. They are economic friction between you and your customer. The closer you are to the reader, the more value there is for you to split between the two of you.

### Treat Your Writing like a Business

Suppose you plan to earn a living from your writing, that means you're starting a business. The authors who learn how to run a business or get help to run their business get further faster. One of the biggest reasons authors fail is the business runs out of money. Any new business takes three to five years to get profitable. Having the money to fund this start-up and support yourself is a real challenge. That being said, I have seen countless authors bootstrap a publishing business. It requires sacrifice and patience. It will take longer than you think. There will be setbacks. This is your journey, and it will all be worthwhile because you did it despite the odds.

### Your Audience is an Asset

Following on from the last point, the connection you have with your community has great value in the golden age of content creation. Creating strong ties and mobilizing them will result in building a larger and larger fan base. This will allow you to leverage this audience to get into other opportunities. Your audience is the source of your cumulative advantage. Cumulative advantage is a force you must master to win in the winner-take-all publishing market.

### It's a Winner Take All Market

Like it or not, creative markets favor the few. While everyone can have a shot at making a career in writing, most won't. As dismal as the winner-takes-all market may seem, it's not. The opportunity to compete in this type of market is far better than a classical market, where supply and demand drive prices. In that market, your work's value is determined by how much competing supply there may be for demand. Your books would just be commodities. Instead, you're in a market where you can use cumulative advantage to get an edge.

Is this a matter of talent? To some extent, but there are many examples of authors finding an audience that loves what the author writes. The old gods don't see that the secret of the new titans is that they are lovers of reading, and they look to write the content they want there to be, not just what has worked in the past. While fortune will favor the few, it's possible to earn a living as a writer in the long tail of publishing. These are the niche markets that others forget to serve. The secret is that if you remember to focus on the reader, you'll improve your chances of success.

### Cumulative Advantage picks the Winners

If it's not talent that drives who will win or lose in publishing, and it's not a first-mover advantage, then what is the divine source of success?

Create stories that connect with the reader and leave them satisfied. Deliver on your brand promise, and they will become your biggest advocates. You see, story connects with our human experience, and when it does this well, it becomes part of our identity. Think about the pop culture you enjoy or the brands you buy. Is it because you've attached your identity to their use?

When you begin to build an audience and that audience associates with your brand promise, they will seek others to form a group of like-minded fans. This becomes the organizing principle to you getting a broader audience that then creates more and more fans.

The secret is that this isn't something that is done overnight. Cumulative advantage is using resources gathered in current rounds to create advantage in future rounds. To be one of the winners requires you to have the patience to build a die-hard audience.

**Substitute Writer for Content Creator**

The macro trends all favor those looking to earn a living from storytelling. One shift in thinking is how you think about what you do. Rather than just being focused on writing stories, imagine your words being the source material for endless entertainment.

As the world population increases in quantity, there will also be also significant quality of life improvements. The world population is also raising the overall education level, creating more people who will be readers. Further to this point, a higher-educated population has more disposable income and free time.

History has shown that with more free time, a person's money typically goes to entertainment. As our civilization advances, so will automation and new forms of media. Automation will create additional free time in your audience and deliver new and cheaper ways to deliver your stories to an audience. All this bodes well for the storyteller.

Rather than think about this business being one of just writing, expand your horizons. Think about how you can create content and experiences for your audience.

**Now will be the Time that the Legends will be Created**

If you associate with this next generation of titans seeking to drive creative disruption, you'll be the stuff of legends. All the pieces are in place for a select group of authors to craft the stories that become the pop culture of the twenty-first century. A generation who inspires future generations with the content created in this golden age. In doing so, you become the father to be usurped by the next generation of even better content and greater opportunity for those who wish to entertain others. Can you continue to hold onto the fire of the envious young son? The longer you do that, the more significant your contribution will be.

# Chapter Six:
# Kevin J. Anderson

**Biography**

Kevin J. Anderson is the author of more than 165 books, 56 of which have appeared on national or international bestseller lists; he has over 23 million copies in print in 31 languages. He has won or been nominated for many awards, including the Nebula, Hugo, Shamus, Scribe, Bram Stoker, Lifeboat to the Stars, SFX Reader's Choice, Colorado Book Award, and *New York Times* Notable Book.

Kevin has written numerous Star Wars projects, including the Jedi Academy trilogy, Darksaber, the Young Jedi Knights series (with his wife, Rebecca), and Tales of the Jedi comics from Dark Horse. He wrote three X-Files novels, including the #1 bestseller "Ground Zero," and he also collaborated with Dean Koontz on the novel "Frankenstein: Prodigal Son," which sold a million copies in the first year of its release. He has written Superman and Batman novels, as well as comics for DC, Marvel, Boom!, Abrams, IDW, Wildstorm, Topps, and Dark Horse.

Kevin has coauthored sixteen books in the "Dune" saga with Brian Herbert, as well as their original Hellhole trilogy, including their newest "The Duke of Caladan." His epic SF series, The Saga of Seven Suns, is a 7-volume opus that topped international bestseller lists; he is currently at work on a sequel trilogy, The Saga of Shadows. He produced and co-wrote the lyrics (with his wife, Rebecca) for two crossover rock CDs based on his Terra Incognita fantasy trilogy. He wrote a steampunk fantasy adventure novel based on the concept CD, "Clockwork Angels," by legendary rock group, Rush, as well as the steampunk novels "Captain Nemo" and "Mr. Wells & the Martians." In a lighter vein, he has written humorous fantasy, "The Dragon Business," and the Dan Shamble, Zombie PI series. He has edited numerous anthologies, including "2113," the Pulse Pounders series, "A Fantastic Holiday Season 1 & 2," "Blood Lite 1–3," "Five by Five 1–3," "War of the Worlds: Global Dispatches," and three Star Wars anthologies.

As publishers of WordFire Press, Kevin and his wife Rebecca Moesta have released more than 300 titles from Alan Dean Foster, Frank Herbert, Jody Lynn Nye, Allen Drury, Mike Resnick, Tracy Hickman, Brian Herbert, and their own backlist. He is a professor and the director of the Publishing MA program at Western Colorado University.

Kevin has a physics/astronomy degree from the University of Wisconsin, Madison, and worked for thirteen years as a technical writer for the Lawrence Livermore National Laboratory before becoming a full-time novelist. He is a board member of the Challenger Centers for Space Science Education and the Lifeboat Foundation.

He climbs mountains, including all 54 peaks over 14,000 ft in Colorado, has completed all 500 miles of the Colorado Trail, and has visited six of the seven continents (only Antarctica left!). Kevin and his wife have been married for more than twenty years; they live in a castle in the Rocky Mountains of Colorado.

His most recent novels are "The Duke of Caladan," "Stake," "Kill Zone," and "Spine of the Dragon."

**Education**

I got a bachelor's degree in Physics/Astronomy at the University of Wisconsin. I wanted to be a writer and took some creative writing classes, but I took classes to have things I could write ABOUT. As I built my freelance traditional fiction career, I worked full-time for 13 years as a technical writer and editor for a large research laboratory where I learned editing, design, and publishing. I then worked as a successful trad author for 20 years and finally went back to school to get my MFA so I could become a college professor. Now I teach a Masters Degree program in Publishing for Western Colorado University.

**Influences**

I wanted to be a writer since I was five years old, so I had many different influences at various stages of my life. My parents instilled a hefty Midwestern work ethic, while some of the writers I read really inspired me as an author—H.G. Wells, Ray Bradbury, Andre Norton, Frank Herbert.

Becoming a successful writer, and now a publisher, was a constant learning process and a synthesis of examples I observed—both successes and failures—and always keeping my eyes open. It was like running around and picking up tokens in a video game.

Tom Doherty, the publisher of Tor Books, was my mentor for many years. He taught me more about traditional publishing than just about anyone else I know, but his knowledge—and frankly, much of my knowledge I'm sharing with you here—while of great importance in a historical sense, might not be all that relevant as the industry and your own situation changes week by week.

What I'd like new Indie authors and publishers to understand is that when I was clawing my way up, there really was an established path, a set of steps and rules that almost every author had to follow in order to become a career traditionally published author. You wrote short stories, you sent them to the major magazines, you got a few pro credits and used those to get a New York literary agent, who would then sell your first novel to a traditional publisher. If you played your cards right, that would lead to future book contracts and eventual wealth, fame, and glory.

All of that went out the window about ten years ago, when the publishing industry started mutating like an alien microorganism, leaving traditional publishers under circumstances similar to the owners of a chain of Blockbuster Video stores—wondering what to do.

Think about the music industry. The first half of my life, the way to listen to music was to buy a vinyl album that you played on your record player. You could buy 45-rpm singles, or, if you really liked the band, you could buy an entire LP album. Oh, there were 8-track tapes and then cassettes, but when CDs appeared, vinyl albums were subsumed with astonishing rapidity. CDs then gave way to MP3, iTunes, streaming services... If you owned a Musicland record store, you were left spinning on black ice, wondering what had happened. Giant record labels that used to control the entire music industry, who would pick and choose which songs or groups became hits, suddenly lost much of their power. Musicians made their own Indie recordings, financed them with Kickstarters... and then had to figure out how to sell their music.

Authors have much the same situation, except we don't get to play gigs at the local bar.

## Path to Publication and/or Becoming a Publisher

I submitted my first story when I was 12, and I gathered 80 rejection slips before I had my first publication. I eventually published almost a hundred short stories in small press magazines, broke into the largest professional science fiction magazines, used those credits to get a major SF agent who sold my first novel to Signet Books, then a three-book contract, more multiple-book contracts, and then Lucasfilm contacted me to write Star Wars books for them, which expanded into editing anthologies, writing comics, working for X-Files, Batman, Superman, and many others while building up a following for my own original novels. I worked with Frank Herbert's son Brian to revitalize the Dune universe, which has now branched out into films, comics, games, and TV. I won't go into further detail here, because it's probably of less relevance to most of your readers.

I was never "just" a writer. I was always good at marketing, leveraging my Star Wars fan base to read my original books, attending science fiction conventions, putting out a newsletter. (For many years, I actually laid out, printed, and mailed a physical newsletter to a couple thousand fans, and many of them are still with me.)

I also paid attention to the publishing industry in general. I completed the prestigious Stanford Publishing Course. I worked a real-world job as an editor, where I learned about book and type design, as well as the printing process. I subscribed to, and read, each issue of *Publishers Weekly* so I could follow the trends and be aware of the changes. And boy were there a lot of changes!

Around 2010, almost a quarter century after I published my first novel, the traditional publishing world was headed toward a giant tangled knot, like an ominous "space anomaly" in an episode of Star Trek. In the space of a couple of years, numerous major publishing houses consolidated down to six behemoths. Borders, one of the primary retail outlets for traditionally published science fiction and fantasy, went bankrupt, and all those stores closed. The mass-market paperback market dwindled and nearly vanished—and that was how I got most of my income, by writing media tie-in books, movie novelizations, and other spinoff projects... all of which went away with the paperbacks.

And while all these bad things were happening, other sorts of turbulence occurred. Amazon released the Kindle, and after literally decades of predictions that "e-books will take over soon," ebook readers finally reached a tipping point. Authors like myself had an entire library of backlist novels, all of them out of print from traditional publishers, but my fans wanted to read them... if only someone made them available again. The technology arose for ambitious authors to do-it-themselves; they didn't need the high priesthood of giant publishing houses. Also, giant libraries of excellent stock art were created and open to the public, so Indie authors could get beautiful cover paintings for almost nothing.

As I saw that crackling, glowing, scary "space anomaly" ahead, I could see that in the next few years my long-established career would be very different indeed. Was I going to be a dinosaur, or a mammal?

By sheer luck, I had sold three substantial multiple-book contracts to traditional publishers, and so I had job security and a guaranteed income for several years—but I could see that space anomaly ahead, and we were racing toward it down a gravity well. That's when my wife Rebecca and I decided to dive into Indie publishing as well and form WordFire Press as a vehicle to release my own backlist. Other authors came to me, because they saw the cliff coming as well.

Now we have over 350 titles published by 95 different authors, and we publish in hardcover, trade paperback, ebook, and audio books.

Unlike my early days of traditional publishing, there is no one set path, and, even after a decade, we continue to try to figure things out, day after day, changing our approach, experimenting, failing, succeeding (preferably more of the latter than the former).

In the normal publishing world, I would be coasting at this point of my career, cashing royalty checks, writing whatever I damn well pleased, and enjoying the success I'd earned. But that's not the case. It's exciting, but it's also exhausting. You can't take your eye off the ball for a minute!

Fortunately, I like to keep learning.

### The Hard Lessons You've Learned

I was on a panel at Superstars Writing Seminars, "Things I wish I could tell my Younger Self," and I put a lot of thought into my answer. I came up with something very important, something I would not have realized if I hadn't been through it.

*Never assume that you have it made.*

No matter how great your last month's earnings were, or how many bestseller lists you've hit, do not let yourself believe it will always be that way.

Early in my career, I studied the rise and fall of MC Hammer, the hugely successful music artist. As the millions of dollars came rolling in, he developed a lifestyle that required the millions to keep rolling in, expanding to need countless assistants and employees, big houses, extravagant spending. But his earnings dropped as his expenses kept rising, and superstar MC Hammer shocked the world by declaring bankruptcy.

Writing and publishing, like music—or anything that depends on the public getting excited about the next thing you produce—is a volatile, turbulent business. Never assume it's going to stay the same. I have reinvented my career numerous times, ridden one wave only to have it crash under me, and then I picked up and charged off in a different direction.

I had done over 50 projects for Lucasfilm, written a bunch of movie novelizations, dozens of monthly comics, TV and film tie-ins, kids' books… and the entire genre of media tie-ins vanished in only a year or two. The huge and lucrative comics industry collapsed to a tenth of its former size.

So I tried something else. I call my writer-self The Doctor because I have regenerated in a different form so many times.

If you have a particularly successful year, then pay off your house, add to your retirement account, fill up your savings. Don't start a Ferrari collection. If your career continues to be phenomenally successful, and the money comes pouring in by the truckloads, you can always buy Ferraris later.

I've been making my living in the publishing industry for decades, and quite successfully, thank you. But I've watched countless colleagues fall by the wayside, unable to adapt and change.

Even today's most successful Indie authors are going to face major disruptions as technologies change, as readers go chasing after different fairy lights, as… who knows, a pandemic changes all the ground rules? I'm sure the CEOs of Blockbuster Video thought they were sitting high and pretty, and snickered at the upstart called Netflix that mailed DVDs to home mailboxes.

When you can, build a cushion so you can ride out the turbulence that is sure to come.

### Where are You Now?

Right now I'm a happy, successful hybrid author, enjoying the various facets of my career. All the different income streams give me not only variety so I can keep loving what I do, they also give me stability, a broad-based all-terrain vehicle instead of a pogo stick.

As a traditionally published author, I have 56 national or international bestsellers, 23 million copies in print in 31 languages. As an Indie author, I've reissued all my backlist as well as a lot of new titles, books that I think were better served by new-model publishing instead of the old-fashioned way. All told, I have 170+ books published.

My wife and I are also publishers of WordFire Press, which has been around for a decade, with 350 titles and almost a hundred authors, so we make some income as publishers, too.

We run the Superstars Writing Seminars, a high-end writing and publishing workshop that's currently in its 12th year. And I'm a professor and director of the Publishing Masters Degree program at Western Colorado University, where I can mentor students, teach what I know, bring in guest speakers for the parts I don't know, get a decent salary, and rock-solid health benefits.

All together, I'm in a pretty good place. Oh, I do have nostalgia for the 1990s when publishers were throwing book contracts at me as fast as I could accept them, and all I had to do was write a novel, send it in, and start the next one. But I can wish all I want; those days are not going to come back. I'd rather keep doing what I love.

### Where do You See Things Going

Well, thanks to the pandemic, I can't predict six months in the future, much less five, ten, or fifty years. What I do know, though, is that people will always want to read great stories. As a species, we enjoy our imaginary adventures, and we'll keep being drawn to them. So the good writer, and good storyteller, will always have a home... somewhere.

The technology, the delivery system for stories, is all just window dressing. Think of all those writers in the 1930s who made their living by writing the radio dramas broadcast into every household. Every evening, families would gather around and listen to the adventures of The Shadow or The Lone Ranger. Radio dramas may have gone away, but people's love of stories didn't.

**Contact Info**

Wordfire.com

Wordfirepress.com

Twitter: @TheKJA

Instagram: @TheRealKJA

Facebook: https://www.facebook.com/KJAauthor

# Chapter Seven:
# Craig Martelle

**Biography**

I retired from the Marine Corps, tried working in government service for a bit and that was a gooned up experience, so I went to law school. After I graduated, I immediately went into business consulting, a bizarrely perfect fit to leverage a lifetime of experience and those things I was good at. But the travel was brutal. After seven years, I retired from consulting. Immediately thereafter, I lit myself on fire trying to burn a pile of deadwood in my yard. I decided since I couldn't be trusted outside, I'd write that book I always wanted to write. Sixty-one days later, I had a robust 100k word post-apocalyptic novel that would later become the first book in the End Times Alaska quadrilogy. Publishing that book was an eye-opening experience. I knew nothing and the resources to help were scattered far and wide and often conflicting.

In walked Michael Anderle, who was realizing some success with his first books, and I followed him to a Facebook group called 20Booksto50k® where I joined him in helping to build something special with a group focused on the business of being a self-published author. Five years later, 20Books is one of the most influential groups in the world with a growing cadre of wildly successful Indie authors. We've kept it not-for-profit and that is a breath of fresh air across the entire community. There are no dues, and the only costs are if someone comes to one of our world-class confer-

123

ences, which are run at cost. We are beholden to no one, yet friends to all. I learn as much as anyone and use that knowledge, and I work with good people who are leaders in the industry to better understand how best to market my brand.

**Education**

Twenty years in the U.S. Marine Corps provided me with the greatest dialogue snippets that have the highest impact. I have received a great deal of praise for the dialogue in my books. Much of it was earned the hard way, while knee deep in some third-world cesspool, trying to realize success in a hopeless mission. I logged those events in my mind and now is a great time to let them see the light of day. As a lawyer, I had front row seats to how the law works in real life. Working as a white-collar coach for blue-collar employees made me best appreciate the hard knocks of the daily grind. I was an enlisted Marine for eight years before becoming an officer, so I saw the front lines from both sides of the game.

I was always a student of human behavior. It helped in my intelligence analyses. It also confirmed one fact that resonates through all my books. I despise bureaucrats.

As for publishing help, I wrote my nonfiction books, the Successful Indie Author series, to answer key questions about self-publishing. It saved me a great deal of time from answering the same questions over and over. I also recommend that every self-published author or those considering self-publishing join the 20Booksto50k® Facebook group. That is the safest place on the net to discuss all aspects of realizing value from your words.

For courses, I recommend Mark Dawson's Self-Publishing Formula (SPF), Ads for Authors course which is what I consider the premier course to teach and remain current on marketing. Buy it once and you have access to all new course material for life. SPF has been in business for a while now, and they grow stronger with each new year. People will get their money's worth.

### Influences

It's important to note that quality of the story is critical for any long-term career as an author. Grinding out word after word of unreadable prose will waste a great deal of time. When starting to write, I tried to model myself after a number of authors—Anne McCaffrey, Andre Norton, Robert Heinlein. My first effort wasn't as good as theirs—of course it wouldn't be—but fans liked the stories. I worked to improve and am pleased with today's level of prose. Only took me publishing more than four million words to start getting things right.

I've always been self-motivated, so there wasn't any external influence to write until my stories resonated with readers. I do my best to keep them entertained. I also liked what I myself was reading. There is a lot to be said when my books can both entertain and educate, and maybe build a foundation for what may eventually be a better society. Who knows what the catalyst will be? "1984" isn't the book we want to model ourselves after. Let's go with some different choices.

### Path to Publication and/or Becoming a Publisher

Most barriers to publication have been removed through self-publishing and knowledge. The group 20Booksto50k® is gold because there is nothing that someone hasn't run across before. There are few surprises left and none in the important stuff.

The important lessons that one needs as a self-published author are:

1.  Help readers to find you—give them a way (website, social media presence, ads pointing them to a way to check you out)
2.  Keep your readers once you find them (get their email addresses and put them onto a newsletter mailing list)
3.  Manage your readers' expectations (underpromise and overdeliver—do not promise a book a month if you can only write one a year. Tell them what you're going to do, and then do it)

Everything stems and builds from those three things. Authors can get creative as to the details, but those are the basics. Find readers willing to pay for your books/stories and then keep them on board. They will become your biggest fans.

**The Hard Lessons You've Learned**

Readers will move on if you don't deliver, and that's why above I said to underpromise and overdeliver. As for becoming and staying successful, that takes great stories. These aren't just words on a page—the words weave a three-dimensional world into the minds of your readers with characters they believe can be real doing things that they can relate to. There are twists and turns, unique ways to engage the readers' imagination. The readers will find themselves hanging on for the ride. A new reader may come for the free sample or the steep discount, but they'll stay because they are entertained. The hardest lesson is to keep writing great stories. Never let your story suffer because you're in a hurry, but don't wait until you're inspired. Sometimes the best words are hard gotten.

### Where You are Now

I am a hybrid. I have four books with an imprint of Simon & Schuster, one of the legacy publishing houses. Those four books do just fine. They are good stories set in a believable, post-apocalyptic world. I have more than one hundred other books in twenty different series that I've published myself or in collaboration with other self-published authors.

There's a new world of Indie publishers, and I'm happy to say that I'm at the forefront of that movement. I have my fingers in all the sectors of the publishing industry. My company, ubiquitously named Craig Martelle, Inc, is increasing market share through marketing campaigns to grow my organic readership as well as consistently providing new and fresh stories, well-written and engaging, keeping readers going from start to finish in one sitting. That is always my goal. A reader who is so entertained will look for my next book. I always have a next book. That's how to maintain and grow market share.

### How do you define success

Varying ways—for me, it's about leading by example. If I'm going to be the Mister Rogers of the publishing world, it's important that I show the way. That means I need to sell books, a lot of books, because my stories are written in a way that they want to read. And then the real success is in leading people to a better life—those writers who can tell a good tale and have the discipline to finish what they start (each book).

### Where do You See Things Going

Digital will dominate. There will be people who buy physical books, but industry titans will make the majority of their money off ebooks. Amazon will dominate for a while longer, but a competitor will rise, or Amazon will be broken up by regulators. Indies will flex far more quickly than traditional publishing houses or those with huge backlists. If I were forced to publish across six or eight different platforms with my books, it would be a significant challenge in time. It would impact new production as I waded through unique formatting requirements and tweaking cover files. But still. I could do over one hundred books in a week, a couple hundred books in two weeks. How long would it take a publisher with tens of thousands of titles?

And this will have to be done. Hopefully, the conversion process will be painless because of improved software. We can hope, but new businesses generally don't play well with old businesses because of proprietary software and other issues where the new player is forced to pay the old. Those are the battles that will be fought beyond the horizon of what Indies see.

I personally believe ISBNs will be replaced by something without an extreme cost or go away in their entirety. The US Government-enforced monopoly of Bowker is not sustainable without the legacy publishing houses, brick and mortar stores, and libraries forcing the issue. A new system will encompass a variety of ways to order books that can be easily adopted by anyone with a computer.

Pay to play. With the influx of new material, it will be increasingly difficult to find a new author who has a small advertising budget. This is where Indie publishers who invest time and money in building cultivated readerships will flourish. In a return to the original days of publishing, where an author had to get a traditional contract or their books wouldn't see the light of day, new authors will probably need a sponsor of some sort or an advertising budget (and an understanding of how best to market their particular book). It will be a golden age of Indie publishers. They will be able to expedite a person's career, but without a million-dollar advance. To make that kind of money, quantity will come into play. New authors won't make huge money with single titles. It'll take a number of books with inspired plotlines and engaging prose to appeal across the broadest marketplace along with a well-cultivated marketing campaign. Going viral will be an increasingly rare phenomenon.

**Contact Info**

https://craigmartelle.com or craig@craigmartelle.com

# Chapter Eight:
# Dakota Krout

**Biography**

My name is Dakota Krout. I am the youngest of four children, second youngest of eight after my father remarried while I was an early teenager. I grew up on a hobby farm in rural Wisconsin before eventually moving to a small town on the edge of Minnesota. Upon graduating high school, at seventeen I joined the United States Army. I served for 8 years, and near the end of my service I moved into the Army Reserves and started attending college. I did my first couple of years at a community college in White Bear Lake, Minnesota, a suburb of Minneapolis. From there, I moved even farther north, ending up in Grand Forks, North Dakota, where I got a degree in computer science from the University of North Dakota. While I was attending the university, I spent some time working in a bioinformatics lab, and have a published research paper from that experience.

When my focus shifted more heavily to the programming side of things, I had a two-semester-long internship at NASA Jet Propulsion Lab, and worked with some of my classmates to design a system for accountability and experience sharing. Since I had joined college late, I was in a hurry to complete my studies. Multiple times, I took over 20 credits per semester so that I could graduate "on time," but it left me with a glut of time my final year in the university. With these large chunks of time, I found that I needed to feel productive. This is when I started to write. I completed my first novel, "Dungeon Born," in roughly three months. At the same time, I was attending classes, had an internship, a job at a restaurant, and a lovely new wife: Danielle Krout. In total that year I had made roughly $11,000. I put out my first novel, never expecting that it would reach the height that it did. In only a couple of weeks, I saw a large amount of income, and, by the end of the year, that novel had made roughly $5,000.

Seeing nearly half of my yearly wage appearing, I immediately applied myself and wrote two more novels in the series. After I had those books out, my wife and I both spent a significant amount of time learning how to improve the process that I had been working on. Better cover art, taking courses, learning marketing, and purchasing tools that would help with all of the above. I started my second series, and, when that took off, I left my day job behind and pursued my dream of a full-time authorship. Within a month, my lovely wife had also left her job, and we started our company: Mountaindale Press. Since then, we have worked with multiple authors who have earned over six figures in just the few years we have been working with them. Our goals now are to help all our authors get to full-time status and produce high-quality books constantly and consistently.

**Education**

Danielle, the CEO of our company, earned her PhD as a research scientist. She now applies her skills in research to our marketing tactics, new avenues in advertising, and best-practice methods. I have a degree in computer science and find that the attention-to-detail mindedness that my degree helped me attain was extremely beneficial. My time in the Army was a wonderful motivator, teaching me that motivation is something that cannot be trusted. Only by doing the work, and doing it consistently, can the books that need to be produced get produced.

## Path to Publication and/or Becoming a Publisher

There are many things that stood in the way and continue to stand in the way of moving forward or expanding. I will touch on one, because I believe I will likely be the only person in this book to have this particular issue. In terms of owning a company, in terms of finding the success that we have in writing, we are very young. At the time of writing this, I am not yet thirty-years-old. This has made for a very interesting experience when discussing writing, publishing, and other business practices. Our research shows that the average age to begin publishing is 50 years old, and owning a company is roughly mid-thirties to early forties. The difficulty comes from not being taken seriously or by being conversationally pushed to the side as the "experienced" authors, publishers, and other business professionals speak.

Typically, there are a few things that can work in your favor when attempting to discuss business: one of those things is the fact that age tends to add feelings of respect or lend weight to the words of the person speaking. I have had many instances where someone will tell me "I do not know what I am doing," "I am doing things wrong," or "I need to change things to better suit the proven methodologies." There have been roughly a dozen people who have come up to me during conventions or conferences and told me specifically that "I should give up on writing, I am still young so I should focus on other forms of work more suited to me." It is very confusing to me. At the time of writing this, I have 18 of my own books on the market and have made millions on my intellectual property. Yet, the only thing that I can do when something like this comes up in conversation is smile, nod, and let the other person feel that they have gained a win.

Over the course of this incredibly interesting time in my life, I've realized that the best way for me to remain happy is to allow people to bulldoze the conversation if they want and then quietly forget them. I'm always able to find the successful people in the room, because nine times out of ten, they are going to be the people who are just standing there listening. A huge goal of mine is to be exactly like that. Quietly competent, quietly successful, and able to work in the way that works best for myself and the people who work with me. Don't let other people determine what is best for you. Listen, learn if you can, take the lessons that work for you, leave everything else behind. Remember that if there was a surefire way to become successful, everyone would do that. Do things your own way, then go out there and blow them away with your success.

**The Hard Lessons You've Learned**

The hardest thing I had to learn was to do things in moderation. Instead of taking on five authors, take on one. Instead of having five series running at a time, have one main series, and one that you work on when you need a break. Allowing yourself to be pulled in too many directions only slows you down. Everything costs money. Everyone has heard the colloquialism "it takes money to make money," but very few people understand what that actually means. A return on investment, ROI, is the largest hurdle to overcome for new companies.

However much you spend, you first have to make that money back, and then more to make a profit. This sounds simple, but in self-publishing, the costs can be astronomical. Depending on the quality of things that you want, putting out just an ebook can cost nearly $5,000. Artwork, editing, tools that you use. Then of course, the dreaded advertising. Social media, newsletter swaps, time investment, courses to better your understanding of writing or business aspects. All of that adds up very, very quickly. Some basic preparation can help almost anyone who is starting this process, but something to remember is that most businesses do not turn a profit in the first two to three years of operating. No matter how else you think of this, if you want to be a writer full-time, this is a small business. Treat it like one, with the same expectations and knowledge of the risks, and you'll be far better served than someone who is walking into this planning on becoming famous.

### Where You are Now

I am an independent publisher and the owner of Mountaindale Press. We are increasing our market share by focusing heavily on very specific genres instead of becoming a broad-based publisher. I have heard on multiple occasions that we are simply a big fish in a very small pond, but my goal with our company is to become the pond. If it is a small pond, but every fish pulled out is one of ours, why would I be upset that we are not expanding yet? Eventually, we will expand into other genres, but we will do it with the same methodology that we practice now. Narrow focus, deep market penetration. Just like a river grows slowly, a deep river will collect more water and expand further over time.

### Where do You See Things Going

This is a very difficult question. As with many jobs, markets, and industries, publishing has changed rapidly and radically over the last decade. I think that there will be a multitude of publishers, and they will be the ones to mainly serve the community. Since there is far less need to have a physical copy of a book, digital platforms will expand further, and book stores will become small places. My personal preference for a small bookstore would be what is essentially a coffee shop. If you want a physical copy, you can order your coffee at the counter and have a printing machine attached to the shop get you your book by the time your coffee reaches your table. No one has ever touched it except for you, and you get that same experience of opening a book for the first time.

I do think that physical books will become more of collector's items, and the digital format will continue to increase. How will that look? Who knows! There is a strong possibility that you will eventually be able to have the book played for you in your head as you walk around, with no indication that you are reading at all.

### Contact Info

We can be found at: www.MountaindalePress.com
www.Facebook.com/TheDivineDungeon
www.Amazon.com/Dakota-Krout/e/B01M2UQD

# Chapter Nine:
# R. J. Blain

**Biography**

My name is R.J. Blain, and I'm one of the many who hate biographies. It's bad enough talking about myself in the first person, but to make me talk about myself in third? *Noooo.* But here we are. I face off with my arch nemesis, the biography.

I was born, and, since I don't remember a danged thing about life before the age of five, I'm grateful it happened. So, huzzah! Apparently, I was born in the state of Maryland, but I only have the words of my parents for that one, and they were the same people who convinced me the floor was lava, so they could have been leading me on about that, too. They happen to have legal documentation supporting their claim, but I stand by my general opinions on this one: they convinced me the floor was lava.

I think the important take away from my biography is one simple fact: I was functionally illiterate until fourth grade. Sports were more interesting than books or math, thank you very much. I did just enough to trick people into thinking I was educated, but that was about it.

This ultimately became a critical foundation for my life as a writer… when you fast-forward to my early adulthood. A special thanks to my fourth-grade teacher who introduced me to Madeline L'Engle's "A Wrinkle in Time." Without that book, I'd likely still be functionally illiterate.

### Education

Ah, education. I *love* educating myself. Researching is one of my joys. If I don't understand something, I love learning about it. Some days, I go down rabbit holes. For example, once I meant to find a new type of tea for a character to drink and ended up reading about tea cultivation practices in different countries. Tea growing is pretty interesting. Unfortunately, very little of the things I read about do me any good when playing trivia games. You'd think it would, but no. But one day, there'll be a question about the different types of tea. When that day comes, *I will be ready.*

As I mentioned in the rather evil biography section, my education flopped until fourth grade. That's a lot on me, but it's also a lot on the society I lived in, where education simply wasn't all that valued. *Everybody* put emphasis on sports, and it was much easier to receive enthusiastic praise for performing well at sports than at book learning. I came late to the education party.

I never finished the education party, either. I dropped out of college during my first semester. That's a "me" thing. I do *not* handle group learning well. I prefer to learn through reading, fiddling, and self-directed education. Part of this is due to aphantasia, or my complete lack of a "mind's eye." (I do not ever have any pictures, sounds, tastes, textures, etc. in my head. Not a single one. I have no visual memory, either. That section of my brain does not activate. I compute things I read a great deal better than listening, and if I don't write it down, chances are it is gone. Forever.)

Aphantasia technically classes as a disability, as it impairs a lot of my day-to-day life. (Just please don't ask me to a play a game of memory or concentration; it's a guaranteed way of upsetting me. I lose… for good reason.)

In good news, I never stopped educating myself. And that was a key part of becoming successful later. I don't know something? Okay, no problem. Where can I learn to do this thing I don't know? I chase knowledge much like dogs chase cars. And like the car, it'll get away, but there are infinite cars for me to chase, so the chasing never stops.

And I like that a lot. That's just me.

The day I stop learning will be the day somebody is tossing dirt onto me. In better news? No final exams.

I take everything I learn and apply it to either how I write my books or how I run my business.

You don't need a degree to do well in life, but you *do* need an education. I just opted to pick up my education in an unconventional manner.

There is no easy way to success. Period. You won't get lucky without putting yourself in the position to become lucky. Never expect life to give you lemons *or* lemonade. If you want it, you need to earn it. Blood, sweat, and tears won't guarantee success, but I'm of the opinion it is better to bleed, cry, and sweat than it is to sit there and wonder why life didn't treat you kindly.

Life isn't going to treat you kindly. Everything I've accomplished, I've done so through the use of my sweat, blood, and tears. That's something to be proud of. But please, please, *please* go in aware that nothing about this is *easy*... and if you think it's easy, you're probably not working to your full potential.

This isn't supposed to be easy.

Also, relearn English. I had to as an adult. Personally, I keep a copy of the Chicago Manual of Style handy. Yeah, you'll have to look up terms to understand it if you don't have a solid foundation, but it's surprisingly useful as a learning tool if you're not clear on how English works.

I know you've heard this a million times by now, but you can't break the rules without first learning the rules. If you're breaking the rules without understanding how the rules work, all you're doing is making a mistake.

That was one bitter brew I choked down, but, once I did, my writing improved substantially.

**Influences**

Without my fourth-grade teacher, I never would have discovered I love to read. Without reading, I never would have discovered I enjoy writing. I didn't really start writing until adulthood. I played with a pen and paper younger as an escape from life. Simply put, I was severely bullied because I wasn't rich enough, I liked reading books, I liked reading big books, and I had a better vocabulary than most everyone else—from reading books.

It always comes back to that one teacher who tried something a little different to see if she could convince me books were worth reading. Everything gradually fell into place, as one day... I realized nobody was writing the kind of books I wanted to read, so I'd have to write them myself if I wanted to read them.

It really was that simple.

### Path to Publication

Once upon a time, approximately ten years before I published my first book, someone told me I couldn't, so I did.

Yeah. I operate on pure spite sometimes.

But seriously, the most critical part of becoming a successful author was the simple act of a jerk telling me I couldn't. Not that I *shouldn't*, but that I *couldn't*. This was a big deal for me. My response was to essentially narrow my eyes and reply, "Pardon?"

At the time, I lived in Canada, and that's a fighting word. Game on.

Since I couldn't write my way out of a cardboard box then, I started with the basics, relearned English, and kept giving it a go. I kept submitting to agents and publishers. One day, the radio silence turned into 25% of all queries I sent out turning into a request for a partial or full. At that point, I figured I'd gotten "good enough" to give it a whirl.

So I did.

I have been on the USA Today list twice on solo ventures; one with a collection of books and once with a single title. The collection of books was the first seven titles of my most popular series, and the single title was book five in the same series. I've also been listed twice as part of anthologies, although I don't tend to count those.

They were hard work, but it was a joint effort between 20+ people, and trust me when I say it's a *huge* difference when you have 20+

people working together versus you and yourself and your advertising budget.

I've since had a few "close but no cigar" moments with USA Today with full-priced books. One day, I will get there. One day. That's a goal I'm currently working on.

But I really started out because someone told me I couldn't. Do I remember his name? No. He was really just some jerk hoping to feel superior on the internet. The internet has a lot of those. But he lit a fire, and I still sit here some days and get pretty smug over knowing what I've accomplished because he told me I couldn't.

Everybody begins somewhere, but my determination truly began when someone tried to tell me I couldn't.

The rest is really just details. Like getting a copy of a good grammar book and picking through the Chicago Manual of Style trying to learn the bazillion rules and exceptions that make English tick. Do I get it right now?

For the most part.

Some readers don't appreciate my style, which is fine. My style is an eclectic converging of several dialects, as I've lived in many places across the United States and Canada. That will never change.

Readers do not appreciate when dialects or regionalisms they're unfamiliar with are used. Too bad. They're not *my* readers, and that's okay.

### The Hard Lessons You've Learned

The publishing industry is brutal, readers often do *not* care about your feelings, and generally, they never will. When they're buying a book, they want to be entertained. They want to walk away with something. Not every reader will like the same book. Get used to it.

That will never change.

But while readers often do not care about your feelings, there are some who will, and they will come to you.

Some will tell you their father died, and your books were what helped them get through it.

Some will tell you they're the victim of domestic violence, and they need help—or at least someone to talk to, because they don't think they'll ever be able to get help.

Some will tell you they're dying, and you've made their last days more tolerable.

Some will tell you their pets died because of a natural disaster, and they didn't have anyone else to tell.

Some will tell you they just lost a child, and you made them laugh when they never thought they could laugh again.

Books forge connections, and I'm not sure anything could have prepared me for the situations listed above… all of which have happened to me as an author.

And then there are the scammers, which I've had my unfortunate run-ins with. Staff who didn't do their jobs. Staff who used my name in an inappropriate fashion. I've had a former contractor attempt to use my name to scam people. Unfortunately, this individual was successful several times.

That sucked.

There have been people who never even worked for me making claims they had, using my name to get new clients. (Confirm references. Seriously. Yes, it takes time, but if someone says they worked for someone, send them a message to confirm it. And ask if they did that work.)

Nothing about publishing is truly easy, and there are a lot of people out there who will make it even harder. And that was a bitter brew to swallow.

### Where You are Now

Right now, I'm an independent author who makes a good living at doing what I love. While I have hit USA Today twice on my own, being able to make a living at writing was the real dream and goal—and I'm there. Staying there will be a challenge, but I've always enjoyed a good challenge.

### Where do You See Things Going

I haven't the foggiest, truth be told. Part of the brilliance of being an Indie author is the ability to change with the markets. I do expect ebook and audio book to claim more and more of the market with every year, with print books being the domain of libraries and collectors, especially as e-ink technology becomes cheaper and more readily available.

But beyond that? I'm looking forward to the adventure. I *do* hope books become even more accessible, and that modern education trends head towards encouraging reading for entertainment. Will it? Only time will tell… but a woman can dream.

### Contact Info

The primary way to reach me is at https://thesneakykittycritic.com; my blog is operated by the Furred

& Frond Management, with Zazzle the Beguiling Tyrant taking the reins most of the time. Princess the Understudy does her fair share of the work, but she's pretty shy and getting older.

I can also be reached on Facebook at https://www.facebook.com/rjblain.author/.

# Chapter Ten:
# Toni Weisskopf

It is hard to overstate the impact that our next Titan has on her company, Baen Books. To the public at large, Toni Weisskopf *is* Baen. She gives selflessly of her time for conventions, gives away mountains of books at Baen Roadshows, publishes good stories because they are good stories and for no other reason, is accessible to authors, and generally makes anyone who knows her glad that they do, and those who don't know her wish they did. Her participation in this work provides critical insight from a traditional publisher who does it right.

### Biography

In 1987, Toni Weisskopf began working for Baen Books, a leading publisher of SF and fantasy. She succeeded founder Jim Baen as Publisher in 2006. She has worked with such authors as David Weber, David Drake, Lois McMaster Bujold, Eric Flint, Wen Spencer, John Ringo, Mercedes Lackey, Larry Correia, Sharon Lee & Steve Miller, Charles E. Gannon, and many others. With Josepha Sherman she compiled and annotated the definitive volume of subversive children's folklore, *Greasy Grimy Gopher Guts*, originally published by August House.

148 | WEBB & KENNEDY

Baen is also known for its innovative e-publishing program, founded in 1999, which has expanded under Weisskopf's leadership to include not only titles published by Baen, but also titles from other publishers, all without digital rights management (DRM) encryption. Other programs begun under Weisskopf include the Jim Baen Memorial Short Story Award (co-sponsored with the National Space Society and administered by William Ledbetter) established in 2007; and the Baen Fantasy Adventure Award established in 2014.

Weisskopf has been a guest speaker at many writers workshops and science fiction conventions across the country, and is well known for her interactive, audience-participation discussion of Baen's books, covers, and artwork, on-going and ever-changing since 1991—and now gone virtual in 2020 (available at Baen's Facebook page and YouTube channel).[64]

Before taking over as publisher, Weisskopf edited several anthologies for Baen, including "Tomorrow Sucks" and "Tomorrow Bites" (science fictional treatments of vampires and werewolves respectively) with Greg Cox, and "Transhuman" with Mark L. Van Name. She also edited "Cosmic Tales" for Baen, two volumes of exuberant hard SF. Her latest anthology project was "Give Me LibertyCon," co-edited with Christopher Woods, a memorial to LibertyCon founder Tim "Uncle Timmy" Bolgeo, with proceeds donated to charity.

Weisskopf was a Guest of Honor at Cascadia Con, the NASFiC in 2005, and the toastmaster for ReConStruction, the NASFiC in 2010. In 2017 she was awarded the Kate Wilhelm Solstice Award by the Science Fiction Writers of America.

---

[64] Editor's note: Where allowed, they are continuing in person in 2021 and beyond.

Weisskopf is a graduate of Oberlin College with a degree in anthropology. She enjoys being the mother of a delightful daughter. She lives in a hundred-year-old house with two cats, too many dogs, and just the right number of polearms. Taking care of those consumes most of her spare time, but she is also interested in space science and was an active participant in the Tennessee Valley Interstellar Workshop (now the Interstellar Research Group).

### Education

Science fiction publishers have to be generalists; a solid liberal arts education doesn't hurt. And I had a good grounding in the arts and science before I ever hit college, going through New York City public schools and finishing up in public schools in Huntsville, Alabama.

At Oberlin, I studied anthropology, a useful topic for anyone interested in science fiction, which can sometimes be described as applied anthropology. But the best practical lessons I got out of my college years were from my participation in Oberlin's extensive co-op system of dining halls. There I learned that political structures were all very fine and well, but you don't eat unless someone steps up and works.

### Influences

Jim Baen, obviously. He was not a great teacher, but he was a good mentor, letting me, and many others before me, learn the editorial and publishing business.

My dad, an astrophysicist, who encouraged my interest in science and science fiction. My mom, a university librarian, one of the best people I've ever met. Her lessons make it easy for me to work with creative people. My brother, always pushing me to be a better person.

Heinlein, whose work also makes you want to be better than you are. My late husband, Hank Reinhardt, who also had that magic about him. One of his favorite sayings was, "A man's grasp should exceed his reach." In other words, keep trying to improve.

### Path to Becoming a Publisher

I started out at the entry level position in publishing, editorial assistant. Which at most houses meant "clerk," but, because Jim took the editorial mentoring seriously, also meant that I received training in editorial matters, from reviewing the slushpile, to soliciting stories for our magazine, *New Destinies*, sitting in on his editorial conferences with authors, seeing how he edited manuscripts, and so on. By the time Jim passed away in 2006, I had been executive editor for many years, leaving Jim to focus on the parts of the job he most enjoyed: acquisitions and art direction. And, of course, he loved Baen's Bar. He was a constant presence on the Bar, interacting with authors and readers, and stimulating conversation. When he passed away, I had to learn how to use what wasn't then called "social media," and that's taken me a while.

Running a business is a constant process of learning new things. We are lucky enough to operate in a dynamic economic system that welcomes technological change—which means that just because you got it right a while back, that doesn't mean you're getting it right now. Learning how to adapt to that change while remaining true to the brand and the company's ethos keeps me on my toes.

### The Hard Lessons You've Learned

When Baen started out, Jim tried a lot of things: computer books, computer games, practical computer programs, thrillers, scientific nonfiction. What he did best at was the science fiction and fantasy, and by the time I joined three years later, it was clear that we needed to refine the brand. Which is what we did. And now, 33 years later, Baen is one of the most recognizable brands in fiction publishing.

For me, the rough and tumble of the Bar was not my natural métier. I've learned to achieve a social media presence, but I prefer to find points of agreement rather than disagreement—a form of rhetoric sadly out of fashion these days. I have been accused of all sorts of things after Jim's passing, but I feel overall Baen's brand has remained the same clear brand it was before he died. I did heed John Ringo's advice and have tried to put more females on the covers than in my first year of art direction—he revealed a bias I hadn't been aware of for scantily clad men.

The worst part of publishing is letting an author know that, while you like their work, you haven't been able to grow their audience and you can't keep publishing them. The best part of publishing is calling a new author to make an offer for their book, then later signing a six figure royalty check after eveyone's hard work has paid off.

### Where do You See Things Going?

It certainly does feel like we are entering into a post-literate society. Authors speak into devices that turn their vocalizations into words on paper; people consume them as professional readers reinterpret those words. So the actual process of reading seems to be going away for the mass market. Nevertheless, the market for *story*, which is what I sell, I think will always be there, no matter how it is delivered. We've already pretty much digitized all there is out there; we're now in the process of turning all there is into audio books. Once that happens, I think we'll see a lull in the market—which means an opportunity for new voices to find an audience. I think the next big medium change will be direct neural transfer—we already have the fundamentals being researched today. I think we'll see it in our lifetimes. And that will combine the full immersive effect of the current crude video games with scripted experiences. But, as always, not all stories are equal. Someone will have to imagine them, someone will have to edit them, and someone will have to sell that to the public. And that's what publishers do.

**Contact Info**

www.baen.com

# Chapter Eleven:
# Rick Partlow

### My Story

I was born in Tampa, a child of the late 60s and a late child for my father, who was in his forties, a WW2 veteran who'd manned the nose gun of a B24 bomber in Europe. He'd been shot down over the Ploesti Oil Fields and bailed out, spending a few months in a POW camp before the Russians invaded from the east and the Bulgarians put all their Allied POWs on trains heading west to surrender them to the Americans.

I cut my teeth on Star Trek reruns and Heinlein juveniles, and, like all kids my age, went nuts over Star Wars. The first thing I tried to write was comic books, and I eventually hand-drew my own comic book adaptation of "Splinter of the Mind's Eye."

As the 70s wore on into the early 80s, my tastes shifted to post-apocalyptic end of the world stories and the first book I attempted to write was post-apoc. I hand-wrote, single-spaced, over 250 pages before I gave up on it. The first book I completed was an 80s-style "men's adventure" about mercenaries and spies and terrorists, which I finished while I was a junior in HS.

I finished a second novel about the time I graduated HS, another action adventure book that was more YA, if I was to put a category to it, also written long-hand.

I was, at that time, set on being an Air Force fighter pilot, and I spent the better part of three years trying to get into the Air Force Academy. During that process, I learned I had an astigmatism in one eye that disqualified me from being a pilot (since at the time, corrective eye surgery was in its infancy and not accepted by the military), and the whole idea lost its luster. Instead, I attended Florida Southern College on an Army ROTC scholarship and was commissioned as a second lieutenant in the Infantry.

I was still writing while in college and began what would eventually become "Duty, Honor, Planet," "Glory Boy," and "Birthright" at this time. Of the three, I concentrated on DHP and had handwritten over 275 pages by the time I graduated and headed to the Army Infantry Officers Basic Course at Ft. Benning. Then, when I went home on leave for Christmas, a maid threw the manuscript away. Which was a gut-punch at the time, but it already needed to be updated because I had made assumptions about the end of the Cold War in the original plot that turned out to be inaccurate.

After I got out of the Army, part of the post-Gulf War drawdown, I decided to get serious about my writing and, by the end of 1996, I had two complete novels: "Duty, Honor, Planet" and "Birthright." I shopped them around and managed to get signed by a literary agent. She spent two more years trying to sell them to a publishing house but had no luck. We went our separate ways, and I gave up on being a published author. I still wrote but never finished anything and wound up with a hard drive full of partial manuscripts.

And that would likely have been it if it hadn't been for the Kindle Revolution. Around 2010, a friend of mine began bugging me about putting my novels on Amazon and selling them as ebooks. I ignored him at first, because self-publishing, in my mind, was vanity publishing, which was something only losers did—people who couldn't accept they weren't good enough to be published and wound up with a garage full of self-published books they tried to sell at craft fairs or some such thing.

But he kept at it and kept telling me about people making hundreds of thousands of dollars self-publishing their work as ebooks on Amazon. So, around the end of July, 2011, I went ahead and put both my books up on Amazon. They'd been edited by my agent, but they weren't formatted correctly, the covers were homemade using images available free on the internet and I'd done the titles on Photoshop. The covers weren't even in the shape of a book cover—they were square. I priced the two books at 99 cents each and forgot about them, figuring at least this way someone besides my friends and family would read them. The only "marketing" I did was to mention on a firearms message forum called ar15.com that I'd put the books out, and they were 99 cents if anyone wanted to read them.

In four months, I'd sold 30,000 copies and given away around 10,000 more. This amounted to $10,000, which was an unexpected and welcome windfall, and enough incentive for me to try to write sequels. Unfortunately, I still had the trad-pub writer's mindset and a nasty pantsing habit that meant book two in the Duty, Honor, Planet series, "Honor Bound," clocked in at 190,000 words and took almost 14 months to write. By which time, all that momentum I'd gained from 2011 was gone. I still made $6,000 in 2012, so I went ahead and wrote book three in that series, which took a year. Making $5,000 in 2013 was heading the wrong direction, but it was still enough reason to write sequels to "Birthright." Another year got me "Northwest

Passage" and another $5,000, but the direction the income was going pretty much assured that writing would remain a hobby, a side gig.

Then, in 2016, I managed to finish book 3 of the Birthright trilogy and had to decide what I was going to write next. The Birthright trilogy was all based on an unwritten war story I'd begun back in high school called "Glory Boy." I'd used bits and pieces of that story as flashbacks in the Birthright trilogy, so I had basically the whole plot constructed. I put those pieces together in what became my first real outline and wrote "Glory Boy" in three months, releasing it in December 2016.

I made $11,000 in 2016, and most of it was in the last two weeks of December. It was a nice Christmas present, and I was happy, but I still didn't know what was about to happen.

"Glory Boy" had touched a nerve somehow, and, fortuitously, it had three sequels already written. In January, I made $28,000. I had fantasies that this would be the haul every month, that I'd arrived and was going to be pulling in six figures a year until the end of time. I didn't stop writing this time, though. In 2017, I wrote six novels and learned all I could about marketing. I started running Amazon, Facebook, and BookBub ads. I made a website, a Facebook Author Page, and a newsletter. I did everything I was supposed to do. In 2017, I made $120,000 and was psyched and ready to become a full time author.

In 2018, I worked even harder, wrote eight books, ran even more ads, marketed harder. And made half as much money.

Okay, I thought, I just had to double-down. In 2019, I wrote *nine* books and made… less. $45,000. I could see how things were going even late in 2018 and I was very discouraged. I was ready to just stop all the marketing, stop writing so many books a year, and just go back to writing as a side gig. Maybe, I thought, I was one of those flash-in-the-pan Indie authors I'd heard about who made a big splash for a year or two and then disappeared. But I made a fateful decision in 2019, one that would change my life. I was casually acquainted with Steve Beaulieu and Rhett Bruno through 20BooksTo50K and the Keystroke Medium podcast, and I knew from a friend that they had started an Indie publishing company, Aethon Books. I approached them with an idea I'd had years ago for a series of mecha military SF books called Wholesale Slaughter.

They got me a good advance from Audible Studios for a six book series, and I wrote it. It was a fun series, and, although I wasn't sure about the whole Indie publisher thing, I figured it was one series and what would it hurt? It sold very well, though not enough to salvage my horrible 2019, so when they asked me in early 2020 about writing another mil-SF series, I said okay.

I had no idea what to write, but I'd written a short story for a JR Handley anthology called "Backblast Area Clear," a short story titled "The Great Wide Open," about a young Marine Drop Trooper who was severely agoraphobic when he was outside of his suit. It was well-received so I thought I could expand it into a series. That series was Drop Trooper, and when "Contact Front" released in 2020, lightning stuck again, bigger and flashier and louder than it had with "Glory Boy." "Drop Trooper" is now going on its ninth book, Aethon bought the publishing rights for three of my other series, and I've written another best-selling series for them called Holy War.

I'm the type of guy who works harder when there's an incentive, and, in 2020, I wrote a million words, twelve separate novels, and climbed back up to $160,000 income for the year. I also came to the conclusion that I do *not* know how to market, but I do know how to write well and fast, and I should concentrate on my strengths and leave the marketing to people who know what they're doing.

As I write this, late September 2021, I've finished seven books and am working on two more. I am going to hit a mark of 50 books written by the end of the year, not counting those two I hand-wrote in high school. Financially, I've already made more through the beginning of September than I made all last year, and my wife and I are about to follow through with a longtime dream of moving to the mountains.

And the cherry on top was that Drop Trooper 4, "Direct Fire," was a finalist for the Dragon Awards in 2021. I didn't win, but I attended the awards dinner and ceremony and got to meet and talk to SM Stirling, Steve Jackson, and Timothy freaking Zahn. I gave Steve Jackson and Timothy Zahn signed copies of "Contact Front." God knows if either of them will ever read the book, but it felt incredible.

Will it last this time? Is this the dream or just another hill to climb, with valleys ahead? Who knows?

But I plan on enjoying the journey.

# Chapter Twelve:
# Tim C. Taylor

It is hard to overstate the generosity of spirit in Tim Taylor's honest sharing of best advice for how to succeed in today's writing environment. The sheer magnitude of his entry tells you all you need to know about not only how much he wants to help others, but also why he is included here. There is more to being a Titan than statistics.

## Biography

I was not one of those authors who always knew they had to write. I didn't pen my first stories until my early thirties. On the other hand, I've always created.

At school I used to write RPG scenarios, mostly for Traveller and The Fantasy Trip. I also wrote music and software. The Space Invaders game I coded in Z80 assembler for the family TRS-80 microcomputer remains one of my proudest achievements. I started a career writing software, but I found time to write and record music and do some game design.

As my career progressed, I cut less code and spent more time writing internal training materials and quality procedures, trying my best to make them interesting reads that fit the needs of specific groups of readers. In other words, nonfiction carefully tuned for a target audience.

The desire to write prose fiction hadn't occurred to me, and yet all these endeavors were aspects of the same creative self. All of them fed into and strengthened each other. I believe that if you apply passion and commitment to each facet of your life, the rewards are often transferable. It sounds hokey, but all those things I did before I began writing fiction were preparing me to do just that.

Author Ian Watson once told me that everything he read and did was research. He just didn't know which bits would make it into his next book. Now I think I understand what he meant.

After two decades, the company I'd worked for let me go, and I decided to take a sabbatical to get some space before deciding my next career move. I'd been writing as a hobby for nine years, with stories placed in a few magazines and some novels work-shopped but not published. I had a literary agent and a few sniffs of interest by publishers.

Solaris is one of the main small publishers of science fiction and fantasy in the UK, where I live. They had requested a manuscript of mine and sat on it for a year before passing but inviting me to pitch my next novel to them because they said they were interested in me as a writer.

That's about as good a rejection as you get. So the initial plan after I was made redundant was to pitch a new novel to Solaris. Sign a contract. Write it. And then go get a proper job.

None of this was a business proposition. Solaris wasn't going to pay big bucks, and even if sales were good, the royalties wouldn't start flowing until after I was back in a conventional career.

This was early 2011. I'm writing these words over a decade later. I'm still on sabbatical and I never did make contact with Solaris. It's the same explanation for both. 2011 was when the Kindle broke big and the world of science fiction publishing (at least in the English language) changed completely. I seized the opportunity.

Since then I've written twenty-one novels and plenty of short stories, published around fifty books by other authors, worked as ebook designer or project manager for another hundred or so. According to Amazon, I've had the #1 bestselling title in space opera, military science fiction, alternate history, and time travel romance. I've also published books that bombed totally. In my best year of publishing, I earned a six-figure income from book sales. I made a loss in my worst.

I never said it was easy.

After a decade plus of doing this, I regard myself as a seasoned "mid-list" Indie author with a smoldering backlist that can spring back to life when I rake the coals just right. By "Indie" I mean a mix of self-published works and books published by new and innovative digital small publishers. (By "digital publisher," I mean ebooks, streaming audio books, and print-on-demand paperbacks).

My ambition is to sell a million copies of my books. True, that's just a number, but it's one that means something to most people, me included. There's a long way to go. I'm only about a third of the way there, but I know quite a few Indie science fiction authors who have hit that million mark, and they pull me onward. Just as they're both inspiration and a source of practical advice to me, I hope some readers will be energized by the words in this book to go forth and win.

## Influences

Dr. Who and Star Wars. Car Wars, Illuminati, GURPS, and other games from Steve Jackson. KISS, Black Sabbath, and Ronnie James Dio. 2000AD comic, David Brin, and Anne McCaffrey. Space Invaders and Jumbo Jet Lander for the Commodore PET. Bass Brewing Co. and the Burton-on-Trent brewing industry.

These are a few key examples of the inspirations that fired up my imagination and set me off wanting to create things myself. I've never stopped.

That's an eclectic mix, but for me the passion to make things that I can look upon and see that they are good comes from the same internal fire. These days, I express that through writing fiction, but all these creative influences are fuel for that creative fire. In more recent years, I've been fortunate enough to have been stoked by inspirational creators as well as the inspirations they create.

And if it seems a bit of a stretch to equate Bass beer with writing novels, think again. In my late teens I developed a love of good beer, which led me to learn about brewing heritage and create my own recipes. For about five years I was all about mash tuns, yeast strains, and diastatic enzymes. It allowed me to appreciate that beer could be much more than just a brown fizzy liquid you chugged out of a tin.

Another five years down the line, and, after thoroughly enjoying "The Uplift War" by David Brin, I had the brainwave of repeating the experience by writing my own science fiction, just to deepen my appreciation. The idea of being a professional writer didn't even cross my mind for many years.

Spending time with people and things you feel passionate about is good for the soul, and you need soul to write good books.

### The Hard Lessons You've Learned

1.   Luck is not a factor.

Here's a classic oxymoron for you: successful people make their own luck.

On the face of it, it's an absurd assertion. Luck by its nature is random. Pure chance. You can't make it.

In the context of successful writers (irrespective of how they choose to define success), the degree to which their accomplishments are down to blind luck is a topic that only comes up occasionally, probably because the debate can rapidly get heated. However, in my experience, people aspiring to a career as a professional writer should regard this as one of the most fundamental questions they should be asking.

I've yet to encounter an author who considered themselves to be successful and says that luck was not a factor in their success. On the other hand, many of them will also say that they made their own luck.

For people who are underwhelmed by the level of their own success, it is more common to assert that "making it" as an author is almost entirely down to good fortune (possibly combined with the "luck" of knowing the right people). The internet is awash with people who hold such opinions. You'll find plenty of them speaking at certain literary conventions and writers' communities too.

It's easy to dismiss both viewpoints as being influenced by a form of cognitive dissonance, which is where you distort your view of the universe in order to feel better about yourself.

The argument goes that the author who makes it will dismiss all the evidence of their lucky breaks and exaggerate the effectiveness of their actions in order to persuade themselves that their accomplishments are earned. The less successful author will look for opportunities to convince themselves that the success of other authors is down to pure luck (and possibly unfair advantages too). If the triumphs of other authors are unearned, then their own lack of perceived success is not their responsibility.

Here's the kicker, though. Plenty of those who say they made their own luck can point to what they did to make it. What's more, many were saying what they were doing to make their own luck *before* they were successful. This is clearly not a question of people being wise after the event to justify their good fortune to themselves.

That's not all. When authors talk about how they made their own luck, the same suggestions keep reappearing. Perseverance ranks number one.

It seems sensible to me to pay attention to some of those things people are saying. Which, after all, is what we hope you will take away from the accounts in this book.

Take "Marine Cadet," which was my breakout novel.

I was lucky.

However, I think that the biggest factors in my luck were the cover art, title, book description, price, and pre-order strategy. None of those were accidents. All were carefully planned.

What would happen if I rewound the clock to December 2014 and re-rolled the dice, setting up the book and the launch strategy exactly the same as before? Would it take off so well next time?

Maybe not. I would still have to roll a dammed good score and there are never guarantees with the dice.

But I believe I had so successfully stacked the odds in my favor that, yes, more likely than not it would still have reached the top few titles of the military SF bestseller list and sell tens of thousands in a few months.

That's making your own luck. The competition is fiercer now than in 2014, but the principle is the same.

Here's how I see this working.

Imagine you're playing a game called "How to succeed in publishing." It's actually a cool game with fun graphics and a much catchier name because it's been designed by Steve Jackson. (If I'm going to play make believe in my head, you better believe it'll be fun, so sue me.)

You've paid your dues learning your craft and are now ready for your debut big-time publication. For the book to be a big success that moves you to the next level, let's say you need to roll 34 or more on six six-sided dice (6d6 for the initiated). That's a likelihood of 0.06%. Don't get too hung up on that precise number, although it feels about right for real life.

At those odds, if you write a good novel every year for twenty years, you're still almost certainly never going to make it. Some people will, and you'll hear about them, but it won't be you.

(By the way, I'm going to assume here that your book is good enough for people to enjoy.)

Here's how you make your own luck.

You get the right cover. Not one that looks good; one that will *sell. +2 to the die roll.*

Prior to the launch, you run a podcast for a year or more involving authors in your field. You get some of your podcast guests to shout out about your debut release. *+1 to die roll.*

Instead of self-publishing, you sell the book to one of the top Indie presses in your sub-genre. *Roll 8 dice and pick the best 6.*

Newsletter, advertising, paying a pro to write the book description, co-writing with a highly successful author first to get your name out, etc. etc. There are many other things you can do to affect the die roll. The effectiveness of each will change over time and depend on what you've written, but you get the idea. Look at ways to make your own luck, consider which ones you have the time and inclination to do, and do them well because the way to win at dice is simple. Cheat. Or, at least, stack the odds in your favor with die roll modifiers.

Oh, and one more thing. And it's a big one.

One of the best ways to load the dice in your favor is to get really good at writing discipline. I'm talking about speed of typing, accuracy of dictation, getting up to write early every morning, avoiding distractions, writing in sprints, finding the optimal way for you to balance the tasks of writing the story and finessing the prose, and discovering the tricks that get you into an efficient flow state where the words come out faster than you can type. That kind of thing.

Get inspired by other writers. Your personal circumstances might mean you can't emulate them in the details or don't want to, but you can still be inspired by them to be a better you.

Like I said, it's not easy. I've been writing and publishing full time for over a decade now and I still find it a hard discipline to get up early and consistently when I don't have a workplace to clock into or a boss to yell at me if I'm late. And that's the most basic work discipline of them all.

Why is this important?

Firstly, if you write faster and more efficiently, you're probably writing *better*. This is counter-intuitive and took me years to understand and then prove to myself. The internet is full of bigots who sneer that if you write four or more novels a year, you can't possibly be writing good ones. Right?

Wrong.

Professional authors who write fast are able to do so because they have learned to flow with story. Not everyone can do this.

The second reason why developing your writing discipline can help you comes back to the making your own luck question.

It's simple. If you write five books a year, you get to roll the dice five times as often as the once-per-year author. Congratulations, you've just increased your luck five-fold.

Not everyone can write five novels per year, but don't despair because less prolific authors succeed all the time. Even if you can shift from delivering one novel every three years, to once per year, you are tripling the number of rolls.

Cheat the clique. What does that mean?

I've been in many writers' groups over the past twenty years. Still am. Online communities, bulletin boards, Facebook groups, physical writers workshops, even an old work-shopping group where you annotated the manuscripts of your fellow writers and then put the updated copies into the parcel and sent by snail mail to the next writer.

Writing is hard and there's a lot to learn. Joining the right writer communities can help significantly. However, I've learned two things about them. They usually tend toward being cliquey, and they usually tend toward a single viewpoint of the writing and publishing world (and more besides).

People who don't fit in by thinking the right way are made to feel unwelcome and are eventually driven away. The notion that there is only one correct viewpoint becomes self-reinforcing, because alternates are suppressed. Without dissenting or critical voices, the ortho-doxy goes unchallenged, no matter how risible it appears to people on the outside.

None of that is going to change, because it's human nature. In my experience, the best way to navigate these tendencies is to acknowledge that this is going to happen and get involved in multiple groups so that you can experience a variety of viewpoints, while keeping a core group where you feel comfortable and supported.

Yes, this could mean being involved with a community where you don't feel at ease with what some other members are saying, but you are nonetheless benefiting from the broadening of your percep-tion. In fact, it probably is good to be challenged.

In the past fifteen years, I've been a member of or involved in the community around the British Science Fiction Association (BSFA), British Fantasy Society (BFS) ,and Science Fiction & Fanta-sy Writers of America (SFWA). Three different organizations, each with a long and illustrious history. In terms of their dominant per-spectives on writing mindset, what they value in stories and what they don't, and political and social outlook in general, all three are essentially identical. You won't experience the benefit of a diverse range of viewpoints by being involved with all three. If these were the extent of your writing community, I would strongly advise to broaden your search.

You can learn a hell of a lot from people who don't look and talk and think like you. I know I did.

One example of a group that carried a different perspective from those three was Kindle-boards Writers Café. This was one of the groups I benefitted from most a decade ago. I learned a lot. We learned a lot from each other because none of us was more than a few months ahead of the others. A lot of key figures were there. I used to chat with Hugh Howey on occasion as his career was really taking off. I remember Tom Edwards turning up one day with a post announcing he was an artist and would anyone be interested in him doing their cover? I'm pretty sure Tom's provided the cover for more science fiction bestsellers than any other artist of the past decade. Exciting times!

It got cliquey, though. It became intolerant of diverse viewpoints. Some of the most successful authors there were harassed until they said, "You know what, I don't need to be here." Then they cleared off.

It's still going (as KBoards—Amazon asked them not to use the word Kindle in the name) and still has a lot of useful things to say. But it's not what it once was.

You can help to keep these groups healthy by avoiding being a dick, and one of the key ways to avoid dickishness is to avoid telling people they are wrong because they don't share your viewpoint. Maybe you're convinced you're right and they're wrong. Fine. Argue your case, if you like. But do so respectfully because you know what? They might *also* be correct. In publishing, there's always more than one route up the mountain.

Even if you can't value a challenging opinion, by making the community unpleasant for people who don't think like you, your dickishness is pushing your group down the path to being narrow-minded and ultimately ignorant. It's not just about being "nice." A community that's ignorant is not going to help you much.

By the way, I'm not suggesting that it is inappropriate to counter mistruths, so long as you default to doing so respectfully. For example, I've encountered many people who've stated that Kindle books read in Kindle Unlimited pay authors less than books that are purchased. Nope. Or that you can only succeed in self-publishing by rapid releasing a book every 2-3 months. Also no. Or that Amazon boosts your ranking if you're Kindle Exclusive, that Amazon boosts your book after fifty reviews. etc. etc.

2.  Weight advice.

No, I'm not talking about the correlation between sitting at my writing desk all day and my waist measurement. All advice is not created equal, and this is definitely true in the world of publishing. So treat it as such. Weight the advice.

We live in a culture that often insists that all viewpoints are equally valid, and if you value one group of people over another then you are a very bad person and need to be punished.

It's so pervasive, and there are so many people on constant alert to scold us for our failings, that it's easy to fall in the trap of not paying enough attention to *who* is giving us advice.

It's nonsense of course.

If my son is diagnosed with cancer, and I want to find the best treatment options, whose viewpoint do you think I will weight higher: the oncologist at the hospital, or the soiled woman sprawled behind the dumpster drinking from a plastic gallon container of cheap cider?

That's not to say the cider-swilling drunk is unworthy of my time and respect, but on the topic of how to cure my sick son, I'm going to weight her advice far lower than the trained, experienced, and (hopefully) sober oncologist.

The same with advice on how to succeed at publishing. Would you give equal weighting to advice from someone who writes in a similar genre to you and sells hundreds of thousands of books every year, or to the author who has been writing for many years but has sold a few hundred books and constantly complains about how unfair publishing is and how the authors who achieve success don't deserve it?

There are considerably more of the latter than the former, and they are allowed to dominate many writing communities.

Of course, just because someone's sold a ton of books doesn't mean that they are any good at giving advice or that what worked for them will work for *you*. And that new kid on the block working up to their first book launch could have exactly the advice you need precisely because they see the situation through fresh eyes. Nonetheless, people with more experience and more success generally give better advice. Weight it accordingly, but don't ignore other voices entirely.

And if there aren't such people in your current circle of friends, make an effort to expand your group.

I suggested earlier that groups tend to become insular and drive out diversity of viewpoints, so it's good to listen to or join groups that are not all the same. This goes far beyond a question of political viewpoint, although that's important too.

3.    Genre is another key thing to consider.

A lot of Indie publishing innovation came first from romance. Has done so right from the beginning, because romance is where the big money and sharpest minds are. The first full-time Indie author I knew personally was making bank in science fiction romance around 2003, back at a time when her ebooks were PDFs on CD, and she made her living self-publishing paperbacks.

When I hear romance authors talking about websites to use in a sale promotion, I switch off. Site promotions are very genre specific, and this is not information that will help me. But when authors in other genres talk about marketing strategies, I listen closely. I might learn something that the core science fiction authors aren't talking about.

Take my breakout novel, *Marine Cadet,* as an example. One of the reasons for its success is that I had the book listed on Amazon for four weeks as a pre-order when hardly anyone else was doing this in science fiction. Consequently, if a reader checked out science fiction books at the Kindle Store and sorted on publication date, I was on the first page for over a month. It was the kind of exposure that literally money couldn't buy.

But the romance people… they had been all over pre-orders right from the start, discussing results from various strategies they had tried. And the reason I was ahead of the curve for science fiction authors was because I made the effort to hang out with plenty of authors outside of science fiction.

Besides, I like to listen to people who are different from me and learn how they think. It's a big part of why I write science fiction rather than other genres.

**Where do You See Things Going**

Competition and branding are the keys.

With digital publishing finally making its long-predicted breakout around 2011 (ebooks, but also streaming audio and print-on-demand paperbacks) there was no longer a reason for titles to go out of print. Every year, new titles would have to compete for consumer attention against an ever-increasing list of titles still available from previous years. And with barriers to publishing collapsing, the number of titles published each year increased enormously.

With the increasing importance of online sales platforms relative to traditional bookstores, the ability of the major publishers to influence which books are sold has diminished. (Amazon.com sells more paperbacks in the US than any other retailer and has dominated ebook sales ever since that medium took off.)

Which is all very interesting (to me, hopefully to you too), but that's the past. We want to be talking about the future, right?

One of the key solutions to these problems is to brand. Consumers can cut through the noise of so many books by choosing books from brands they recognize and trust.

Smart Indie publishers have been trying hard to establish branding for the past decade. In the relative backwater of science fiction, successful Indie small publishers have now achieved this. The Chris Kennedy Publishing imprints, Aethon Books, and Galaxy's Edge Press are brands that readers follow because they promise something tangible. Readers want to know what they're getting, and they demand quality. These brands deliver.

Indie romance established bigger brands and did so earlier, of course. It's usually the case that if you want to see where Anglo-American publishing is headed in five years, just look at where Indie romance is now and extrapolate to the rest of publishing.

Traditional trade publishers have branded in the past, but in recent decades have done so sporadically and mostly in the romance and academic areas. Baen Books is about the most non-traditional of traditional publishers, being possibly the first publisher in the world to make a success of ebooks. They have always branded. From the logo, the cover art style, to the focus and style of the prose inside, readers know what they're getting and keep coming back for more. This is where the imprints of other major publishers are headed, but it will take another decade or more for them to catch up with the likes of Baen.

I just used the term "trade publishers." This is how traditional publishers refer to themselves because they sell to the "trade," meaning bookstore chains such as Barnes & Noble. Their primary business is not selling to readers; it is selling to book retailers. A lot of readers are surprised by the notion that book publishers don't sell to them (or, at least, direct sales to readers are a secondary consideration at best). However, it is the explanation for why over the coming decades trade publishing will resist the shift to becoming consumer-oriented businesses. They will remain curiously uninterested in satisfying the expectations of large swathes of potential readers.

Nonetheless, one of the biggest themes over the next two decades will be traditional publishers learning how to sell to readers. They will be dragged by their corporate overlords, kicking and screaming that this is the *wrong way to sell books*. But they will get there in the end. Or die.

So far, they're taking baby steps. The week before I wrote these words, Penguin Random House announced that several of its major imprints would switch to using the classic Penguin logo on all their paperbacks.

On the other hand, I just checked the websites for all the major science fiction imprints. Other than some general platitudes about publishing new talent and some standard corporate statements about diversity and inclusion, there's absolutely no attempt to say what distinguishes them from every other science fiction publisher. They don't stand for anything. None of them. The idea doesn't even occur to them. Until they do, their brands will remain weak.

Over the next few decades, a major source of fireworks for western trade publishers will be their increasing intolerance and narrow focus. It will be an opportunity for Indies too.

People who work in trade publishing are overwhelmingly educated to degree level or beyond, live in a big city (probably London or New York), never had a career outside of publishing, are politically left wing (especially what they would describe as "progressive" or Marxist), are female, and frequently use social media to scold people who don't follow their political agenda.

None of those characteristics are unwelcome in publishing. Well, maybe that last one. The real problem is that trade publishing rarely includes people from outside that list. It's becoming more intolerant of people from other groups at the same time as it draws from an ever-narrowing range of people (although, to be fair, ethnicity is slowly becoming more diverse). The quality of writing dwindles as the pool of talent becomes stagnant and shrinking.

The authors of tomorrow who might have been published by traditional publishing ten years ago won't get published today. Those who sneaked through in a more tolerant era will be canceled because they don't "share our values."

In 2016, one of the new stars of Harper Voyager, Nick Cole, was dumped with extreme prejudice because he gave a character a backstory that "deeply offended" his editor. Cole returned to self-publishing and established himself as a million-selling success. This signaled the end of an early phase of the "ebook revolution" that ironically Harper Voyager had pioneered. It had seemed for a while that trade publishing would use the new self-publishing, with its sales visibility in Amazon bestseller ranks, as a feeder league from which they would acquire new talent. That's much less common now.

Amazon's own publishing imprints still do this, as do several audio book publishers, such as Podium. However, Nick Cole was one of the more prominent early examples of how trade publishing has become so exclusionary that it is culturally unable to work with many successful Indie authors. This trend will intensify.

In 2020, staff working at Hachette UK refused to work on a forthcoming book from left-wing activist author JK Rowling because of comments she had made that took a feminist stance on trans issues they disagreed with. The attempt to cancel the most successful novelist in the world was widely supported across the western traditional publishing industry, many of its workers joining in with the toxic abuse heaped upon the author. That same year, new books from several less lucrative authors were cancelled before publication after complaints by people who had largely not even bothered to read advanced copies before condemning the authors.

By 2025, I extrapolate that "problematic" books published in previous years will start to be retroactively canceled by their own publishers because they no longer "share the values" of the editorial staff. Authors will be dropped unless they actively endorse the cultural agenda of their publishers.

By 2030, there will have been attempts by the multimedia conglomerates that own trade publishing to establish new imprints that can encompass the "toxic" points of view that have been driven out elsewhere. (Most likely this will be attempted first at News Corp, which owns HarperCollins, and whose owners also run Fox News.) These will largely fail because staff who could accommodate such diverse viewpoints will have been so thoroughly driven out of trade publishing.

By this point, there will appear to be a permanent divide between traditional trade publishing and Indie publishing, although Indie authors with a good fit with trade publishing's political and cultural viewpoints will still move between the two.

But by 2035, cancel culture will come for those Indie authors and Indie publishers who are accused of not sharing the political agenda of trade publishing. Amazon will de-list huge numbers of offending titles and cancel thousands of publisher accounts. They may find it easier and cheaper to simply shut down their Amazon KDP operation altogether. Attempts to establish rival sales platforms will be de-platformed after lobbying of web hosting services and payment platforms.

To be honest, that final speculation might never happen. Or it could come sooner. The crucial factor will be whether a few key individuals at Amazon are willing to commit to widescale censorship.

If Amazon ever does pull the plug on its Indie publishing business, or censors it to death, then there will remain a flourishing Indie movement right up until the final moments when the lights go out. Ironically, the same pressures that may push Amazon to kill its KDP operations are what will make it flourish until its final days. Namely, the increasing insularity of trade publishing and its willingness to vilify its own potential customers.

Traditional publishing has always had a fundamental problem. Editors, agents, marketeers (and critics too) don't share the same cultural background and reading taste as the majority of readers. Their job is to source and refine products that will appeal to people who are not like them.

It's a problem that will never go away, but it has become more acute as trade publishing becomes increasingly detached from large sections of society.

I saw that with the Brexit referendum vote in 2016. I personally know many people in trade publishing or in closely aligned fan groups. None of them could understand how our country had voted to leave the European Union. Many of them posted social media comments along the lines of, "I can't understand it. I mean, I don't know a single person who voted to leave the European Union."

Cross the Atlantic in 2016 and ditto, Donald Trump.

*I don't know a single person who voted that way…*

That admission is why, now that the barriers to establishing a publishing business have fallen, small publishers and Indie self-publishers will continue to thrive for as long as Amazon allows them to. They will succeed because they are more willing to stand for something, their authors come from a wider pool of potential talent, and because they are prepared to write to a more diverse range of readers, including those the trade publishers despise.

### Subscription is coming…

Apple Music, Disney+, Spotify, Amazon Music, Kindle Unlimited, Netflix, Xbox Game Pass, and Audible Premium Plus. To young consumers today, the very concept of a record collection or even a DVD collection is bewildering because the norm is to consume your entertainment media (and more besides) through a monthly subscription. And for TV media, the coolest shows are on Netflix and Disney+.

Here in the UK, even though BBC TV is free (well, not really, but that's another topic…) viewers under 30 spend more time watching Netflix, which costs £120 per year in its standard package.

The subscription business model is coming to books too, and that will be a huge deal over the next couple of decades.

It has already begun with ebook services such as Kindle Unlimited, Overdrive (for libraries), Pearson+ (educational ebooks), and Kobo Plus.

I predict that book subscription from the major trade publishers will take several missteps before hitting the winning formula and leading to another transformation in publishing.

The most likely stumbling block will be getting enough critical mass of titles to encourage people to spend their $12 per month or whatever on the subscription. HarperCollins, for example, wouldn't cut it on their own. But Penguin Random House + Hachette + HarperCollins = millions of subscribers.

The obvious losers in this shift will be physical bookstores. There used to be record stores in every town in the country. Not anymore. The same will happen to generalist bookstores.

There will be strong resistance from the trade publishing industry against signing the death warrant of their traditional business partners, but the numbers are already in that point to this being inevitable.

Back in the 2020 pandemic lockdowns, publisher sales through UK and US physical bookstores collapsed. Publisher book sales revenue through all channels was down but not profits. Profits shot up. It turns out that if you shift book sales from physical retail stores to online (and this is true for printed as well as ebooks), your profit margins will rise, and people will *still be able to find the books.*

One after the other, all the big trade publishers found this to be the case and made their numbers public for all to see.

Who knew?

Well... actually thousands of Indie authors and small presses have realized this for years but now the evidence is there on tradpub's bottom line. And despite traditional publishing being about the most reactionary business on the planet, the "Big Four" (assuming Penguin Random House's purchase of Simon & Schuster goes through) are owned by media conglomerates Bertelsmann, Hachette, Holzbrinck, and News Corp. And the main boards of those conglomerates won't allow forever what amounts for special pleading that books are somehow different from other forms of media and entertainment because... reasons.

### The International Perspective...

In my publishing home turf of science fiction and fantasy, the digital publishing revolution has largely involved authors and publishers from America, Canada, and the UK. Also, Ireland, Australia, Israel, and New Zealand. Not all, certainly. But a large majority.

Those countries are home to less than a third of the world's English-speaking population. Most of the other English speakers live in countries with much lower average incomes.

You see where I'm headed with this...?

To be fair, proportionately more people in those countries lack the education and middle-class luxury of spare time to develop a passion for writing that could lead to a career. But the relative affluence of the West is decreasing all the time.

India's the best example but there are others too. Pakistan and Nigeria are not far behind. How about the Philippines? Those four countries have over half a billion English speakers between them.

They're potential markets. But to many readers of this book, I suspect they are more important still as potential producers of novels. That means a bigger pool of talent, more varied viewpoints, and ultimately a more vibrant set of books for me to read.

Having seen something similar develop twenty years ago in the software industry, I can see one way this will develop is in contract development of novels.

Take, as a thought experiment, the Battlestar Galactica TV series that ran from 2004-2009. Imagine instead that it had been produced between 2024-2029. In anticipation of success, the producers might contract a series of tie-in novels to be launched simultaneously with the show. The TV scriptwriters might write the series bible, outline some of the novel storylines, and provide series editing for the books. There's nothing new about any of this, except that in the near future the hard work of writing the novels might be done under contract in India.

And if the TV show is a ratings success, the producers can simply triple the order for tie-in novels the following season.

None of this is restricted to tie-in books. Nor do the owners of the intellectual property have to be western.

Here's another angle. Imagine a series of fantasy novels that are hugely successful in China. The authors write them in Mandarin. Today there might be translated editions where the rights are bought by a US publisher who then organizes and pays for translations. But what if a Chinese publisher produced their own in-house translations into English and distributed via Amazon KDP?

Alternatively, imagine the Chinese publisher will subcontract translation of its books to a Nigerian business.

How long to translate a book? A month?

The average monthly income in Nigeria is currently around $160 USD. I imagine this would be a highly paid task, but even so, if high quality translations cost a few hundred dollars per book, the Chinese publisher wouldn't have to sell many copies in the West to make a profit.

Will English translations of foreign language genre fiction really win followers among US readers?

It's already happened with LitRPG, a sub-genre of fantasy and science fiction popular throughout the West that originated in its current form in Russia around 2012, (pertinent to this discussion, the LitRPG movement in Russia was sparked by Russian translations of Japanese light novels that would today be labelled LitRPG). Many authors from western countries have tried to jump onto the LitRPG bandwagon, but it's still the case that many of the most successful series are written in Russian, and their US ebook and print editions are not published by US publishers (audio books generally *are* licensed to North American independent publishers such as Podium).

Then there are authors or publishers working in English and doing exactly the same as their Indie peers in western countries. They're just doing it from a different part of the world.

A friend of mine, Yudhanjaya Wijeratne is Sri Lankan. His first books were published by HarperCollins India and self-published in other territories via Amazon KDP. Building on this success, a subsequent novel was published through small US publisher Aethon Books, hitting the top of the audio book charts with Nathan Fillion as narrator.

He hasn't needed to leave Sri Lanka to achieve this. All you require is an internet connection and to be able to write in English, and you can live anywhere in the world. And talent. You still need that, of course.

Some authors from non-western countries will be reading these words now. Hi, there! I wish you power to your words and good luck in your endeavors.

For those of you who live in USA/ CA/ Ireland/ UK/ NZ/ Oz, English language books from outside those countries are today overwhelmingly translated from foreign language under license from the original publisher.

That is going to change.

**Contact Info**

Find Tim C. Taylor at www.humanlegion.com

# Chapter Thirteen:
# Lydia Sherrer

Everyone who knows Lydia Sherrer uses the same phrase to describe her: "Lydia is a force of nature." Pick your natural event and it fits: rainbow, tornado, hurricane, earthquake, or a field of flowers blooming in an Alpine meadow. What this abstract phrase attempts to describe is Lydia's relentless drive, both in business and in generosity of spirit. She truly wants other writers to succeed, to know the joy she has found in writing books. If you need *prima facie* evidence, her entry here is over 9,000 words. That's not merely sharing, that's pouring out your heart to help others. That's what Titans do.

**Biography**

My mom was reading me The Hobbit by the time I was five and had read me the entire Lord of the Rings trilogy by the time I was eight. I grew up reading so voraciously that my parents had to take my books away from me and lock them up so I would do school, eat, and sleep. When the 5th Harry Potter book came out, I took it and hid in our barn loft on our farm so my mom couldn't find me, then read the entire thing in one afternoon (after which I had a massive cry and book hangover. If you've read Harry Potter, you know why).

Needless to say, I grew up loving fiction and storytelling, so it was natural for a creative like me that I would start making up stories of my own and writing them down. I never even considered the idea of publishing, though, until I'd written about 30,000 words of a book for my little sister during my college years. I stopped one day and thought about how many hours I'd spent writing, and decided it would be a darn shame if she were the only person who ever benefited from all that hard work. I realized for the first time that what I longed for was to create something that made other people feel as amazing as I did when reading my favorite stories.

That was the first time I ever thought about the idea of publishing. But, for the next four years, I went through college expecting to be a career translator (I double majored in Chinese and Arabic language). Yet, life had its way with my plans, and, after college, I ended up at home taking care of my grandparents instead of pursuing my career. Though disappointing at the time, it was a blessing in disguise. I have an entrepreneurial spirit and a strong creative drive, so it took those post-college, what-the-heck-do-I-do-with-my-life years for me to figure out I'd never be happy working for someone else. Once I realized that, I started searching for something I could make into an independent career.

I tried selling Mary Kay first (yeah, I know, it was as insane as it sounds), then tried starting an art business. I soon discovered, though, that I loved writing much more than I loved drawing. Around that time in 2012, a good friend, who had recently started self-publishing his own stories, handed me a copy of Writers Market. Reading that turned on the light switch in my brain, and I finally started making plans for how I could one day write for a living.

Through the next four years, I wrote and rewrote the first three-fourths of my first novel—which I am embarrassed to admit started out as terrible Twilight fan-fiction. It will never see the light of day. But it got me started writing, so I am thankful. I wrote a few short stories, and even got one published in a magazine. All this time, I was exploring the idea of Indie publishing versus traditional publishing and trying to make a business plan for how to achieve a full-time income as a writer. After doing a lot of research on the trad market, I concluded that Indie publishing was a vastly easier, quicker, and more sure route for a go-getter like me. I finally settled on a marketable storyline, and in December of 2014, I started writing the first book in my now bestselling urban fantasy Love, Lies, and Hocus Pocus universe.

During this time, I was working a corporate 9-5 to pay bills and spending hours upon hours reading up on self-publishing, subscribing to newsletters, taking free courses, and finding author groups online (mostly Facebook) to ask questions of. I made a business plan and presented it to my husband, and we made a budget for living off one income. It wasn't fun, but we were both used to being frugal, so we made it work. In October of 2015, I quit my day job and started working full-time to publish my first books. In the beginning of 2016, I kickstarted and published my first two Love, Lies, and Hocus Pocus novels. The following year, I did the same for the next two novels in the series. After that, I was making enough money from book sales that I could fund subsequent books on profits instead of needing to crowdfund them. For me personally, that was a huge achievement, and it proved to me that what I was doing was a viable career path.

Most of my sales in the first two years came from physical books. We did as many author events as we possibly could, following my "see and be seen" strategy—the principle that to make it in the publishing industry (or any industry), it was vital to network, meeting both professionals in our field as well as customers (readers) face-to-face. My goal has always been to find people successfully doing what I want to do, find out how they did it, then adapt that to my own situation. I'm an extrovert and a people person, so I did well with face-to-face sales and that helped my publishing grow to the point that I could start taking paid marketing courses to up my game.

In 2018, I knew the next step was to figure out the whole online marketing thing, because I could passively sell way more ebooks online than I could ever sell physical books in person. I took several courses over the next two years. Most useful were Mark Dawson's Ads for Authors course, and Steve Pieper's AMMO course. I applied myself to studying and implementing an online marketing strategy that would be diverse and independent enough to weather the changing tides of online marketing and Indie publishing. This involved setting up my own storefront website, using Facebook ads to drive traffic to it, collecting email addresses for my own newsletter, setting up a marketing presence on multiple platforms—we're working on Amazon, and I plan to move to Youtube next—and lastly, diversifying. Diversifying consisted of building a Patreon following (an ongoing crowdfunding platform that trades monthly support for monthly content), and breaking into the traditional publishing sphere as a stop-gap against any sudden or disastrous changes to online platforms like Amazon.

My ultimate goal was always to be a hybrid author, meaning someone who is both independently and traditionally published. The real money is in Indie publishing, hands down. But traditional publishing offers vital advantages in reputation, networking, and professional development.

My strategy to becoming a hybrid author began with "see and be seen." I hoped to become a known face in my own little corner of the publishing industry by helping and teaching in any way I could, so that when publishing opportunities came up, I was a person that would come to mind. That is, in fact, why this account is in this book, because I met the publishers at a convention and did panels with them (i.e. I networked and gave up my time to teach and help others).

In the case of my traditional publishing contracts, those came about because I attended LibertyCon where Baen Books has a large presence. While there, I had a table selling my Indie published books in a professional and compelling manner. They caught the notice of a Baen author, John Ringo, who later asked me to collaborate on a book series with him. Signing for that book series with Baen opened other doors, including multiple short stories in various anthologies, and an open invitation to submit any manuscript to their senior editor for consideration. All of this happened because I was committed to seeing and being seen—as an enthusiastic and authentic reader, as well as a professional writer and business owner.

By late 2019, I was making more than my engineer husband, and so he was finally able to quit his corporate job and come work in the biz with me. He has taken over as marketing director so that I can focus on writing more books and managing and exploiting our intellectual property.

So here I am in 2021, with so many wonderful things behind me, and decades of amazing things ahead. I have big plans for the future, and my only problem is that there aren't enough hours in each day. That, and the fact that my body needs sleep (I wish it didn't, but it does).

### Education

I read a great piece of advice early on in publishing which I will paraphrase here: find people doing what you want to do, figure out how they got there, and do what they did in as much as it fits with your own situation. That's what I've been doing from Day 1.

In the early years, the authors I followed the most were Mark Dawson and Joanna Penn, two amazing, humble, insightful Indie authors who were making it big when Indie publishing was first exploding on the scene. Both have podcasts and lots of content and resources to share. I eventually took Mark Dawson's Self Publishing 101 course, as well as his Ads for Authors course. Both were very useful and worth every cent.

Two years ago, I discovered Steve Pieper's AMMO course (from a Facebook ad, funnily enough). It was a big investment, money-wise, but it would teach me how to become independent of Amazon and optimize my ads on Facebook using data, instead of being driven by guesses in the dark. Steve's course teaches the sort of marketing that huge companies like Coke and Nike use, and it brought us (hubby and I) into a small group of motivated, professional Indie authors who were all doing the same thing we were. That marketing group has been just as vital to our success as the information the course taught, and we do a weekly marketing call with them to discuss what is currently working (and not) and to exchange tips and tricks.

And, to address the elephant in the room, Facebook ads are responsible for eighty percent of all our gross book sales. Facebook is THE NUMBER ONE most powerful marketing platform created in the history of humankind. Their extensive data mining on individuals, coupled with their advanced targeting algorithms, open doors that are not possible and never have been on any other platform.

Now, that *is* changing to an extent with privacy pushback and the development of other platforms. But for an Indie author who wants to control their own sales instead of trying to game Amazon's algorithms or pay Amazon to sell your books in addition to giving Amazon a cut of the books they sold for you, you have to make Facebook part of your marketing strategy. The most crucial importance of Facebook marketing that sends people to your own site is collecting email addresses so that those people become your own customers. Any marketing directly on a book retailer platform does not give you that point of contact with the reader, leaving all the power in the hands of the book retailer.

Now, some authors just do well on Amazon, either with ads or organically. That is really, really great for them. But you can't expect to be the exception. Wide versus KDP select is an entirely separate topic, but I'll just say that I am not and would never be comfortable relying 100% on Amazon for my income by leaving all my eggs in the KDP select basket. For long-term stability, I think diversifying is the way to go.

The last big source of education I'll mention is a no brainer: my readers! The sooner you think about your book publishing as a *business*, the sooner you'll start to realize what a wonderful, direct relationship you can have with your readers. It is not icky or off-putting to ask your readers about their preferences so that you can write and create things that they love even more. I use my newsletter, my Facebook groups, and my Patreon platform to regularly ask my readers opinions on things (conducting market research). I ask things like what kinds of stories they want, what artwork they like best, which characters they want to see more of, and what format details they like most in my paperback books. I encourage my readers to chat with me directly and send me emails, and get a lot of great feedback about my books. The comments on my Facebook ads are invaluable, because they tell me what my readers liked (or didn't) so I can do more of that. Lastly, I have cultivated a list of about 60 trusted readers from my current fan base who beta read for me, and the diversity and scope of the feedback they give helps me immensely to see things from my reader's perspectives and catch things I never would have thought of on my own.

My readers have taught me a lot, and I'm eternally indebted to them.

**Influences**

My dad is my biggest influence. He and I are extremely similar in our entrepreneurial spirit, and he instilled my work ethic as well as the understanding that the world doesn't owe you anything. The only way you are going to achieve anything is by going out there and humbly trying to learn as best you can and work hard toward your goals. My dad has always done his own thing, working for himself, and shown me that with the right attitude, hard work, and not giving up despite setbacks and difficulties, you can pretty much achieve whatever you want in life.

He also taught me gratitude.

Without gratitude, life is a dark, resentful, anxiety-filled mess. It's all too easy to become jealous of fellow authors' successes and let that eat at you or mess with your head, holding you back from achieving your fullest success. You should never, EVER compare yourself to other people. Only compare yourself to who you were in the past. You are unique, and any comparison between you and someone else with a totally different life, past, experiences, and current situation is invalid. So instead, look at yourself yesterday, last week, last month, last year. Look at how far you've come, be grateful for it, and figure out how you can do even better in the future.

One last mindset I will mention as essential to my success has been my insatiable desire for constructive criticism. I've been blessed with a natural urge to seek and implement feedback, probably a mix of my love of learning, outgoing nature, perfectionism, and people-pleasing tendencies. I absolutely love knowing exactly how and why something is good or not good, because then I can take that knowledge and build something better with it. Constructive feedback is, in my opinion, the lifeblood of any creator who desires to become better at their craft.

For constructive criticism to be of any use to you, however, you must cultivate humility, a thick skin, and the wisdom to sort the good feedback from the bad. It is important to understand *who* is giving you the feedback and what perspective they are coming from. You can pretty safely ignore a horror reader giving you negative feedback about your romance story; an avid romance reader's opinion would hold much more weight. Though it takes time, you will also develop an instinctive understanding of your own voice and craft and can make an informed decision on whether or not to take advice that sits wrong with you.

Most important is to maintain a humble mindset. Ask for advice. Seek feedback. Humbly listen to the feedback given and do not argue with it, just ponder it, sort out what is useful to you, and discard the rest. Never assume you know more about a topic than someone else, and never assume you are right simply because you have had some success or have been publishing for a while.

In this industry, there is rarely ever a "right" way to do things. There is just the way that works for you, the way that makes enjoyable stories that your fans like reading and will keep paying for. Oftentimes the people in the profession who are making the most noise know the least about what they're doing (and I say this as a raging extrovert who loves talking, haha! But then I don't really know what I'm doing either, I've only just scratched the surface). It is the quiet humble ones that you should go talk to, make friends with, and treasure above all else.

### Path to Publication and/or Becoming a Publisher

Since I already covered the timeline of my publication in a previous question, I'll focus here on obstacles. Each of these obstacles could have been overcome in multiple ways, so I can only speak on the ways I used, which may or may not fit your own situation. So keep that in mind while reading.

**Obstacle 1**: Time. This was the main frustration that led me to choose Indie publishing over trad, though there were other factors as well. But what it came down to was: did I want to spend significant effort to convince someone else I was worthy of publishing, then *still* have to market myself, or did I want to spend significant time building my own business and professional brand and have all that time with my book already out and already gathering readers?

**Solution**: Independent publishing. In the end, I had exactly zero desire to wait around for someone else to tell me I was good enough to make readers happy. I knew I had the skills, or the intelligence to learn the skills, to create a product that readers would love. I'm a go-get-er and a do-it-myself-er. If that's not you, then Indie publishing might not be as good of a path. You may decide that you'd rather spend more of your time writing while you wait around to hear back from editors and agents, then take that time and put it into building a business. One thing is irrefutable, though: Indie authors make vastly more money per book sale than trad authors. So you have to sell way fewer books as an Indie than as a trad author to create the same amount of profit. And, in today's day and age with so many free tools and information at our disposal, I personally am not thrilled at the idea of handing over the rights and control of my intellectual property to someone else. It's a lost opportunity, and I love exploiting opportunities.

**Obstacle 2**: How to pay for professional editing, formatting, and cover for my first books when I was poor and had no money for it? I was absolutely determined that my books should look as indistinguishable from trad books as humanly possible. For me it was important to do things professionally, to take myself seriously, and to treat my endeavor as a business from the get-go.

**Solution**: Crowdfunding. I hated the idea of asking other people for money, but I came to terms with it in the context that I wasn't asking for charity, I was simply running a pre-order campaign. Plus, I was giving my friends and family a way to support my dreams in a tangible way *and* get some fun rewards out of it. At the time (2016), Kickstarter seemed the best platform to use because of their all or nothing model. An important principle in marketing is the sense of urgency. The urgency of knowing if I didn't hit X goal, I would end up with zilch, motivated me—and my supporters—to do all the more. I spent many months researching successful book and comic book kickstarters, figuring out exactly what their campaigns looked like and said that made them seem professional and compelling, from the images and phrasing they used to what rewards and support tiers they offered.

**Obstacle 3**: Learning how to become my own publisher. Yes, it is daunting, and there is so much to know and do: editing, formatting, covers, ISBNs, distribution (KU or wide?), social media campaigns, other promotional campaigns, building a website, building a newsletter, audio books (its very own can of worms), taxes, business formation (LLC? Corp? Sole proprietor?), budgeting, conventions, and on and on the list goes.

**Solution**: GOOGLE IS YOUR FRIEND!!! I can't keep track of the number of times I've had aspiring authors come to me and ask "how do I self-publish?" When I get that question, I have to pause and rub my temples in exasperation as I wonder if said person has ever heard of a nifty thing called a search engine. I don't know— maybe it was just me having a Dad who was an IT professional—but growing up his mantra was either "look it up in the dictionary" or, as the 90s turned into the 2000s, "what does Google say?" I was always, always, always taught that if I had a question, I needed to go find an answer. That doesn't mean you shouldn't ask people for advice; far from it. But when asking for advice you *must* be specific. I always respond to that "how do I self-publish" question with "Google it and read as much as you can, and if you have any specific questions, feel free to ask!"

You cannot make it as an independent author unless you are willing to teach yourself everything there is to know. You are literally starting a publishing business to publish one author: you. How does one become a publishing house? By doing a butt-ton of reading, research, and asking *specific* questions of people who've done it before you. I used Google back in 2013 when I started researching it, because there weren't a whole lot of self-publishing how-to books written at the time. There are lots of those now, but, honestly, you don't need to spend money on them unless you really want to. There are enough blogs, podcasts, and free courses out there you can learn everything you need to know to get started without paying a cent. When I started, I read a lot by Joanna Penn, and a little later Mark Dawson, though he wasn't as big until about 2015 or so.

One monumentally helpful resource that is worth millions, literally millions, of dollars, that wasn't around when I started is the 20Booksto50k Facebook group. If you aren't on Facebook, you need to make an account and get on there *just* to be a part of this group. It is the largest collection of professional Indie authors (50,000 and counting) who freely share advice and experience, and who are actually there to help each other. A rising tide lifts all boats, is the philosophy in 20Books, and Craig and Michael who started it are some of the most helpful, hardworking, and humble people you'll ever meet. They are absolute gold. That group alone and the years of posts you can search through by keyword, not to mention the free resources and documents you have access to as part of the group, could easily be sold for hundreds if not thousands of dollars for all the valuable information it gives. So, if you want to Indie publish (or even trad), and you're not a member of that group yet, stop reading right now, put down this book, and go join it before you read another word.

Okay, did you do it? If not, stop reading and *go do it*.

Right, so, you've joined. Once you're approved, be sure to read all the intro stuff they suggest, and follow the group rules religiously, or you'll get tossed out. They are too big of a group to tolerate any drama or carelessness.

Use the 20Books FB group like you would Google. Think about the question you have, for instance "should I buy ISBNs for my book or are they worth the money, can't I just use a free Amazon one?" and go search for key terms from that question. It will pull up dozens of past posts on the topic. Scroll through, pick the most recent ones that seem to address your question and that have a lot of comments, and start reading. Yes, you will have to do a lot of reading, but you are learning to become a publisher, remember? Don't expect it to be easy. If, after you search past posts, you still can't find a specific answer to your question, you can make a post to ask that specific question and should get lots of helpful answers. Obviously you'll have to learn how to sift through advice to use what is useful—discard the rest—but that's all part of being your own publisher.

**Obstacle 4**: I have a full-time job, how do I find time to write? When should I quit my day job?

**Solution**: It's complicated and takes a lot of hard work.

First let's address time: you will make time for whatever is important for you. Period. I hear so, sooooo many aspiring authors complain about not having time to write the book they've been working on for forever. All I can do is smile but internally shake my head.

As with anything in life, achieving your dreams takes sacrifice. Imagining you can make it at this career without sacrificing something for it is delusional, so come to terms with that right now. I gave up important things, like hobbies that I loved and meant the world to me, and I gave up unimportant, but addictive things, like watching TV and playing video games. You have to evaluate your life, make a list or become aware of what you spend your time on, and then decide what is important and what has to go. You can also look for unused time, such as lunch breaks during work, commute times, etc. Some people use dictation software and dictate while they drive to work or while they exercise or do chores. It doesn't matter how you do it; it only matters that you must *make* time for writing or it will never happen. You must prioritize it, you must hold that time sacred, or other things will encroach.

For me, I wrote during my lunch breaks, and in the evenings 3-4 days a week. My husband and I decided to delay having kids for a few years so I could get established with publishing before we had that extra difficulty to contend with, and that was crucial in my success. Being able to completely devote myself to writing and getting things off the ground helped me get started with some good momentum, so that, when I did start having kids, I had the resources to afford childcare so I could treat my writing like the job that it was. How you manage this is extremely unique to your situation, so I can't offer much advice on it. Just remember:

1. Expect to make sacrifices.
2. If you don't prioritize it, it'll never get done.
3. An author career is a marathon, not a sprint. Look at the long game—years, not months—when you're doing your planning.

As for quitting your job, they always say don't rush to quit your day job. I'd agree with that, with one caveat: If you are married and have the ability to live frugally on one person's income, absolutely quit your day job and devote your full focus to getting those books written and published and your momentum rolling. That's not a possibility for most people, but you can get closer and closer to your goal by being wise with your money, living frugally, and putting every spare cent into savings to give you a fall-back for that time when you do quit your day job and are relying on your publishing income, which will always have seasonal fluctuations.

**Obstacle 5**: Self-doubt. I'm a terrible writer, no one will ever read this crap. I'll never succeed, why am I even doing this? Everybody will hate this; there's no way I'd ever be brave enough to let someone read my work.

Believe me, it's not just you having to battle these thoughts. Everyone, and I mean everyone, thinks these things at some point or another, to one degree or another. Even successful, established authors, including me. When you're first starting, though, the self-doubt can feel insurmountable. One bad review can wreck you. One person you care about dismissing your dream to be an author or speaking badly about your work in progress can absolutely crush you and make you walk away from your dream. It's hard. So, so hard.

Unfortunately, I don't have a silver bullet solution. But I do have a quote for you to ponder (author unknown): "If you can stop writing, do it. If you can't, you're a writer."

People have a lot of different reasons for wanting to write stories or be a professional author. Unfortunately, not all of them are good enough or strong enough reasons to get you through the difficulties. And that can be okay. Maybe you just want to publish something to say you did it or for your family to enjoy. Maybe you'd love it if your books took off, but you have a fulfilling 9-5 career that you have no intention of giving up, and so you're not too worried if your books make you big bucks. That is one-hundred percent okay. It is completely fine to want to publish as a hobby.

But, if you want to make it a career, you really have to want it. You have to be *driven*, or it is much harder to overcome that self-doubt. There's no easy way to say this, but some of you will be faced with difficulty and will give up. And some of you won't give up.

It's as simple as that.

How can you be more likely to not give up?

**Solution**: Research and practice positive thinking. I don't care what you've heard about positive thinking, throw all of it out the door, including your pride, and start training your mind to think positively. Our minds are so malleable, we can literally convince ourselves of the most insane delusions if we tell ourselves the same lies for long enough. You can literally create "truth" of a sort through the power of your thoughts. So, if your thoughts are that powerful, in what insane reality would you *not* take control of them and harness that power to make yourself succeed?

Self-doubt is ALL in your head. It is almost NEVER based in reality or objective standards, but is almost completely a product of your past, your upbringing, and the way you were, or were not, encouraged to foster confidence in yourself growing up. I'm a very confident person naturally, but even I have to fight self-doubt.

Having self-doubt doesn't make you weak or less talented, it just makes you human.

A slight caveat here: I know there are a lot of authors out there facing mental health challenges such as depression, anxiety, and much more. If this is you, please, please, please get professional help and DO NOT BLAME YOURSELF. Being neurodivergent or having something like clinical depression is not your fault. Your job is to accept that you are who you are, love yourself for it, and find the strategies that work for you and your unique situation to conquer the difficulties facing you. Yes, your road will be harder. But you can use your unique experience facing those challenges to become so much stronger and more determined than a person who never had to face those challenges. Plus it gives you unique insight into the psychology, emotions, and life of a kind of person that many would connect with, and you can use that to write super authentic characters that your readers will sympathize with and love!!

So, back to self-doubt and positive thinking.

The first and most important thing is to immediately reject negative thoughts. They have no place in your brain, no function, no worth, and you are too awesome a person with awesome goals to waste your time on them. Yes, you may feel like a fraud saying, "No, I'm a *great* author and people will *love* my books." But think of it this way: you are going to do your darndest to study your craft and write your heart out to make the best book possible, so, even if your statement isn't objectively, quantifiably true quite yet, it will be, because you will work hard until it becomes so. That positive statement isn't about it being one-hundred percent true *right now*, it is about framing your mindset and trajectory. If you frame your trajectory up, that is the direction you will go. If you frame your trajectory down, that is also *exactly* where you will go. That is scientific fact backed up by decades of clinical research.

So, reject negative thoughts and counter them with a positive one, whether the positive one *feels* true or not.

If you are really, really struggling with feeling like a fraud saying a bunch of positive things, you could take baby steps by starting with a practical or realistic statement like, "I'm not a terrible author, I'm probably just average, and I know I'll get better." That is still aiming your trajectory up, so it's a good first step if the whole positive thoughts thing is difficult (as it was for me).

In time, you'll gain life experience that you can pull on to fight that self-doubt.

Yes, I still feel like I'm a terrible author all the time. But when I think that, I remember the hundreds of face-to-face interactions with fans who absolutely gushed about my books, or the over two-thousand five-star reviews I have for my book series. They can't *all* be wrong, so my books must be objectively good, at least to my target audience. Obviously it is hard in the beginning because you don't yet have that validation to lean on. Which is why you should hold onto every little positive bit of feedback you get, because you need that ammunition to fight your self-doubt.

Lastly, as much as you can, surround yourself with supportive people. Whether that is a spouse, a parent, other family members, a good friend, or a writing group, find people who care about you and want to cheer you on, and keep them close. This is a hard career, and you will need that support. Even when you succeed, you need that support, because success breeds pressure and a special kind of self-doubt and imposter syndrome that is a beast to fight.

If you have a person close to you who is not supportive and you have no way of staying away from them, then do not feel bad about avoiding the topic entirely. It is healthy to make boundaries for yourself and to be smart about how you engage so that you don't provoke opportunities for that person to discourage you. You ain't got time for that, I'm tellin' ya! Yes, hopefully they will come around, especially once you find some success and can show them solid wins. But don't waste energy or emotional reserves fighting with them or trying to convince them your dream is worthy. Your dream is worthy simply because it is your dream, and you don't need anyone to validate it. (Even though it is helpful and I hope for your sake your loved ones validate it!)

My hubby is not only my best friend and business partner, he is my biggest fan and better than a whole cheerleading squad. There is no way I could have gotten where I am today without his help every step of the way. I'm so grateful and humbled by his support, because I certainly don't deserve it.

### The Hard Lessons You've Learned
1. **You can't edit a blank page.**

For real, though, you can't. This is the most fundamental truth that should be the fire under every author's posterior. "Writer's block" is just a fancy phrase for lack of discipline and motivation, because you can ALWAYS write something. Always. So what if it's total crap or nothing like what you wanted. At least you have somewhere to start, and you can edit it to make it better. Perfection is the enemy of completion. Professional authors don't just write when they "feel" like it. They don't just write when the inspiration strikes. They write regularly, consistently, and in volume, because that's their job, and they treat it as such.

It is totally fine if you just want to write for fun. Nothing wrong with that. But if you have any dreams of making money writing, you have to treat writing like a job and figure out what things motivate you to write when you don't want to. There are all sorts of strategies, and what works is different for everybody.

A big thing for me is movement. I think and write better when I'm moving, so when I feel stuck I'll go write at my standing desk, put on big headphones, turn on some really catchy music, and start dancing to the tunes. It activates my brain and gets the juices flowing. Another thing I do is take walks in the park behind my house and dictate on my phone. This is my preferred solution whenever I feel stuck with a plot point or don't know what to write next. Something about the physical movement seems to unblock everything and gets my thoughts flowing freely.

Other times, your difficulty in making yourself write may mean you need a break, or need to do some other activity for a while to give that part of your brain a rest. Go exercise. Bake. Make a cup of tea. Do a puzzle. Take a bath. Then come back, glue your butt to the chair, and write whether you want to or not. In the end, you just have to do it, and if you don't do it, then maybe you need to rethink your motivations.

### 2. Never design your own cover or do your own editing.

Unless you have trained professionally to do either of those things, do not try and do them for yourself, and don't hire a friend who isn't a professional either (honestly I wouldn't hire a friend period, no matter if they are a professional or not; there's just a difficult conflict of interests there). The only person you should want designing your cover or editing your book is someone who does it for a career and is aware of current publishing trends and, especially for covers, what genre-specific cues and styles are in at the time.

I designed my first edition covers. I didn't do the actual artwork myself, I hired someone for that, at least. But I designed the idea and told my artist what to do and what it should look like. The artist, while a fantastic artist, was not a cover designer, just someone great at drawing. So they had no idea if what I was telling them to do was a good idea in terms of marketability.

As it turned out, the covers weren't too bad, and the books did sell. But two years later when I had my covers redesigned by a professional, my sales spiked significantly.

Moral of the story: don't design your own covers, and, if you have to for budget reasons, then get them re-done by a professional as soon as possible who has a proven track record and who can show professional knowledge of the genre you write in.

3. **What you like isn't necessarily what your readers will like.**

Oooh boy, this is a big one for me. Yes, it is true you should write what you know, and it is true that most authors write the same kinds of stories they themselves enjoy reading. All that is fine. I'm talking more about the marketing aspect when it comes to cover design, marketing images, ad copy, book descriptions for Amazon, etc.

While you might enjoy what you yourself are writing, you are not necessarily your own target audience. Plus, you are only one person, and if you expect to sell to millions, your own personal style and preference may be far off from the average that you will need to appeal to the largest block of target readers you are aiming at.

Back to my first edition covers.

I had a vision in my head of what I wanted them to look like and the feel I wanted them to have. So, that's what I created. The problem is, my preference for covers (illustrated) was NOT the preference of the vast majority of my target audience, which I honestly didn't have a good grasp on at the time I started publishing anyway.

Another fun example is my magic system. In my books, I have a very practical and science-based magic system. In my head, I disliked the really tropey, cliche urban fantasy stories where the magic is flashy, and there's crazy stuff and creatures popping up everywhere. Everything is dialed to eleven and it all feels so unbelievable and campy to me. It was a personal turn-off. So I set out to make my magic system the opposite of that and uber realistic.

But, what I ran into over and over again was that my books didn't feel "magical" enough. They were in danger of being boring because there wasn't enough magic and "fun" things happening.

What I eventually realized was that even though there was a place for realism and solid worldbuilding rules that were actually followed, people read books to have fun, period. And flashy magic is fun. Crazy magical creatures are fun. Wild and unrealistic things are fun.

I still don't have pineapples tap dancing across any desks or self-washing dishes (if you're a Harry Potter fan you'll get that reference). But now I look for ways that I can make my magic system a little more flashy and interesting than I'd originally intended, while not worrying too much over the answer to my own internal question "but how does this actually *work*." I've made a little room for the inexplicable, the fantastical, the wondrous, because my readers taught me that if I wanted to be a career author, it was more important to write a story that was fun and that people enjoyed than to write something that completely and totally avoided my own pet peeves.

So, moral of the story: do market research, hire professionals to do the job that you don't have experience for, and seek out as much feedback from your readers as you can possibly get.

### 4. Be humble. Really, just be humble.

Never talk yourself up, let others talk you up, otherwise you're just going to embarrass yourself.

It may not surprise you, but I've put my foot in my own mouth on many an occasion, and every time I say to myself "Really? *Really*? Why couldn't you have just kept your big mouth shut?"

I'm a high-energy and high-emotion person, so I have a tendency to get excited and get carried away, forgetting to filter. I've also had times where I say something that seems completely fine in my head, but once it comes out, it is quickly very clear that it is *not* okay. I certainly don't go around singing my own praises, I have a husband for that ;). But I do enjoy talking about myself just as much as the next person, probably more.

I have learned through painful experience that you should talk about yourself as little as possible, and, if you can manage it, only when people specifically ask to hear it. If you do talk about yourself, always focus on sharing things that are helpful for the person you are talking to. Pour into them, offer perspective and *humble* advice. It isn't as fun as talking about all the amazing things you've done that you are honestly and sincerely excited about, but it will build much stronger, more lasting relationship bridges that will serve you well in your career. Plus, you won't come across as an arrogant, self-absorbed jerk, and that's pretty important too, especially when making connections with other professionals and with trad publishers.

P.S. Obviously this is very nuanced and situation specific. It is perfectly fine to be enthusiastic about your own work and the things you are doing. Just be careful to not make it about you and stroking your own ego, but make it about the joy of the art itself and the ways it can delight others and be of benefit to them.

5. **If something isn't working, don't keep doing it hoping it will magically start working.**
This is a constant, repeating cycle, and unfortunately it will always be. When it comes to marketing, nothing ever stays the same, and

what worked yesterday might not work today. The landscape is constantly changing, and you have to be aware of and at peace with the fact that you are always going to have to keep changing things up, no matter how annoying it is. You have to constantly re-evaluate and think outside the box. See what others are doing that is working. Find other authors with books similar to yours and humbly ask for advice or insight into what is working for them (and offer to showcase their books to your audience to thank them for their time).

Obviously timeless marketing principles will always apply, but the platforms and strategies to implement them constantly changes.

6. **If at all possible, keep your audio book rights (and other rights).**

In 2018, I sold the audio book rights to my first four Love, Lies, and Hocus Pocus books to Tantor Media because I had just had my first baby and knew for a fact I would never make time to find a narrator and produce those audio books myself. It just wasn't going to happen, and I was really insecure about picking a narrator. Tantor did a great job with them, got me an amazing narrator, and I'm really grateful for that whole process.

Now, however, my audio books are making A BUNCH of money and I'm only getting a fraction. Tantor took the risk, and they are getting the reward. Looking back, I still probably made the right decision based on my circumstances. But, at the same time, if I'd just held on for another year until I had some breathing room and tackled it then, I could be making much more money now. I've done the next books in my series on my own, now that I have a reliable narrator and know how the process works.

So, if at all possible and if applicable, do things yourself instead of selling your rights. There are exceptions, of course, like movie rights, but that's a whole other ball game that I'm still figuring out myself.

7. **If your books aren't selling, yes the problem is probably you, not everybody else.**

I see this so, so often, especially in the author groups on Facebook. They almost ALWAYS say something along the lines of "I've already redone my cover/description professionally, those aren't the problem, the problem is that readers just aren't buying/Indie publishing doesn't work anymore/FB advertising is a scam and doesn't work," etc.

Except, when you go look them up and see their covers, it's pretty clear their stuff does not look professional.

So, if your books aren't selling, the first thing you should look at is your cover and book description. It might not even be that what you have is bad, but that the genre is changing. Maybe you could do with a fresh cover and blurb, even if the previous ones worked fine at one time. Or maybe it isn't that, maybe it's your first chapter, or first page, or first line. Maybe you don't know your target audience as well as you thought. Maybe the platform you're trying to advertise on isn't the best place to find your target audience. Maybe you aren't as good at running those ads as you thought (or maybe you were, and now things have changed. It happens all the time).

But the solution is never, ever, ever to blame other people/things for your failure. There are so many people doing this now, and making a lot of money at that, the problem is never that it can't be done, or that readers aren't buying books, or whatever. You are the factor that needs to change, and you need to have the humility and honesty to keep searching for a solution that works, not blaming others.

So, keep it real, be business-minded, not ego-minded, and get it done.

### Where You are Now

Right now I'm a USA Today and Amazon bestselling author with a dozen titles to my name and a growing fanbase who are desperate for more books. Unfortunately, with two kids, I only manage one or two a year (though the sacrifice is worth it; I love my kids!). If I could write a book a month, I'd be making seven figures NET profit easy peasy. As it is, we are in the five figure range and edging to six figures in net profit (yes, that is net, not gross sales). I prefer talking about net/take home rather than gross sales because gross sales can be misleading. Saying I made a million in gross sales is a lot less impressive if my marketing costs eat up 90% of that gross profit. So just keep that in mind when people talk numbers, it's helpful to know if they're talking gross sales or net profit.

Chenoweth Press LLC, our publishing company, currently only publishes my books, but we hope to start publishing my husband's books as well in the coming years. I have no plans currently to do more than that. We love our creative pursuits and don't feel any itch to publish other people's works. We prefer to focus on exploiting our own intellectual property (IP).

We plan to maintain our position and increase our market share by:

1. Keep writing books in the series I've established, giving my growing fanbase exactly what it wants.

2. Expand into traditional publishing to reach a larger audience and establish long-term connections in the industry, setting ourselves up to take advantage of opportunities as they come along.

3. Expand where we are advertising. We're focusing on Facebook and Amazon at the moment, but we will be looking at Youtube and Google ads in the future. I strongly believe in diversifying to better hedge against abrupt changes in the landscape in the future as platforms change.

4. Expanding our IP by creating art, merchandise, and other related content to turn fans into superfans and give them more things to spend money on. This isn't a big money-maker right now, but it does engender loyalty and enthusiasm among readers. Just think about the Harry Potter franchise and all the ancillary products they have available. Plus, it's fun to do, which keeps the creative juices flowing.

5. Continue networking and making connections in the entertainment industries, specifically looking for opportunities to pursue movie/TV deals. We've also thought about adapting to graphic novels, but don't think it would be profitable enough at this point to make it worth the time it would take away from writing more books.

### Where do You See Things Going?

In the next 5-10 years, I predict it will still be very similar. Authors will still be writing fun books for readers who want to enjoy

212 | WEBB & KENNEDY

them. Technology will have changed somewhat, but the major mediums will still be some form of print, electronic reading, and audio listening, though the platforms and technology of how those formats are consumed may change slightly.

I also predict independent publishing is only going to grow, along with the growth of small, Indie publishing companies that operate on a very flexible and quick-reacting model. I don't think the big trad companies will go away, but they will certainly consolidate and those that survive will have to adapt, or they'll keep ossifying.

I hope, though I don't know if this will happen, that trad publishers will start treating their authors as valued and respected assets, rather than cash cows to be milked and tossed aside.

In fifty years, who can say? I don't think paper books are ever going to disappear; I think they will always be popular. I think there will be a rise in virtual and augmented reality experiences. I predict that in fifty years, you won't just be able to read a book, but *live* it, perhaps passively just as an observer, perhaps by becoming a character in it as a sort of choose-your-own adventure melding of books and video games.

But the basic paperback, ebook, audio book will still be there.

I think in the future it will become ever more important for Indie authors to build their own tribe of readers, fans they connect with and can respond to. Advertising is only going to become more and more competitive, especially if we have a growing backlash against it as people advocate for more digital privacy. So social media and platforms like Patreon where you can cultivate your own fan family are going to get more and more important.

## Contact Info

My home base is at www.lydiasherrer.com. There you can read about me, my books, and sign up for my newsletter.

Check out my books and merchandise at https://store.lydiasherrer.com/.

Enjoy cute cat pictures and book talk on my Instagram and Facebook pages www.instagram.com/lydiasherrer and www.facebook.com/lydiasherrer or join my VIP reader group at www.facebook.com/groups/LydiasVIPReaderGroup.

My books and audio books are on all major book retailers and many of the minor ones. Just search for me by name. You can also look for my books in your local library system. If they don't already have them, you can always ask your librarian to add them to their catalog!

If you have any *specific* questions I can help you with, or if you'd just like to chat, I'd be delighted to hear from you, shoot an email to lydia@lydiasherrer.com.

Thanks for reading, and remember success = sound plans + hard work + never giving up.

Good luck!

# Chapter Fourteen:
# Kevin Steverson

There are things Kevin Steverson has never done, like being a professional race car driver, flying a Fokker DR-1 triplane, or writing the code for a machine that might take over the world; it only *seems* like there's nothing he hasn't done. In sharing his Titan views, Kevin was specifically asked to focus on one part of his story by the editors, which is why it varies in form from the responses of our other Titans. True to character, Kevin worried that he might appear arrogant. Anyone who knows, or knows of, Kevin Steverson realizes how absurd that sounds.

But Kevin does have a unique story, and the editors felt it should be told.

**Biography**

There is no one path to becoming a successful writer.

I am the Unicorn.

I've been called such by several author friends as well as readers with a familiarity of the writing and publishing side of stories and books. I don't mind. It's all in good fun and makes for eye-opening stories when I'm at conventions on panels or talking to attendees at my table or in the halls.

Yes. The first story I had published was the military science fiction novel, "Salvage Title." Yes. It was published by the first publisher I contacted about it. Yes. It was still ranked well, sitting at number 660 on all of Amazon thirty days after release with no ads. Yes. Six months later it was still ranked in the 10,000 range. Yes. The second and third books in the Salvage Title Trilogy were released inside those six months and they broke the number 800 barrier in ranking... still with no marketing ads back then.

Yes. The trilogy has been picked up for development into feature film. The script on the first movie has gone through three drafts and the CEO of the production company feels good about it. The final script is near completion. In his own words, "we are making a movie."

Yes. I didn't start writing until after I retired from the military in 2017. Yes. I have only been published since September 2018. Yes. There are now seventeen books in the *Salvage Universe*. These include my own, anthologies, and novels by others invited to write in it. Yes, by the time you read this, I will personally have nine novels and twenty-six short stories published. Oh, and four anthologies I helped edit. All in three years.

I am the Unicorn. Now, having written all this let me tell you what I did to make it all happen on my end.

No. I didn't get hit with lightning and develop some kind of magic aura. No. I did not make sacrifices on a moonless night to an ancient entity in another dimension. No. I did not make a deal at a crossroads in the middle of flyover country. No. I am not the luckiest son-of-a-gun you ever heard of.

### Path to Publication and/or Becoming a Publisher

I did a lot of research. I looked into self-publishing, weighing the pros and cons. I looked into trying to land an agent and go for the Big Four publishers to be traditionally published. I looked into being a hybrid author. After much deliberation, I decided to find a small press. One that would publish my work, yet let me maintain a bit of control on what I write and when. It also let me not have to worry about a middle man, an agent.

Then came a lot more studying and I found the one I thought would publish what I wanted to write. Chris Kennedy, of Chris Kennedy Publishing. I loved his writing style and the types of books his company was publishing. I bought his book on self-publishing and got to work. I built my website and did several other steps in his book. Once I obtained his email, from an open call for short stories in one of the universes he publishes, I was good to go.

I did my homework, and I sent the email. I knew what he was looking for. I knew what he liked, and I was able to intelligently answer his questions in our correspondence. Yes. He was the only publisher I reached out for my novel, but the move was deliberate on my part. So, yes, the first publisher I contacted said "yes." I would not be where I am without him. He and his editors have helped me grow as an author, and I could not be more thankful.

### Influences

On writing: I am, like the vast majority of writers, a reader. I always have been. I distinctly remember being questioned on the story we were reading in fifth grade in class, because the teacher caught me reading another story three quarters ahead in our reading book. I answered her questions thoughtfully and went back to reading ahead. She never chastised me about it again.

I love to read and, over the decades, picked up what I liked best in stories. The characters, plot development, styles of writing, all the things which make a good story... good to me. When I write, it is what I would like to read. I will never be considered a literary author. I'm fine with the distinction or lack thereof. Nor will I ever be considered a hard science fiction author. I enjoy the works of several who are; it's just not in me.

I write for the common man or woman. I am a story teller first and foremost, a writer second. I had to learn to stop using crutch words and brush up on grammar. I am still working on it. I will always learn more and keep working on it.

When I came up with the idea for "Salvage Title," I thought: "Everyone knows of salvage titles on vehicles. Of restoring them and getting them registered. Readers may not have done it themselves, but they knew of the concept. Why not with a ship? One capable of traveling between star systems. The authorities trying to keep my man down? The struggle to overcome it. A loophole? Perfect."

Thus it began. Once again, I write for the common person.

I spent more than twenty-one years in the military and retired as a senior NCO. I don't force my writing. I am not one to work with outlines. Maybe a sentence or two for a chapter and I'm off to the races. When I write dialogue between characters, it has been noted to seem natural. I feel that is a great compliment. I try not to write what I think they would say. I simply let my fingers type what they say in my head. Do I hear voices? Maybe, I guess. Don't all authors?

When I started writing my first novel, I cut scenes to give the reader a glimpse of the other side during the action. Much like a movie does. I have been told it is like watching one. It is deliberate. Decision makers in the film industry didn't have to imagine what a script could be like. It was there for them the first time they read my book. I also made sure to have finality at the end of each book even though it was a trilogy. Within the books, I write so a reader can't put it down at the end of a section or chapter, but I don't do it at the end of a book.

A series sells books, but when being considered for a movie, the decision maker is not looking to read five or eight books to see what happens in the end. They move on to the next potential product. That is why I try to avoid cliff hanger endings yet still have a series. From the beginning, I had my eye on movies. If it didn't happen, I would have been fine with it. It's all about the stories. A movie would be icing on the cake. Of course, I like cake with icing as opposed to without.

So, yes. I am the Unicorn, but it didn't just happen. I had to work towards it. I write every single day to build a backlist and become known to more readers. I have written many short stories in anthologies to reach new fan bases. I now advertise. It is something I wish I had done from the beginning. I didn't and it was a mistake. I am working on it and on building my subscriber list for newsletters. It could be another year or two before the first movie comes out. I plan on being known to many before then as I keep working at the craft and the marketing side of it all.

Yes. I rose to this point quickly. I can fall from it just as quickly. It took work to get here and I plan on working to stay and rise more. I do the business side of the house in the afternoons and I write through the night. I go to bed at six in the morning and sleep until noonish. Even Unicorns sleep. It's just at odd times.

### Where Do You See All of This Going?

I think self-publishing/small press is going to be the future. It is inevitable. Computers, printers, Amazon... it all leads to the conclusion. The days of the big press gatekeepers are gone. Social media allows anyone to become known. Yes, it may take some money and ads but there is no one to tell a writer, "no one will read this."

There may come a time when nearly all literature is digital. It must be good writing with well thought out plots and characters people will relate to, but there is no one stopping a writer from introducing it to the world. In the past, great works were pushed to the side and never saw the light of day because of the gatekeepers. No more.

# Chapter Fifteen: J.N. Chaney

**Biography**

I was born in a small town to a working class family of entrepreneurs. My dad and his father sold cars for a living, while my mom sold insurance next door. I grew up learning how to run a business. As I got older, I discovered science fiction and found comfort in the escape those stories provided. Eventually, I decided I didn't have much interest in cars or insurance, so I went off to college to see what the whole writing thing was about. My dad disowned me for a while (he didn't believe in school, having dropped out in seventh grade), but he eventually came around and accepted it. After working full time while getting a BA in Creative Writing, I decided I needed a few more years of education, so I joined the Air Force and got my Master's. During that time, I saved half of every paycheck, knowing I would leave the service and begin my writing career. When I finally became a civilian again in late 2010, I had an MFA, $27,000 in savings, and a will to succeed. Everything I have now, I grew from that initial investment.

**Education**

Personally, I didn't get much out of college as it pertains to writing (your mileage may vary, though). It did allow me the time I needed to develop my craft, but the most useful knowledge came from books like "On Writing" by Stephen King or the other popular plot structure books most people recommend. From my experience, the real wealth of useful knowledge lies in conversations with people who are more successful than you are. Seek them out. Ask them what they did and how they did it. Ignore specialized courses from failed so-called gurus who claim to know the secret sauce. Chances are they're just repackaging old information at a premium cost. You can find the same information from Google or Facebook. Ask around. Go to conferences and meet people. Find your tribe and develop relationships. Talking to people is remarkably affordable.

**Influences**

I view my job as two sided. On one, I'm a writer and storyteller. On the other, I'm a business owner. Each of these requires a different skillset. For the writer half, I learned most of what I know from reading. Orson Scott Card's early work had a massive impact on me ("Ender's Game" is the reason I wanted to be a writer), Kurt Vonnegut helped shape the way I write, and Robert Heinlein showed me that big ideas can take your story a long way. I was also influenced by the likes of G.R.R. Martin, Stephen King, and many others. When it comes to business, I always took pride in my grandfather's story. He dropped out of kindergarten and somehow managed to start a successful car dealership. Because he couldn't read or write, he signed with a large "X" when he went to the car auctions. He kept no notes, so every bit of information had to stay locked in his head. He had an incredible memory, and he always took time for his family. I used to spend most of my afternoons and weekends at his house, listening to his stories about his life and how he grew his business, and I like to think I took something away from all of that. As I got older, I found I had an interest in building things, so blending writing with entrepreneurship just made good sense.

### Path to Publication and/or Becoming a Publisher

Money is always one of the big things, but the truth is that you can do this for cheap if you really want to. I was living off my savings, so I had to make budget calls constantly. I found someone to do my first series' covers for free (that same guy is now my company's Art Director), and I asked a few friends to help edit my book. It took me five years to write that first one, a year to do the second, six months for the third, and so on. At one point, I wrote a book in two weeks, which went on to become my first major breakout hit. I'd like to tell you that the first few took a long time because I was still learning, but the truth was that I just wasn't determined enough. Once I sat down and said "I'm going to do this," things changed rapidly. I went to bed with a keyboard in my hands, then woke up and immediately started writing again (I wrote in a small room on my TV, so I had to use a wireless keyboard and mouse in my bed). I'm talking 15-16 hours of writing a day. I became totally fixated on my goal, completely unmovable. If you want to do something, you have to want it more than anything, and you have to be willing to give nearly everything up in order to see it done. That doesn't mean you'll have to quit your day job or go without new clothes like I did, but it does mean saying "no" to going out with your friends from time to time so you can stay home and write. And maybe it means turning off the TV to go edit that chapter.

Becoming a publisher was probably just as challenging as becoming a successful author. It was expensive, time consuming, and required a lot of difficult decisions. I have always believed in a quality-first approach to writing, perfectly happy to delay a book for a full year if that's what it takes to make it good. When your name goes on something, you want that name to represent a certain level of quality to the reader. If they pick it up and hate it, you'll never see them again, so every hour you spend working on it to make it better is an investment. And it's important that the co-writer believes in that same philosophy. I've worked with a few people who wanted to turn in a first draft and then walk away because they aren't interested in editing it, and that's fine, but it's not how I operate. It's taken a lot of trial and error to locate the right authors with the same quality standards who are just as hungry for success as I am and who believe in the power of a good story. When you add on the requirement that we have similar writing styles, finding the right collaborators becomes a very tricky and time consuming task.

### The Hard Lessons You've Learned

The biggest lesson I've learned is to listen to readers. They'll tell you what they want, whether it's in the comment section of a post or the reviews on Amazon or Goodreads. You can't just ignore them, no matter how scathing the feedback might seem. I've reached out to people who 1-starred my books and asked them for more feedback or to beta read the next book, because I saw value there.

Ever since I decided I wanted to write for a living, I've told myself I could be better. No matter what story I was working on, I sought out someone smarter than me to explain what I had done wrong. It's something I've maintained to this day, that no matter who you are or how much you've achieved, you can always be better. You always have room for growth.

### Where are You Now?

It's been seven years since I published my first book. In that time, I've released 120 others, hit the top 100 on Amazon multiple times, and I'm still writing. I also run Variant Publications. I'm engaged to an awesome lady, and we have a dog named Misa and a cat named Meatball. Life is pretty good, but I still work more than 40 hours a week, and I still delay books when they don't hit the quality standards I've set for myself. You can't get lazy in this business. You have to keep going. There's still so much work left to do.

### Where do You See Things Going?

As more and more writers crowd the market on Amazon, the company's KENP rate will continue to drop. This has been happening for the last few years, so I expect it to continue. I think many writers will either quit, scale back, or just accept the new normal and earn less money. The bigger authors are going to move away from Amazon and establish themselves in separate spaces. You'll see more of them sell from their own websites or use other services that give a better ROI. I think Amazon helped kickstart the movement of independent authors, but eventually they're going to get left behind as those same authors continue to evolve. Maybe Amazon will pivot and find a way to keep people around. They're always looking at ways to improve. Still, that might not be enough for some authors, so an exodus may be inevitable.

I also expect audio to continue to grow over the next 10 years. I'm sure this comes as no surprise to anyone. At the same time, thanks to programs like Audible Plus, we will likely see a more competitive space where newer authors have an even harder time breaking out.

This business has, since the early years, become more and more competitive and expensive. I don't see that changing. In fact, I see it getting even more difficult in the coming years.

More and more authors will continue to sign with small publishers who understand the market and how to push their books for them. Traditional publishers will see more of their market share diminish, replaced by these smaller groups.

### Contact Info

You can find me at www.jnchaney.com.

# Chapter Sixteen:
# Martha Carr

As of September 2021, Martha Carr had nearly 250 books available for sale on Amazon. Calling such a backlist Titanic would not be a stretch, and, in fact, would likely be the most accurate term. That's a lot of books. Yet even a cursory glance at her ratings shows that readers don't merely like her books, they *love* them. Quantity and quality do not always go hand in hand, unless that hand belongs to a Titan like Martha Carr.

**Biography**

I started writing in the dinosaur era when computers were brand new and large and sat on a desk and the printers made a loud clacking noise. Even that seemed revolutionary. No more typewriters or white out. (Something invented by Mike Nesmith's mom and bonus points if you already knew he was in the Monkees. I used to carry around Davy Jones' picture from the back of a cereal box in my plastic wallet when I was six. I take the Monkees very seriously.) I wanted to write from the time I was five years old and discovered libraries. We didn't have much and to find out there was a place that would let me borrow as many books as I could carry (my father's rule), read them, and bring them back for more, well. These must be the most benevolent people in the world. I've had a love affair with libraries ever since—and writing.

I spent my teen years in the DC area and thought of the Washington Post as my local paper. When I started pitching them stories in my late twenties, it never occurred to me I wouldn't get something over the transom. They took my very first story—a long piece about surviving an abusive marriage, losing weight, and training to run a marathon—and only changed one word. Of course, that last part never happened again, but I went on to become a stringer for them and wrote a lot of pieces on topics from rock concerts to the federal highway system to sweat lodges. Each time there were about three different editors who reviewed and had questions, and I quickly learned to tell subjects, "I may call you back with more questions." It was such a great training ground for looking at things from every angle, just listening, working on something till it was right, and learning how to tell a complete story without a lot of adjectives.

I went on to sell pieces to every major print outlet—the Wall Street Journal, the New York Times, Politico and more. Eventually I landed my own national column on politics with the syndicate Cagle Inc that ran in newspapers across the country twice a week, with four million readers. Along the way, I got a thriller, "Wired," published, as well as a nonfiction book on US orphanages, "A Place to Call Home," that gave me the chance to stay at different orphanages all over the country over a two-year period. What a wonderful life in a lot of ways.

However, money was never plentiful, and I got really good at stretching a dollar as a single mom of the fabulous and now grown, Louie. Finding a five-dollar bill in my wallet was cause for celebration. I had all the critical accolades and "Wired" had even sold well, particularly to libraries, but no big paycheck.

Until…

The world changed and Indies became a force of their own. And I heard about this guy—Michael Anderle—who had just started writing five months prior and was already making six figures—in fiction. That was supposed to be impossible. I went to hear him speak with the hope I'd at least hear a couple of good marketing tips.

Halfway through, I realized he had noticed something the rest of us had missed. Partially because he was already in online marketing and partially because he is a voracious reader—what we call a whale reader. He wrote what he wanted to read and fast, and it worked.

After he finished, he said he'd stay as long as anyone had a question. Out of almost a hundred writers only three of us went up to him and only one stayed in contact. That was me.

Here we are, almost 250 books later, having a great time and selling a lot of great books, interacting with fans and building a strong financial base. My five-year-old self would look back over the entire career and say, this was even better than I imagined. Well done. Let's see what else you can do.

**Education**

Writing articles for old school publications was a great training ground. I learned how to be direct, concise, hit a deadline no matter what, and work with others. Plus, I made a few dollars and saw my work in print pretty quickly.

One of the best things I did as a new writer was to form a writing group with about four other writers that met once a month in someone's home. We had to send our latest chapter at least a week in advance and the group would critique it. There was a basic rule that there were no critiques on whether you liked the genre or story, but only on whether the plot held together. Did we believe the characters? It created an artificial deadline and helped me continue to grow as a writer as well as make some life-long friendships. "Wired" was work-shopped in that group.

The other thing was that a few writer retreats were led by an accomplished author/teacher in some remote place that had no TV and one phone. This was pre-cell phones. (Yes, I'm that old.) There was a rule that we couldn't even say hello to each other till two in the afternoon and at night the author would go over what we had written, and we'd read some of it out loud and drink some wine. There was even an inner tube ride down a river on one of the days. I wrote so much each time while listening to the sounds of other writers through my open window. One guy had even brought an old manual typewriter. That's a wonderful sound.

Each of these things were nourishing, encouraging, and brought necessary critiques with them that helped me grow as a writer and gave me courage to keep going.

Once I did start making money as an author, it became harder to get away, and I'm about to set out for a personal retreat in the woods of Wisconsin. My first in about three decades, and I can't wait.

### Influences

Two influences stick out for me. The first was a cousin of mine. My family has roots in the South and even a third cousin twice removed is Family with a capital F. This cousin, Virginius Dabney, or V as a lot of people called him, was a Pulitzer Prize-winner for his columns on segregation in the 1960's as an editor of The News

Leader in Richmond, Virginia. He was not lacking in courage, and he didn't suffer fools well, even if he was one of the kindest people I ever knew.

He and his wife, Douglas, (who used to greet me every time with how we were related, running through all the past relatives till she got to us) told me stories about V's early days as a young reporter, newly engaged. At the time, I was a newly minted single mother with a baby and terrified of making it on my own. Apparently, when V was new on the job he was hanging around the newsroom when a shout went out from an editor telling him to go cover a bank closure. Someone muttered something to him about probably not using the piece and so, V took no notes. Well, they did want the piece, and V had to type up something fast from memory. His lead was that the bank president had embezzled the funds. Too bad no one actually said that. It wasn't until after the paper was in print that V realized his mistake and was sure his new career was over. However, it turned out—it was true! He had gotten his first big scoop, completely by accident. They were both laughing when they told me the story. Life has a way of working out—keep going.

But the rest of my family thought writing was the dumbest idea I'd had in a long string of dumb ideas. I mean, look where I was for proof. A young, single mother who wanted to be a writer. But V understood. He took one of his most popular books and wrote inside, "to my cousin, Martha. A great writer. Virginius Dabney." It was before I had written a single word. It was my gold ticket and made the rest of the family shut up just long enough to get started.

The other influence was William Styron by proxy, sort of. He was my literary hero and the reason I finally sat down and started writing "Wired," after reading "Sophie's Choice." In one of those darker economic years with a young son, I yelled out loud to the cosmos, "I'm gonna need a sign here. Do I keep going?" I was at one of my lowest points. V had passed away, and I was out of cheerleaders. Maybe I should quit.

But, that same day, I got an invitation in the mail to the opening of the new state library. The speaker would be William Styron. Wait, it gets better. My cousin, William, was going to introduce him. Turns out his mother, Lucy Kate, grew up with Mr. Styron and William was writing his official biography. Facts I was completely unaware of.

I showed up hours early and talked my way in using my cousin's name. I was determined to get a front row seat and sit right under Mr. Styron's nose, which I did, listening raptly to him read from "Confessions of Nat Turner" and tell stories about being a writer. Afterward, I got in line to get a book signed, barely able to take a deep breath. When I got to him, I quietly told him I was an author too with one book to my name. "Wired." He looked up at me, his eyebrows going up and smiled. "Oh, I read that. Good book. You should keep writing." Turns out my cousin had given him a copy.

I stood there for a moment, holding my breath, waiting for him to sign my copy of "Sophie's Choice" before floating away to the middle of the packed crowd. My hero told me to keep writing. The universe had answered.

### Path to Publication and/or Becoming a Publisher

I have a math learning disability—discalculus, which means I don't recognize numbers easily or follow along with the logic of math. That means for me, doing ads successfully is not going to happen. I could let that be a permanent roadblock and a woe is me, or I can pair up with someone—like Michael Anderle who's very good at that part of things—and keep going. I made a lot of something that is shared instead of keeping a little, tiny pile. And I have someone to share the highs and lows with who understands better than anyone else.

### The Hard Lessons You've Learned

I've been both traditionally published, and I've been an Indie on my own, and then lately teaming up with Michael to co-create the Oriceran Universe. It's all been good and a lot of fun and frankly, that's my guiding principle and constant question. Am I having fun?

If not, what can I change? What do I need help with? What am I willing to let go?

The reason I think the collaboration has worked is because of the acronym, WAIT. Why Am I Talking? I hear it float through my head all the time. In the past, old insecurity might have me wanting to interject with some nugget of useful info just to show I deserved a seat at the table. But, I already had a seat and a lot of the time being quiet is more useful. With the Post editors, they had so much more experience—they didn't need to hear from me. And with Michael Anderle, he was already financially successful. Maybe I just keep saying yes and see what happens. Both times, that tactic paid off rather handsomely. The first time with what I learned from everyone at the Post and the continuation of assignments, and the second time with a financially and creatively successful collaboration.

### Where are You Now?

I am a bestselling Indie author living in my dream house with my secret garden out back and nearly 250 books and counting having a hell of a time. The Oriceran Universe continues to grow along with the fan base, and it's given me the freedom to think about other outside projects without the financial fear.

### Where do You See Things Going?

The old style of publishing with brick and mortar buildings will probably go away and be replaced with a more virtual hybrid that will look a lot like a collaboration but with more back office people. Indie authors will continue to thrive and do some books with these hybrid publishers to gain more readers and access to bigger marketing budgets, as well as do projects on their own.

Indies in general are very clever, creative, business-minded people. Many of the innovative ideas that will change the way the industry operates will probably come from this group. Indies have more flexibility, and now, enough capital to try something new and tweak it quickly or abandon it fast and go on to the next idea or build on a good one.

### How do you define success?

Success for me means balance. Do I have enough time to pursue what I want to do at home and at work? Do I have enough financially to expand my business, travel, have some fun, retire well, build a garden, leave something behind?

That does require me to ask a few questions after I spot some of the Facebook posts that have a detailed list of things another author is doing to reach their new heights. Is it useful for me? Do I have time (even with a great assistant)? Am I already on a good track? Do I even want to do that? That keeps me from getting dazzled by someone else's shiny object and staying grateful for where I am and what I have.

TITANS RISING | 235

**Contact Info**

You can find me most days at www.MarthaCarr.com and email me at martha@marthacarr.com. I'm also often hanging out in https://www.facebook.com/groups/MarthaCarrFans giving away stuff, planning fan events, Pizza Fridays, and lots more.

# Chapter Seventeen:
# Mel Todd

It is no exaggeration to say that Mel Todd is one of the biggest names in urban fantasy today, but in so saying, the trap is to limit her by that success and measure her by the inherent deception behind mere numbers. Reading the lessons that she so generously shares here is a reminder that while Titans make it look effortless, they all have their own trials and tribulations to fight through that are most assuredly *not* effortless.

### Biography

I was born and raised in California—but we are talking Northern California, not Southern. Both of my parents were teachers and we had a small ten-acre farm. While I never remember going hungry (at least not outside me refusing to eat dinner) I know there were years where money was scarce. I went to college in Oregon, falling in love with Portland in the 1980s and 90s (I miss that Portland). I worked in a variety of jobs and places: Portland as a construction secretary, Connecticut as a nanny, Northern California as a substitute teacher, Southern California in a Rape Crisis center, Ohio as an IT tech, Atlanta in IT. Life led me to Atlanta, Georgia, in 2002. That was where I met the man I'd marry, Ash Lovins. Of all the places I thought I'd end up living, the South wasn't one of them. My parents moved out to Georgia in 2005 and I had a pretty good life. When my husband was killed in a car accident in 2016 I had to pick myself back up again and find a new life. It's been a wild ride and I'm just waiting to see what the next chapter in life brings me.

### Education

Having two parents that are teachers is a blessing and a curse. A blessing in that I was encouraged to read and challenged to explore. Curse in that you didn't get away with not doing your homework. I have read all my life. I can't remember not being able to read. I grew up on a small farm so I always had chores and animals to take care of. And that is a special type of education. Animals don't care if you are sick: they need to be milked, fed, let in/out. Weeds need to be pulled, vegetables picked, fruit processed, even when you are bored, angry, or just tired of everything. I think you learn more with that than what any school can teach you. I earned my Bachelor of Science degree in Psychology in 1997. It took me ten years of working full time and going to school part time to get that degree. And yes, it is a Science degree because calculus was less work than a foreign language. Since then I have gone to writing conferences, read books, had friends and betas shred my books, and, through it all, I try to remember the lessons of my childhood—if you don't do it, then it doesn't get done, and it has to get done.

### Influences

I have so many writers that I could say I want to write like them, and these are the authors that provided me hundreds of hours of distraction in a life that wasn't always perfect. But I don't think any of them inspired me; they were all pillars that I looked up at and worshiped. I honestly have to say the person who convinced me I could sell my weird stories was Evan Currie, a fellow fanfic author. We were talking in 2011, and he had just got a deal with 47North. He told me I should write the original stories and see what happened. It took me a while to believe him, along with a lot of self-doubt. But the fans and friends I have gained via fanfiction convinced me that I could write a story people wanted to read. The stories I wanted to tell. From there I started writing. Oh, the mistakes I made, but my husband believed in me, and I was pretty sure I was telling good stories. So, I kept trying.

He was killed in 2016, and I took most of that year off. I wrote some novellas about widowed people finding love, but that didn't help me. I said screw it and decided to write stories I knew he'd love, fantasy, sci-fi, and urban fantasy. I haven't looked back since I started writing what I'd grown up reading. So I guess the final person to kick me over the hump was trying to give my husband stories to read.

### Path to Publication and/or Becoming a Publisher

I've been a writer for a long time. I've found manuscripts that I wrote in high school and college. It's something I've always done and never figured they were good enough to attempt to do anything with besides entertain myself. In 2003, I was introduced to fanfiction, though I'd already written my own Star Trek fanfiction in 7th or 8th grade, and I dove in. Over the years, I wrote over 500,000 words of fanfiction before I ever thought of writing original stuff. The novel that I originally published as "No Choice" was written from scratch three times. The reason changed, the story changed, the characters changed, but I finally had a book I liked.

But, before that, I was a Romance Writers of America® (RWA) member in my local group. That led me to attending an RWA convention where I listened to Bella Andre talk. At that time she was Indie and earning seven figures a year. She had a comment that I never forgot—"Start out like you will be earning a million a year; that way, when you do, you'll be ready."

I've kept that philosophy and so I started a company, not an author, not a brand, not just a series. I want Bad Ash Publishing to be a small press people come to, knowing the types of stories they will get.

By far, the death of my husband was the hardest, but it also convinced me I could do anything. "You never know how strong you are until you have no other choice."

### The Hard Lessons You've Learned

*Write in a genre you love, not the genre that is hot.* Everyone says write to market, and I kinda disagree. If you suck at writing erotica, I don't care how hot it is, you won't have fun writing it, and your readers will know. I say look at the market and see if you can twist or amplify what you like and center it in that. For example, I am not a huge fan of zombie novels—after a while they all seem to run together—but I love aliens. If I saw the zombie market getting hot again I'd twist it, make them aliens that have invaded humans, or an allergic reaction to aliens, or a plague to wipe us out so they can terraform. I'd still be writing a zombie novel but it would be more of something I love.

*Talk to people.* I can't say that enough. I hate trying to introduce myself to people or putting myself out there; I'd rather hide in the corner with some whiskey and watch. But, by talking to people, taking a chance and asking for a favor, miracles happen. Most of us don't have a problem giving a helping hand to someone trying. Just make sure you say thank you, are polite, and then do it for someone else.

**Be patient.** I'm sure there are going to be people saying I'm an overnight success. And maybe I am. But I've been publishing regularly since 2013. It wasn't until 2020 that my sales took off. You can never tell what will catch spark and fly.

**Be where the readers are, not the authors.** Look I love my author groups. I love learning and seeing what they've done, but here is the honest truth—we don't have enough time to read. No matter how much we want to support other authors, we know we need to spend the time writing. So if you want to get people to find your books you need to be where the readers are. Facebook groups, book clubs, even Goodreads. Remember, other authors are your friends and competitors. Readers are your livelihood.

**Plan to fail.** I know that sounds very anti-positive thinking and everything else. But I mean it. Just because a book did great, doesn't mean your next one will. Always plan that everything will go wrong, and then, when something does, you're ready for it. If you have planned to fail, then you are ready to succeed.

Last one, promise. **Don't downplay your success.** Writing a book is impressive. Publishing it is hard. Making money off it is harder. Failing and trying again and again is something most people don't do. Be proud of what you've done and don't use words like "just" or "only." You did this, own it.

## Where are You Now?

Lol, the smartass answer to this is I'm a Unicorn. [Editor's note: this book contains a herd of Unicorns] The honest answer—I make low six figures right now publishing me and one other author. I have plans to expand in the next few years and find other authors that I want to publish. It is always an uphill battle, but I'm proud of my company, Bad Ash Publishing, and myself. I kept at it and persevered. Now to see where I am in five or ten years.

## Where do You See Things Going?

The industry has changed a lot. And I think it will change even more. Gazing into my crystal ball here is what I think.

- More audio and computer read books. I think this is going to expand more and more as people realize they can ingest story and do other things. The appetite for entertainment is not going to lesson.
- Niche publishing. I think the big publishers are going to die. They are too bloated. I think you will see more and more like Baen or Hard Case Crime, where the publisher has the loyalty.
- New Media Types. We know about digital and audio, but I'm expecting more virtual storytelling, immersive things, maybe even holodeck-like. I see the VR gaming technology grabbing stories and running with it.
- More niche genres. While, personally, I think there should be six genres (mystery/thriller, horror, romance, nonfiction, wonder, self-help) the reality is genre is a marketing thing, so as we have more freedom to write the stories we want, the more genres there are going to be.

**Contact Info**

I'm on Facebook, Twitter, and Instagram all as BadAshBooks. It makes it easy. You can find my website at www.badashpublishing.com and I'm at various cons each year. My newsletter is the best way to keep track of me.

# Chapter Eighteen:
## Colonel Jonathan Brazee, USMC (Ret.)

### Biography

I was born in Oakland, California in 1958 to a working-class family, the middle of five children. We moved around quite a bit in California, Mexico, Maryland, Connecticut, and Iowa. I had skipped a grade in school, so I was the youngest in my Des Moines high school class, and the second youngest in my class at the US. Naval Academy.

I had initially intended to be a biology major and work in the Navy's Marine Mammal program, but the Academy dropped that major the year I arrived. I shifted to Far Eastern Studies, but more importantly, I decided to take my commission as a second lieutenant in the Marine Corps.

I became an infantry officer, serving in infantry, anti-tank, recon, air delivery, logistics, and lots of staff billets throughout my career. My final billet was as the liaison to USAID in Iraq during the war. I retired as a colonel.

I worked a number of jobs before joining the military, always hustling to make a buck. Besides the typical paper route, McDonalds, and busing tables, I started a number of small companies to sell things door-to-door, mow lawns, shovel snow, and contract out industrial work. I've been a university professor and the Director of International Business for a large Thai manufacturing company.

245

Sports have always been important to me. I wrestled and played tennis in high school and wrestled at the Naval Academy. It was there where I discovered my love of rugby. I played for the Academy, for several civilian teams, and for the Marine Corps team when we took the military championship. I've also run several marathons and have multiple national championships in equestrian events. While in Iraq, circumstances forced me to shift from running to weightlifting, and I've kept that up to this day.

I am married and am the father of three-year-old identical twins, now living in Colorado Springs.

**Education**

I've got a bachelor's, master's, and a doctoral degree, the first in political science/Far Eastern Studies (Chinese), the second two in business fields. The first degree was mostly a general engineering degree despite the title, but I took a class in Creative Writing as an elective. It helped formulate my writing style and resulted in the first story I ever published. It also gave me a good background in Asian history and culture, which I further expanded with over twelve years being stationed and later living in Japan, Korea, Thailand, and the Philippines. Several of my books take advantage of my experiences in Asia.

My advanced degrees were in the business arena, and, while the courses I took may not have had a huge influence on my writing, the research required to earn a doctorate has been a boon as I research my own books.

The military has been extremely influential, too. All of my military-themed books reflect on my experiences and the experiences of others. I believe those experiences allow me to create a feeling of verisimilitude, even if the military action is in the far future.

I've always been a student of the human condition. I've travelled extensively, having been to over a hundred countries, and that has given me a broad background from where I can pull different cultural aspects for my writing.

I am not a person that attends many workshops. I signed up for one but got sick upon arrival and spent most of my time in my room. However, I was invited to attend the first 20Booksto50k in Las Vegas, and, as I was living there at the time, I went. It was an amazing event, and I did learn many options on how to further my writing career. Since then, I have attended every 20Books conference, and I learn something new each time. 20Books is at the top of my list, but I have also learned ways to improve my writing and the business of writing at the Science Fiction and Fantasy Writers of America conferences, the Romance Writers of America National Convention, and Novelists, Inc.

While not formal workshops, I do get together with other writers to socialize and pick each others' brains. This has been beneficial in furthering my writing career.

One of the ways I've tried to learn is simply to read other books. There are amazing writers out there, and, while I won't copy anyone, I try to figure what I like or don't like about a particular book, then try avoid what turned me off and emulate the techniques for what I liked.

### Influences

My father was my earliest influence as I grew. He was the person who taught me honor and discipline, traits that I have tried to maintain throughout my life, and I think that reflects in my writing. Later on, while at the Naval Academy, then Captain Gary Parks, USMC, (later Lieutenant General Gary Parks), exemplified those traits, and he was largely the reason I chose the Marines over the Navy.

I can count a dozen Marines who have impacted my life, and the core trait among them was probably discipline. Not the "do what you're told" discipline of boot camp, but the discipline to do what's right and just get it done. That discipline is what has enabled me to produce the millions of words I have under my belt to date.

My brother introduced me to the wonders of science fiction. I had been reading "adult" books since I was seven, but he gave me a copy of Andre Norton's "Star Man's Son." I was utterly gob smacked that a writer could make up their own universe, and that was a huge allure. With my brother urging me on, I first read every Norton book published to date, then I went through most of the Golden Age of Science Fiction and fantasy books I could find, reading Heinlein, Asimov, Pournelle, Niven, Simak, Harrison, Williamson (whose book, "Darker than You Think" gave birth to my love of werewolves), Schmidt, Tolkien, and Pohl. Later I graduated to McCaffrey, Brin, Resnick, Cherryh, Le Guin, Dickson, Bujold, McIntyre, Tiptree, and Pashin, among others. It would be difficult to say who might have influenced me the most, but I think it was all of them as a group, helping me slowly develop my own imagination and ideas.

### Path to Publication and/or Becoming a Publisher

I wrote and published my first short story while a midshipman back in 1978. During my military career, I published a wide variety of nonfiction articles and books. It wasn't until I was in Iraq in 2006 that I wrote my first novel. I never dreamed that anyone would want to read it, so in 2009, I went to a vanity press so I could get twenty copies that I could give to family and friends. The vanity press put the paperback on Amazon, and over the next several years, I made $98 in royalties, and I thought that was amazing.

In late 2012, I saw my first Kindle at the United lounge at LAX, and I mentioned that I had a book on Kindle. The guy looked me up and told me I didn't. I called up the vanity press and was informed that I needed to pay them another $70 for the book to be uploaded as an ebook.

By this time, I had read a few articles about self-publishing, so I decided to give it a go. I put the price of the book at $0.99—I mean, who would pay more than that for an unknown like me? To my utter surprise, over the next few weeks, I sold 400 books. The next month was 700. I was shocked.

After a few months, I started getting emails asking when the sequel would come out. As I'd killed off half the characters, that was a problem. But I wrote another, then a third. All were still at $0.99, so I wasn't making a mint, but I was happy that people were reading them.

I wrote another military fiction trilogy, taking place in Iraq during 2006, a general science fiction book, and an historical fiction, and I was making good hobby money. It wasn't until 2014 that I went back to my true love, science fiction, that my career took off. My first military science fiction took off, as did the subsequent series.

I had all the usual suspects of missteps, to include horrible covers, paying exorbitant fees to editors, and blurbs that were lukewarm at best. But I paid close attention to my reviews. When several mentioned the theme of "Forget about the cover, the book is actually good," I took it to heart and redid the covers. For one series, I redid them twice. I was constantly online with other writers, listening to their triumphs and failures, then seeing what might work for me.

As my backlist grew, my income grew, and, in January of 2017, I quit my job in Thailand and came back to the US to become a full-time writer. I was nervous, but it has worked out well for me.

I turned down two trad contracts when I realized they weren't going to do much for me that I couldn't do on my own. I flew to London to discuss a contract with a large publisher there, but that fell apart due to a lack of knowledge on how Kindle Unlimited worked (in this case, my ebook sales had dipped that year when I went into KU, and my explanation of page reads and the fact that my revenue had increased seemed to fall on deaf ears).

I have increased my short stories, publishing both in traditional magazines as well as in anthologies that are technically traditional publishers, but publishers with an Indie mindset. I've done audio books both through ACX royalty share and with a publisher, and now I'm branching into hiring a narrator so I can retain full rights.

### The Hard Lessons You've Learned

I am not sure I have many hard lessons. I've always had a strong work ethic, and I think that is one of the major reasons for my success.

Relating to writing, I don't think I initially realized that a good cover was so important, but I think that had more to do with the fact that I didn't dream I'd be writing books that others wanted to read. I think my mindset was that as this was more of a hobby, spending the time and effort on a good cover wasn't really high on my list of priorities.

Also, because I was successful without any marketing, I think I may not have put that much emphasis into learning how to market my books. I had sold well over 100,000 books before I even started a NL signup. As the marketplace became more congested, and as it started to become easier to get lost in the static, I was well behind the eight-ball in learning marketing skills.

### Where are You Now?

I am a full-time hybrid writer with emphasis on Indie publishing. I have about eighty-five titles published, of which over fifty are novels. Most are military science fiction, but the reach extends to science fiction, paranormal, military fiction, historical fiction, and nonfiction.

I am a USA Today Bestseller, a two-time Nebula Award finalist, and a two-time Dragon Award finalist.

Except for a brief hiatus after my girls were born, my sales, and, more importantly, revenue, continue to climb each year. Part of that has been due to starting to make strategic marketing decisions, something I ignored for most of my writing career, and part has been because of co-writing with other successful writers.

2021 will be my best year ever, and I hope I can keep up the momentum moving into 2022.

### Where do You See Things Going?

I think the industry will continue to become more and more decentralized on the production of books on one hand, but more centralized in the distribution, especially in the US (this assumes no major anti-trust actions). There may be more venues through which producers can distribute their products, but the vast majority of the books will find their way into readers' and listeners' hands through one or two platforms.

Producers who want to make a good living in the industry will need to keep ahead of the trends and diversify their products to make full use of their intellectual products.

I think that as programs for editing and animation become better, more and more producers will be able to branch out into clips to promote books first, but, before too long, the ability to create visual content will allow short stories, and eventually, novels, to be made into features for a reasonable cost—by the writers themselves.

**Contact Info**

http://jonathanbrazee.com

jonathan@jonathanbrazee.com

jonathan@semperfipress.com

https://www.facebook.com/jonathanbrazeeauthor

# Chapter Nineteen:
# Nick Thacker

### Biography

I'm a hacker—meaning I don't like to play by the rules, and I don't like to do things the long way if I determine there's a shorter way to do it. I used to think it was laziness, but I've come to realize that it's probably the exact opposite: a severe case of loving the work more than the outcome. I would gladly spend the time learning a programming language, writing code, and developing an applet to autofill fields in Excel instead of just doing it all manually, even if ultimately it cost me far more time.

I treat books the same way—I *could* write faster, but there's something really profound about trying to improve craft and being iterative. I never set out to be a writer but writing found me—I'm just trying to embrace it!

### Influences

I started writing because I love to read. Authors like James Rollins, Matthew Reilly, and Dan Brown got me into the action-adventure/thriller genres. I still read vehemently, but I've expanded my reading to include science fiction, technothrillers, and plenty of nonfiction (I'm a sucker for a good biography).

### Path to Publication and/or Becoming a Publisher

Publishing was a necessary (and inevitable) step along the writing process. I never set out to start a publishing company, but, then again, I never set out to do half the things I've ended up doing. When I finished my first book, I didn't want to waste time querying agents and waiting around—I wanted to see if the book had legs, and I wanted to know immediately. (As it turned out, the book sucked but I learned a lot!)

When I wrote and released the next few books, I realized something—this whole "author" thing is a business, and I was an entrepreneur. For me, that was a good thing: I don't think I could simply write words all day, every day. As such, I enjoyed (and still enjoy) the non-writing parts of the business: bookkeeping, marketing, sales, etc. I've improved and streamlined these systems over the years, and when we started Conundrum Publishing, everything just came together.

I think one of the most important things to keep in mind, whether publishing your own work or publishing someone else's, is that this is a business, and it's a volatile one, especially at the beginning. When you can check your sales every hour, you tend to want to extrapolate that ("if this continues, I'll only make $X this month! Oh no!"), and this is a very unhealthy way to run a business. These numbers change so quickly, and so often, that checking income and sales as often as possible just because we can is cancer to our business model. Instead, check them once a day—or even once per week. Your mental health will be far better because of it.

**The Hard Lessons You've Learned**

Writing as a career is an isolating job. Even if you're clinically introverted, locking yourself in a room for days is unhealthy. I found very quickly that I missed the camaraderie of having an office to go to with other people around—even if I only spoke to a few of them during the course of a workday. I came down with a *very* powerful run of anxiety and even started having panic attacks. I blamed my lower income levels, but the truth of it was that I felt alone.

These days, I try to take walks to get outside more often, and I go to a gym to work out. Once or twice per week I get my writing done at a local brewery or coffee shop, just to get the "background noise" of other people. It helps to feel like I'm still part of human society!

**Where are You Now?**

After 30+ books between myself and cowriters, I'm a USA Today Bestseller, but I care less about the title and more about what writing and publishing consistently has done for me. My family and I own a home on some land in Hawaii and Colorado, which never could have happened with a traditional day job. I still write and release my own books, but I'm publishing others' books as well through our company, Conundrum Publishing.

We publish thrillers exclusively, and after working with traditional publishers for my own work, we've created a traditional publisher that doesn't operate at all like other traditional publishers—and that's a *very* good thing. Our process is set up to reduce costs, produce far better (and more salable) books, and we actually invest in advertising and marketing, unlike many publishers.

### Where do You See Things Going?

I believe the book world is at the cusp of artificial intelligence and machine learning changing the way we (authors) do things. My company, Conundrum Publishing, is already making strides in using AI-based editing, AI audio narration, and other models to create and produce content faster. Using these technologies for creative work may be a point of contention now, but I believe it's not a question of "if," but "when."

Furthermore, I think we are seeing a severe lack of quality recommendations engines, and that will change in the next 5 years. For example, my Kindle knows exactly when I read every day, and for how long before I fall asleep (how long has he been stuck on this page?) If they wanted more of my money, they would advertise books that are exactly like the kinds of books I like to read, right when I pick it up to read at night before bed, right *after* I've just finished another book. To seal the deal, they could even tell me something along the lines of, "We know you read for about this long every night before you fall asleep. This book has chapters that are just the right length, so you'll fall asleep in just the right spot!"

### Contact Info

You can find me at nickthacker.com, on Twitter and Facebook (just search for my name!), and if you're interested in publishing a thriller, do check out Conundrum Publishing (www.conundrumpub.com).

# Chapter Twenty: James Rosone

**Biography**

I'm the oldest of three kids; I have a younger sister and brother. Something most people do not know about my story is that my family was technically homeless for a short period of time during our childhood. My parents were in the process of building a new home in Wisconsin and we had sold our existing home in Illinois, when suddenly, our homebuilder failed to finish our new house. Lawyers got involved, but in the meantime, we ended up living in a campground, various hotels, people's living rooms, and eventually a rental home for fifteen months while my parents struggled to get our new house built.

I remember seeing how tough the circumstances were on my mom and dad. They did their best to make it an adventure for us kids, but it wasn't always pleasant. We slept in a campground even when it rained, and our sleeping bags would get soaked. Eventually, it snowed, and we had to leave the campground. We stayed with some friends until we found somewhere else to stay for a few months. It was tough—my dad's money was tied up in trying to get the new house built so we couldn't afford two rents at once and my mom had to take care of us. It was a super difficult time for us as kids.

I think that tough childhood helped prepare me for some of life's adversities I've had to go through as an adult. When I graduated high school, I started college, just like a lot of young people do. However, I struggled in school. My uncle was a full-time member of the Wisconsin Army National Guard, and he talked to me about joining the Guard. I ended up joining the local unit in my city. It turned out to be the best decision I could have made. I was eighteen, floundering, and not sure of what to do with my life. The Army changed that. They gave me discipline and a purpose. I might have been a National Guardsman, doing this on the weekends and working in my community for the time being, but it paid for my college while giving me some military experience, training, and leadership skills I never would have gotten elsewhere.

Prior to the events of September 11, 2001, I had wanted to go into banking. My plan was to stay in the National Guard for twenty years and be a full-time banker. Then the Twin Towers went down, and the direction of my life changed. I decided to go into the military full-time, and instead of going full-time in the Army, I changed directions and went into the Air Force.

I was originally accepted into the Air Force as an officer. I was waiting to start my officer training when the Air Force initiated a force-shaping process. The military hadn't changed its direction post-9/11 just yet, so they were still downsizing. I ended up losing my officer billet because I was not going in as a pilot. I had to wait another year and go in as an enlisted person. This became a screwed-up mess because I was prior enlisted, meaning I had previously served in another branch of service, something the Air Force didn't like to accept into their own. Luckily for me, I had worked as an intern for the powerful congressman, Paul Ryan. He made a couple of calls, and, 24 hours later, I was in the Air Force and kept my rank as a Staff Sergeant.

I wasn't happy with the job I'd been assigned to in the Air Force, but I knew once you were in, you could easily cross train in a couple of years, so I sucked it up. Eighteen months in, my opportunity came. A call came out, asking for volunteers to assist the Army in a special duty assignment as a military interrogator. I jumped at the opportunity. For me, this was a way of being able to directly contribute to the war—to finally hunt terrorists. I'm not going to lie and say the training was easy or that deployment was easy. It was the hardest thing I've ever done, but I know beyond a doubt we made an impact in the war. I saved lives. I lost lives, I took lives… I lost a huge part of myself in that war, and it dramatically changed me…

The Iraq War made me into a better person in some respects and a not-so-good person in others. It took me a long time to get over what I did and what went on in the sandbox. Truth be told, I almost lost myself completely.

I've been very open about my journey with PTSD. I struggled to find the right help for many years—the medicines the VA gave me did make things better, but it also made it hard to stay mentally "on," and I ended up losing several jobs in a row. This led to a very deep period of depression. Writing may have very literally saved my life.

I began to pour myself into my hobby of telling stories. That spark gave me something to work toward, and it was an excellent escape from the cycle of negative thoughts that kept trying to consume my mind.

At first, writing just made a few extra dollars on the side, but over time, it grew and grew, until eventually, it became a legitimate way to support my family. After a while, my wife, Miranda Watson, who co-writes with me, even had to quit her day job as a nurse so that we could keep up with the production schedule.

Now that I've achieved a certain level of victory over PTSD, I try to help my fellow vets as well. I have been able to do a few TV news specials with our local Fox affiliate about writing therapy and stellate ganglion blocks, and I am currently working to mentor a few veterans to help them get started in launching their own writing careers. It is my belief that having a new mission and purpose in life can have a major positive impact for many others.

**Education**

Believe it or not, I never went to a formal primary education. I grew up in the 1980s and early 90s, and my parents homeschooled me before it was cool (and before we had the internet). It was a lot harder back in those days. Despite that, I obtained double undergraduate degrees from the University of Wisconsin, earned an MBA while in the Air Force, and I went on to graduate school at the University of Oxford, Said Business School. My past never slowed me down or stopped me from attending the #1 university in the world or achieving the kind of education I wanted.

The program at Oxford taught me how to think critically, how to understand business, and how to write. We had to write a *lot* at Oxford. It's ironic—I was sitting in class one day when I decided right then and there, I was going to publish a fictional series. I had already written my memoirs of the Iraq War, but now I wanted to create books about the kind of subjects *I* like to read about. Little did I know, it would take three more years before I'd actually publish my first book, but I believe that class—right then—that's when the idea was born for me to be a published author. I just hadn't moved 100% in that direction yet.

I'm a big believer in continuous professional development. When I am not writing my own books, I continue to read. Now as I dig into a book, though, I am not merely a passive observer of the stories; I make mental notes of what I liked and didn't like from each author. After working with a professional editor for several years, I now see things that I missed in previous reads, such as point-of-view errors or places where dialogue should have been used instead of narrative.

I like to network with other authors, and I'm fairly active in several writers' groups online. These connections are invaluable. With so many ravenous readers in the world, I do not feel intimidated by the other authors out there—we can only produce so much content in a year, even if we increase our productivity. Instead, we are a community that can support one another, and help each other learn from our triumphs and mistakes. In that spirit, I have also traveled in person to attend various networking events in person, such as the yearly conference for NINC, 20Booksto50k, and the London Book Fair. These opportunities have led to fantastic personal connections that have launched me forward as an author.

The nature of the genres I write in is that they are heavily research-driven. I have received more than one one-star review because I made a mistake about the number of rounds a certain weapon can fire or missed an update in the current weapons systems being used by a specific military unit. I've taken that feedback and incorporated various layers to help avoid those errors in the future. I spend a lot of time researching various units, geographical areas, weapons, ships, et cetera—and I firmly believe that my time at Oxford that was so intensive on research gave me the skills I needed to be more effective in this venture. There are times I can spend three hours delving into that world before writing a single scene. I also have a very active group of advanced readers, many of whom have served in various branches of the military. They are very quick to key me in on any potential pitfalls in my work.

When the occasion calls for it, I've also been known to travel for research. In 2018, I attended the Politicon conference in Los Angeles with my wife. The information we learned there dramatically altered the course of the Falling Empires series that we wrote when we found out that advancements in blockchain voting technology were far less susceptible to hacking than we previously believed, and that the weakest link in our elections system was actually mail-in balloting. Without this trip, "Rigged" would have been an entirely different book.

### Influences

I have read a lot of Indie books. One of my jobs had me traveling six months of the year, so I was reading between four and ten books a month. Although the stories were interesting, I didn't find them to be as well thought-out or developed as I'd like, at least not in the genres I enjoyed. Eventually, I got frustrated enough I said, "Forget it; I can write a better war book than this." And that's what I set out to do.

The biggest writer influences that have helped me succeed and shaped my business and my writing would be Mark Dawson's Self-Publishing Formula course, Masterclass.com, and the book, "The Bestseller Code."

Mark Dawson taught me the art of writing as a business. Without that, I'd just be writing books and hoping they sold. I've made a lot of money because of what Mark taught me, and for that, I am eternally grateful.

Masterclass.com gave me access and insight into some of the best writers in the industry. For me, I want to hear from these masters and figure out what little nuggets I can find and make my own. As an example, David Baldacci talked about how you have to make the first couple of paragraphs so compelling it causes the reader to have to keep reading, but then the last couple of paragraphs, especially that last sentence or two have to grab the reader by the throat and not let go—it has to force them to turn the page to find out what's going to happen next. That's the essence of a real page turner.

Dan Brown spoke about reader promises. When you make a commitment to a reader to tell them something or explore something, you have to follow through, even if you are leaving breadcrumbs. You have to keep going and let them unravel yet one more layer to that onion.

Lastly, "The Bestseller Code" taught me that there is an absolute science to writing a bestseller. The human mind is predictable, and so is human behavior. Once you know and accept this, you can craft a book that feeds those obvious patterns of desires. The authors, Matt & Jodi, have documented thousands of books and found distinct patterns of what makes a book a bestseller versus what doesn't. Once you see the pattern, you go, "Wow, it's that easy?"

I'm not lying when I say I've leveraged the tools from "The Bestseller Code" with the last fourteen books I've written, and in that timeframe, those fourteen books have gone on to generate more than seventy percent of our entire writing income. Every book we

264 | WEBB & KENNEDY

run through this process becomes a bestseller, and they all go on to hit over one thousand reviews within the first six to nine months. It's not magic—it isn't hard, but it's a process, and it requires work.

Digging into this process requires you to have some tough skin and realize you might have to tear your book apart to rework it to make it fit within the parameters of what a reader wants. At the end of the day, you have to keep in mind, this is a business. I pay my mortgage with my book sales; I feed my kids and pay my student loans with this money. Yes, it's something I love, it's a passion and enjoyable—but it's also work. It's my livelihood and I never lose sight of that.

### Path to Publication and/or Becoming a Publisher

I actually published my first book in 2008 as I was leaving the Air Force. I had worked as an interrogator during the Iraq War, and I felt that I had a unique story to tell. However, at the time, I did not get set up with the right publisher.

While I was in Iraq again, working as a contractor, my wife handled most of the submissions to publishers. Eventually, we received an offer from a company by the name of Tate Publishing. What we didn't know at the time was that Tate Publishing was essentially vanity publishing—they help you to get your book in print, but the assistance they provided in terms of editing was very minimal, and they really didn't put any of their own ad dollars into it in terms of marketing—in fact, they were always trying to sell us further packages for marketing the book. Years later, Tate Publishing would actually fold after a class-action lawsuit. Needless to say, my first book failed miserably.

Sure, my memoir had been published on Amazon, but that didn't mean anything. It wasn't earning royalties, and it wasn't doing well. At one point, it felt like I was practically selling the thing from the trunk of my car. It was an expensive lesson learned.

Later on, when I was in graduate school at Oxford, I decided to give it another go. I ultimately wrote three books that were a total of 350,000 words, but I never ended up publishing them. Between work, job loss, and relocating from Europe back to America, it just never happened. It wasn't until I was unemployed a second time in 2015 that I decided to get serious about writing. I sat down and crafted the first official book we would self-publish. When "Prelude to World War III" came out, it started slow, but it kept building each month. I then discovered a site called fiverr.com. I leveraged this site for marketing help until I eventually took the time to self-teach myself how to do Facebook advertising via YouTube.

Publishing is tough; it's hard work. Writing a book might seem like an insurmountable obstacle, but trust me, writing the book is the easiest part of the process. Marketing and selling the book; now *that's* what's challenging. That is the piece to the puzzle I've had to invest the most into learning about. At first, I didn't know what I didn't know—I hadn't realized I'd need to know about copy writing, search engine optimization, website management, email list building, Facebook ads, Bookbub submissions, Amazon marketing, writing effective back matter, Instagram, and a whole host of other things. But over time, through networking and constant self-development, it all became clear.

When I first started self-publishing, that income was just on the side. I was unemployed when I wrote the first few books, but then I had to manage continuing to write while moving across country and working full-time in Chicago, with three hours of commuting every day. Unfortunately, writing on the train wasn't really feasible either, since I became carsick when typing on a moving vehicle. So all the writing I did during that time was at nights or on the weekends. And during that period, I didn't have a separate office space, so I wrote most of the Red Storm series on a recliner in the living room. I was blessed to have an understanding wife who took the children on many adventures by herself to give me time to be productive. She would often stay up late with me as well, helping to craft scenes or edit.

When I lost that job, it really was almost like a miracle occurred. The preorders for "Battlefield Ukraine" and "Battlefield Korea" took off. I looked for other work, but nothing was really coming through. If that series hadn't taken off when it did, my personal story might be very different.

### The Hard Lessons You've Learned

The biggest mistake made by most new authors is they do not maintain the view or position that writing professionally is not simply a hobby or something we do for enjoyment. It can be, but ultimately, this is a business. And a business needs to generate money to pay both you and the operating expenses.

Each day when you wake up, you have to determine, "What am I going to do today that will move my business forward? Am I going to work on content creating, like writing the book or series I'm currently engaged with?" This is something you should probably do daily or very close to daily.

Next, there's marketing and/or fan interaction. You need to develop a loyal reading base—people who are going to buy anything and everything you publish. One of the ways you do that is by being reachable to your fans. Letting them know how they can get in touch with you through your book's back matter, staying in touch with them, and finding ways to let them be a part of the stories you are creating. People love that kind of thing. By bringing your fans into the creative process, you are letting them be a part of the story. That causes them to tell their friends and family, who may in turn buy the book to support you. Doing this doesn't cost you a dime, but it does cost you time—so you need to figure out how much time you want to devote to this.

The next biggest challenge I faced, which likely plagues every other author, is time management. There are a lot of distractions in this world—a lot of things and people that will constantly try to draw you away from what you should be doing. What really turned things around for our writing business was going all-in and realizing there was no plan B. Either we made this work, and we'd succeed, or we were going to be homeless living in our car or with family. When you burn the boats, you have no other choice than to take the island.

One of the biggest mistakes we made as authors was in the end of 2018 going into 2019. We did not properly plan how we were going to end one series and then start a new one. Up to that point, we had relied heavily on pre-order sales. At the end of one book, we'd have the next one up for pre-order. This allowed our readers who finished one book to immediately jump into the next book or in this case, the next series. When we finished "Battlefield China," which was our sixth book in the Red Storm series, we took several months to work on crafting the next books and getting that series ready to go. In this case, we made a couple of very big mistakes that likely cost us at least six figures in income. The first was we didn't have book one of the new series ready for pre-order at the end of book six of our final series. That meant the tens of thousands of readers who had finished book six didn't have a new book to jump into. So instead of just carrying the audience over from one series to the next, we lost them. We then had to spend tens of thousands of dollars to try and find them again.

Our second mistake was our covers. We had chosen some book covers that, while looking great, really read a lot more like a nonfiction book than a fictional thriller. This turned away a lot of potential readers and cost us sales.

I cannot harp on the importance of book covers enough. If you are unwilling to pay for a quality cover in your genre, then how do you think your book is going to compete against other authors who are? The cover is like the outside of a house. When you go to sell your house, you don't leave the yard to go feral, or the roof to look like it has a hole. You fix it up, you make sure it has that curb appeal that invites a potential buyer inside. You want them to pull up to your house and go, "Wow, I like this place already." That's a book cover. It's the very first impression they have of your book, and if it doesn't tell a story and knock it out of the park, then you've already got a strike against you.

In the beginning, we did not have enough capital to purchase the best quality covers, but we did the best we could with the funds we had at the time. However, as our revenues increased, we realized we were leaving money on the shelves and invested in higher quality covers. This change dramatically increased our sales.

Next, book descriptions. Again, wow, authors struggle with this. And not just some authors—even the great authors struggle with this. You look at their book descriptions, and they are two pages long. A description is not supposed to be a synopsis. It's supposed to be full of hooks—little nuggets that cause someone to want to learn more.

When we first wrote our descriptions, we totally fell into that trap, thinking we needed to include more of the book's content. However, I came to learn that adding too much information just tells the reader, "I already know what's going to happen, so why buy it?" There is a very technical science to this type of writing, and you can see the math in terms of sales conversions. When we updated our book descriptions, the amount of clicks we would have to get to achieve a sale went way down. If you'd like to learn more about effective book descriptions, I refer you to Brian Meeks, who now handles *all* of our book descriptions.

### Where are You Now?

Each year we've been writing, with the exception of 2019 when we made that huge mistake with preorders, we've grown in sales. By the conclusion of 2020, we should surpass the $500K mark in sales for the first time. My goal for 2022 is to surpass the $700K mark. That's going to be incredibly difficult. It means finding more readers, and it means creating more content.

Increasing our sales that much will also mean not forgetting about our backlist and doing what we can to keep promoting it. We now have three completed book series—we have to keep marketing and promoting those books. A common mistake authors will make is they promote the newest series they have and forget about their backlist. I can safely tell you that in 2021, our backlist still generated $120k in royalties—that's revenue that likely would have been lost if I had only focused on our newest material. As I get ready to close out another series and then create a new one, I can never lose sight of how important it is to continue marketing our backlist books.

As to increasing our marketing share, that all comes down to creative marketing—figuring out how to best leverage our marketing tools and dollars to continue finding new readers while always working to retain our existing ones.

### Where do You See Things Going?

I think the book industry is going to continue to evolve. One of the biggest changes I think we'll see is a deal will likely be struck between the major traditional publishers and Amazon to allow them to place their books in the Kindle Unlimited program. This will likely result in a lot of books and content being added to the KU program but will ultimately tank that program in a negative way for us Indie authors.

I think the book publishing business will grow in the coming years, but I think it's going to be increasingly harder and harder for us Indie authors to scratch out a living. Unless you are able to create a lot of really good, compelling content and then have the financial resources to market those books, it will become more difficult to get your foot in the door.

What most people do not realize is that each year, we are seeing thousands of new authors join the KDP platform. Each of these authors is competing essentially for the same group of readers in their specific genre. That means instead of five authors competing for the attention of a hundred readers, you now have ten, or fifteen, or twenty. So, unless people are reading more quickly, or unless KDP/Amazon find a way to acquire more readers, it's going to become incredibly hard to make a living writing books if you are just getting into this business. That's not to say you can't or shouldn't try, but you need to temper your expectations.

### Contact Info

I can be found on Facebook at https://www.facebook.com/RosoneandWatson/

My author website, where you can subscribe to my mailing list is https://www.frontlinepublishinginc.com/

# Chapter Twenty-One:
## James Hunter and Jeanette Strode

James Hunter and his amazing wife, Jeanette Strode, created Shadow Alley Press out of a hope and a dream. Like every Titan in this book, newer writers are advised to follow them on social media, to read their books, and, if you run into them at a conference or traditional Sci-Fi con, listen to every word they say. Representative of the other Titans who have created their own publishing companies, they are disruptively innovating how books are provided to and consumed by readers.

**Biography**

James Hunter is a full-time ink slinger, a former Marine Corps sergeant, a combat veteran, and the bestselling author of over thirty novels, including the Yancy Lazarus series, Rogue Dungeon, Bibliomancer, Vigil Bound, and the LitRPG epic Viridian Gate Online. In addition to writing, James also runs Shadow Alley Press with his wife, Jeanette. On the publishing side of operations, James is the CEO of Shadow Alley and the creative director, responsible for content creation and book acquisition, as well as commissioning all the amazing art Shadow Alley produces. He self-published his first book in January 2015 and hasn't looked back since.

Jeanette Strode is a former chemist turned rogue publisher, who has made it her mission to massively disrupt the publishing industry, help authors achieve amazing things, and make good money while doing it. Jeanette left her job behind to take on the marketing, finance, and administrative control of Shadow Alley Press in 2016. With her at the helm as COO, Shadow Alley has grown from a modest-sized company to a million-dollar-a-year publishing house with over a hundred and fifty titles and fifteen active authors.

## Education

### From James:

Where publishing is concerned, I have no formal education—no publishing degree or MFA. Not even a bachelor's degree in English Lit. I'm just a fan of stories, of books, and of great characters that can sweep me away on a journey. But I have cultivated a Learner's Posture, which is to say I am constantly trying to learn and grow as the industry evolves and technology and reader habits shift. In the early days when I first started publishing, I read everything I could find on self-publishing from David Gaughran's "Let's Get Digital" to "Write. Publish. Repeat." by Sean Platt and Johnny Truant. I scoured the internet, digesting blogs and listening to podcasts, cobbling together a patchwork knowledge of the industry.

I will say that the learning curve for Indie publishing is awfully steep, and getting a handle on it requires a ton of legwork, but there are great resources for authors looking to get knee-deep in the publishing bog. 20Booksto50k is a wealth of great information—both the online presence and the physical conference itself. Mark Dawson and his various self-publishing courses have likewise been an invaluable resource on our journey. Some of the most valuable nuggets of wisdom I've picked up came from conventions. The 20Books conference in Vegas has always been a great place to network and talk shop with other knowledgeable folks, and I also attend Superstars Writing Seminar every year, hosted by the awesome Kevin J. Anderson. DragonCon is also a yearly staple, and I've learned more at the Westin Bar over drinks than I have just about anywhere else.

**From Jeanette:**

When I think about my education in terms of publishing, it really comes down to self-development. Are you going to do what it takes to grow and become who you need to be to achieve your goals or not? We are in an industry that is, in every aspect, in its adolescent years. Kindles are only 10 years old. Companies like ours are forging the way forward. No one before has had ebooks, audio books, and paperbacks to work with. It's an exciting time. "The Book Business" by Mike Shatzkin is a great resource in terms of what changes the industry is going through.

Though it is a fresh and exciting time, that can make it even easier to get off track, to get lost in the newness. Resources like Mark Dawson's courses, NINC, 20Booksto50k, and David Gaughran's books, including "Let's Get Digital" and a handful of others, are what have kept me focused. One of the most important things in terms of educating yourself in a new area like this is to remember that not all things you read are good or valuable. You must be able to test, discern, and use (or not) the things that sound like they will work, and move on if they don't.

Lastly, networking at conferences is invaluable. Four years ago, when Michael Anderle was becoming a big fish with his LMBPN publishing company and 20Booksto50k, I saw that he would be at Boston Fantasy Fest (BFF). This was the year after the inaugural 20Books Vegas conference, which was large at the time with 400 people. BFF was promised to be an intimate event. I saw it as the perfect time to connect with Michael. So, James and I flew to Boston from Colorado for the sole purpose of meeting him and sneaking some of his time. We ended up in a basement area waiting out a fire alarm together. It is moments like this, opportunities like this, that may only come around once. That moment changed our lives and our course forever. Who is in your genre or industry that is a must-meet person? Are you doing what it takes to have time with them?

### Influences

**James:**

I think there are two major influences that shaped me to be able to succeed in this business. The first is, without a doubt, the Marine Corps. I could never distill everything I learned during my time in, but there are a couple of lessons that have stuck with me through the years, lessons that have helped me to thrive as an Indie publisher.

The first is do more with less. The Marines are always getting the short end of the stick—never enough funding, gear passed down from the Army, barracks deemed unfit to be lived in by a brood of wild hogs. Yet, the Marines are known for their ability to do more with less. In Indie publishing, especially when we first started, we were dirt poor and had very little money to invest, but by being tenacious and putting in sweat equity, we were willing to stretch the little we had into enough to launch what would go on to become a multi-million-dollar publishing company.

The Marine Corps also taught me to Improvise, Adapt, and Overcome—an adage I still cling to. In Indie publishing, things are always shifting and changing. What worked yesterday might not work tomorrow, and what works tomorrow might be obsolete in six months. If you want to make it, you need to constantly be willing to learn, grow, and change, because the market always is. The last lesson the Marine Corps taught me that might be worth passing down is perspective.

I served from 2005 to 2009 and deployed three times in four years, including two combat deployments—one as a heavy machine gunner in Iraq, the other as a pirate hunter with CTF 151. Those deployments were painful and hard, but they also taught me one of the most valuable lessons of all: perspective. Sometimes this business can be grueling and difficult in its own way—honestly, I work more hours now than I did when I was in an actual combat zone. But when things get rough, and I feel like quitting, I remind myself that even with all the ups and downs, this is the best job I've ever had, hands down. I work from home, I get to make my own schedule, no one is shooting at me or trying to blow me up, and I get paid damn well for my work. Perspective matters.

The other major influence is my wife, Jeanette. We're high school sweethearts, and we've been together through just about everything. Deployments, the death of parents, the birth of our children. She stood by me even when I was in the grip of PTSD. She never once stopped believing in me. Never stopped supporting me. True, when we started Shadow Alley, I did everything—I wrote and ran the business side—but I was only able to do that because she walked with me every step of the way. She sacrificed her time to give me the space to write and willingly went without so we could save the money I needed to publish. What we have is only possible because she always stood with me. There is no greater help than a supportive spouse and possibly no greater obstacle to overcome than an unsupportive one.

**Jeanette:**

The following people have been invaluable:

Danelle Delgado, Amanda Hodgson, and Ed Mylett for helping me believe in myself and our business. For helping me learn about branding, marketing, mindset, and everything else that's needed to succeed. The moral of this story is to find mentors, people that can shake you to your core and get you back on the right track.

Michael Anderle, Mark Dawson, and my husband, James Hunter for helping me to understand the writing side of the business, how readers work, and how to integrate that into my business knowledge.

Also, my husband (again) for always standing by my side, even when I have another crazy idea, another crazy place we need to fly, another crazy challenge we need to undertake. For letting me take nights away to get caught up, for laughing with me as our children do yet another soul-crushing thing. I would be nowhere without him.

Numerous marketing and business professionals that have taught me to embrace the hard work rather than run from it. That money and time spent on growing yourself is the best investment you will ever make, and you'll never succeed without doing so.

My mom for being the most stubborn human on the planet and teaching me how to take a challenge like "you can't" and crush it. Tenacity and persistence are traits that I am grateful to have, and they most certainly came from her. In this world, you've got to be able to look a challenge in the face, make a plan, and execute.

My dad for instilling in me from a young age that when you work for yourself, you do what YOU want, not what someone else is telling you is good or necessary. That even though business is ridiculously hard, the moments of breathing it all in are worth it. Those quiet moments in Bali, when you walk into a room that perfectly captures all of your hard work, and tears come because you know that all of the work has been worth it. I dreamt about times like that. For years. When they come, they never compare with what you imagined. They are infinitely more. I'm getting chills just writing this.

If you want to achieve your soul's desires, the things that you know you are capable of, listen carefully. If you don't have people surrounding you, lifting you up, you are making your journey 1,000 times harder than it needs to be. Find a mentor, a coach, a relentless friend, and go be the best you you can be.

**Path to Publication and/or Becoming a Publisher**

Our publishing journey starts back in 2014 and halfway across the globe in a concrete townhouse, filled with cockroaches, in a Thai-Chinese neighborhood in Bangkok, Thailand. I'd toyed around with writing during high school and then again while on deployment to Iraq in 2007, but I never got serious about writing until my wife, Jeanette, and I packed our bags, quit our jobs, and decided to relocate with our three-month-old daughter as missionaries. I wrote my first novel, "Strange Magic," in 2014, and, after looking into traditional publishing—and deciding it wasn't for me—I dove headfirst into self-publishing.

We were dirt poor at the time and had to save up money for nearly seven months to be able to afford editing and cover art, but, during that time, I learned everything I could about the industry and came up with a game plan. We published that first book in January of 2015, and I had healthy expectations: I wanted to earn our money back within a year. That would be a wild success. Instead, everything seemed to hit just right, and we earned our money back in the first week. Realizing we might have something real on our hands, I started working on the next book, which we published three months later. Another hit.

At that point, I still thought it was a fluke and had no intention to write or publish books for a living. But, in 2016, we had to suddenly relocate back to the States because of a family health crisis. Suddenly, my wife and I were jobless, with a toddler and a new baby on the way. Publishing was our only option, so we doubled down. That first year was lean (Jeanette here: $36,000-in-Denver kind of lean), and there were plenty of times I thought we wouldn't make it, but thanks to Jeanette's savvy financial budgeting we squeaked by. We consistently reinvested 10% of the money we made back into publishing. The rest is what we lived on. In late 2016, Jeanette came on board full-time, taking on the business side of things, which allowed me to significantly ramp up production. In that third year, we went from barely squeaking by to making a healthy six figures.

With me writing and Jeanette at the helm of marketing, we'd become accidental experts in publishing. We had some writer friends who were great authors but terrible self-publishers, so we offered to take over the publishing side of things for them. We never intended to become a "publisher," but we found more success and picked up more authors on the way.

But it hasn't been all sunshine and rainbows, either. This is one of the most rewarding jobs I've ever had, but it's also incredibly difficult. On the writer side, producing seven plus books a year takes a toll, and I've tiptoed on the edge of burnout more times than I can count. Working long hours with young children at home is always a challenge, and even more so during COVID. Working with authors, scaling up, and dealing with the pain of book launches that just *flop* are all part and parcel of the game. There's a lot of stress that comes with the territory, but there is still nothing we'd rather be doing.

### The Hard Lessons You've Learned

From James and Jeanette: This business changes constantly and specific strategies that focus on marketing or book launches or genre are liable to change before this book is even published. So, instead of trying to home in on specific lessons, we wanted to look more broadly at some of the most important hard-won principles that we've taken away from seven years of publishing. We've worked with a lot of authors, and these are the things we've found to be true, time and time again, if you want to achieve success in this business.

First, don't be a jerk (edited to be PC, but anyone who knows us knows what we actually say here). Strong language, I know, but this is perhaps the most important rule of all, so strong language is warranted. Although publishing may seem like a huge behemoth, it isn't. It's a small, relatively tight-knit community, especially within your given genre, and, if you cause trouble, make drama, or are unpleasant to work with, word will get around. Be kind, generous, and helpful, and you'll already be 90% better off than most people.

Second, and this one is on the writing side of things, not every person is going to like every book. If you try to write books that will be beloved by everyone, you will end up writing a mediocre book that everyone will be indifferent to. Find your place, find your tribe, find the readers who will enjoy the kind of stories you want to tell, and then write for them and no one else. Engage with that tribe consistently, give them what they want to read, release content regularly, and they will reward you.

Third, people often ask what the best kind of marketing is and our answer will always be the same: The best marketing for your current book is your next book, so WRITE MORE BOOKS FASTER. Seriously, the best thing any writer can do for themselves is sit down and put the work in. This is the new age of pulp, and although there are a handful of Indie writers that find success with only publishing a book a year—and good on 'em—most Indie writers need to write a lot to make this work. Make time every day to write and remember that little efforts performed consistently over time lead to big results.

Fourth, it's all about momentum. When everything is telling you to pull back, you should push harder. A little story. We like to go for family bike rides. Our daughter had just learned how to ride without training wheels, and one day we were headed down a steep hill, followed immediately by a daunting uphill battle. My daughter got scared going down that hill and pumped the breaks, but then didn't have the momentum she needed to make it up the incline. Such is publishing. There are going to be valleys and tough inclines you will have to overcome, but if you capitalize when everything is coming easy, when you're on that nice downhill, you will be much better suited to handle those daunting uphill fights.

Five, persistence is king and it's important to remember that Indie publishing is a numbers game. Lots of Indie writers give up when their first book doesn't immediately launch them into stardom. Or maybe they give up when their first trilogy doesn't allow them to quit their jobs. Everyone needs to know going into this that the road to success for most Indies is all about numbers. Heck, even if you have a breakout book one, that's not the end. It's the beginning. We tell all our authors this: You can't build a career off one book or even one series. If you are in this for the long haul, it means you will need to keep writing. Indie publishing is, in large part, about shots on goal. The more books you write, the more funnel points you have, the more opportunities there are for readers to find you and for one of those shots to hit big.

Lastly, set goals and seize opportunities even if they seem impossible. This is a business where impossible things can happen, but only if you put yourself into a position where they can happen to *you*. It's a bit like getting hit by lightning. True, there's no way to guarantee where it'll land, but you can optimize your chances by going to where there's a thunderstorm and running around covered in plate mail while waving a metal club overhead. Sometimes your dreams and goals will seem outlandish, but if you start pursuing them, you'll be surprised what is actually possible. This means that when you get that twisting feeling in your stomach, when some big opportunity comes up, the answer must be yes. Doesn't matter what it is. Doesn't matter if you have the resources. Just do it.

**Where are You Now?**

We are an Indie publisher, Shadow Alley Press, and we have a men's pulp fiction imprint, Black Forge Books. As of November 2021, we are on the road to our second million-dollar year in publishing. We currently have 15 authors and are closing in on 150 titles published. We've sold over 300,000 units on audio and well over half a million copies of ebooks and paperbacks, which includes a total of over 250 million page reads in Kindle Unlimited. We are currently looking to exploit our intellectual property in the gaming and TV/movie industries. Our focus has always been on quality products that can compete with any other book out there, including big-name traditionally published authors. Shadow Alley Press—Great Genre Fiction Done Passionately.

### Where do You See Things Going?

Our prediction is that we will see the "book bubble" burst sometime in the next five years. Audio may hold out another 10 years or so. This isn't scary, it's exciting. We view the business world as waves (thanks Mike Michalowicz). There will always be a new wave, you just need to spot it. What is coming? We think we are going to see an amalgamation of the entertainment industry. More so than what exists today. Books that are movies that are drama cast audio productions that are interactive that are on Alexa. Whatever you can think of, it's probably coming. VR that allows you to play through books. We predict that intellectual property (IP) will become a HUGE deal. Much bigger than it is now. Voice actors needing to protect their sound, authors needing to trademark their worlds/ideas. As content wars continue, the race to create and protect IP will become more important to the success of individual authors and publishers alike.

Be prepared to grab opportunities as they come. It's about to get even better.

### Contact Info

Jeanette Strode
Facebook https://www.facebook.com/jstrode18
Email at jstrode@shadowalleypress.com

James Hunter

www.AuthorJamesAHunter.com

Facebook https://www.facebook.com/writerjamesahunter

Email at jamesahunter@outlook.com

Patreon—https://www.patreon.com/JamesAHunter

Shadow Alley Press

www.ShadowAlleyPress.com

www.BlackForgebooks.com

www.facebook.com/ShadowAlleyPress

www.facebook.com/BlackForgebooks

# Chapter Twenty-Two:
# Rhett C. Bruno

**Biography**

I went to Syracuse University for Architecture and practiced for five or so years after graduating. At the same time, I've always written. Wrote my first series at 16 and signed an awful deal with a vanity press because I didn't know any better. But I went on to publish with Diversion Books, Random House, and Audible Studios before moving on to publish myself. So basically, I've seen it all, and three years ago used that experience to start Aethon Books alongside my friend and co-author on a few series, Steve Beaulieu, with a goal to help other authors earn off their writing when they were struggling themselves. Aethon has since grown to publish around 200 sci-fi & fantasy books a year, with a varied list of authors from both Indie and traditional backgrounds.

**Education**

Like above, I did go to architecture school. Which isn't really relevant to writing, but also is in a lot of ways. Architecture programs are famous for being grueling. A lot of late nights and very harsh critiques. And nothing has improved my writing more than critiques from readers and critique groups like critters.org. Even working with editors and analyzing their work to learn how to improve my craft.

288 | WEBB & KENNEDY

Basically, in an art school program like that, you learn how to fail, and when it comes to publishing others that is a big part of the equation too. Failures happen, and learning from them is the best way to grow.

### Influences

Like most authors, I have my favorite writers. I was always a fan of the golden age sci-fi authors, and the energy in every word of Robert E. Howard's Conan. The classic stuff. But I don't really find myself influenced by them career-wise. I learn better from people I know, and so I was immensely influenced first by my High School English teacher, who really encouraged me to write and took a lot of spare time to work with me. And honestly, mostly, my parents. They fully supported me loving to tell stories from the very start. Did they want me to leave a steady job to go into publishing? I'm sure they didn't, but they never wavered in their support. My dad built his business from the ground up as well, which was a huge influence on me with Aethon. His guidance has helped us grow and smartly adapt to situations we could have never predicted.

### Path to Publication and/or Becoming a Publisher

I took the traditional path to getting published. That meant working with publishers, submissions, etc. The first obstacle was getting taken advantage of a vanity press as basically a kid. With no knowledge of the industry and being so young, I had no way of knowing. At the time, there were many predatory presses like this, but luckily, with the creation of KDP, Amazon has slowed their growth.

As I grew and found bigger, better publishers, I had to go the route of getting an agent. My first agent marriage just… didn't work out. It is always hard to measure expectations, and I tend to prefer working fast. Finding great personal matches in an industry where earning a living can be so hard is not always easy. Even with my publishers. When you sign with Random House, you expect to become a star—99% of the time, that doesn't happen, though, and you have middling to no success. I had to learn from that.

In the end, publishing just isn't for the faint of heart. As a writer or on the publishing side of things (I do both, which isn't that common) this isn't easy. The arts never are. And for as many great partnerships authors can find out there, there are a TON of scams. They can be hard to identity, so do your research.

### The Hard Lessons You've Learned

The hardest lesson I've learned as a publisher is that sometimes, a series fails. That sucks. For us, for the author. And it can be so hard to come to terms with the idea that not everything can be a hit and sometimes doing our best is all we can do.

And so, we've built Aethon on a foundation of honesty. Of preparing authors with realistic expectations and doing our best by them with very favorable and honest contract terms. Of trying never to over promise and under deliver. Basically, we are blunt with the truth. And I think that really has helped us become so successful because that open relationship with authors is so crucial in building trust and relationships. And that, more than the content of the books themselves, is what this is all about. Working WITH authors, to do the best by them.

290 | WEBB & KENNEDY

### Where are You Now?

I myself am a USA Today, Washington Post, and #1 Overall Audible bestselling author. I've also been nominated for a Nebula Award and won numerous other book awards. Basically, as an author, I've accomplished most of what I've set out to do (though getting a film wouldn't hurt...). As a publisher, we're just getting started. Aethon publishes 200 sci-fi and fantasy books a year, and we have many bestsellers across the ebook and audio format. We work with authors that are debuts and experienced, Indie and traditional. Basically, we want to work with great people who tell great stories. We even published the debut novel by actor Lou Diamond Phillips.

So, that is our goal. To keep growing as an independent press who is open to authors from every background imaginable.

### Where do You See Things Going?

Whew, this is tough. I think audio will continue to grow as it has, with other serious players coming in to challenge Audible. On the ebook side, I don't see anyone dethroning Kindle. But I think the Big 4 will begin to take a more focused approach to the ebook side. There will always be print readers, and the Big 4 dominates that market, so it's not one I'd be able to make predictions in.

But basically, Kindle and Audible have such a big following these days, I only see that growing. And, as more authors discover all the publishing options out there, I believe we'll see a lot of traditional authors become more hybrid.

### How do you define success?

Pretty simply. For me, it's being able to do what I love, full-time.

But success for others is a moving target. Every author we deal with wants different things. Some want to be full time authors. Some just want to be published authors, and that's really all. Every career in writing is vastly different. In the end, if you're doing what makes you happy and finding satisfaction with it, that is success.

**Contact Info**

www.aethonbooks.com

www.rhettbruno.com

# Chapter Twenty-Three:
# Kevin McLaughlin

If there is a temptation to begin every one of these introductions with a variation of the words "if anyone exemplifies a Titan, this author does," an apt food analogy would be that Kevin McLaughlin's writing career is a slice of apple pie grilled in butter, with rich vanilla ice cream melting over the top. In addition to writing at a pace that some authors find incomprehensible, when asked to contribute to this work he cheerfully said "yes" and went to work on his entry right away. Like every contributor in this book, McLaughlin deserves to be here. He deserves your attention. He is a true Titan of 21st century Publishing.

## Biography

I was a precocious reader and began reading my first children's picture books at age three. By the time I was five years old, I read "The Hobbit," so it was a fairly rapid acceleration! My kindergarten teacher spotted me with the book and told me, "You can't read that."

I clutched the book to my chest—my memory of this event is very strong—and told her, "Yes, I can. My mom said I could!"

At that point she clarified: she was expressing surprise that I was capable of reading the book. I read her a passage to demonstrate, and... well, life was never really simple after that.

By age seven, I was composing my first short stories. I believe I was the first science fiction author to write a tale about the Earth flooding due to global warming, back in 1979... Won a school contest with that one, too. I was at that point falling asleep every night listening to my mother, an aspiring writer herself, typing away at her IBM Selectric. She in turn gave me her old manual typewriter, which I used to draft page after page of extremely amateur prose, most of which has unfortunately not survived to this day. It would have been nice to re-read some of it, forty years on!

My first official publication credits were nonfiction, writing and editing for my TaeKwonDo organization's newsletter. First published fiction came a few years later, while I was in college. It was a nice story called "Trial By Fire"—not the most creative titling in the world, but the story won an award and earned me my first writing paycheck.

But then I sadly bought into the idea that writing as a profession was all about luck, not skill—to be fair, that was much more true in the 90s than it is today—but even then, dedication and effort mattered quite a lot. I do sometimes wonder what might have happened had I pushed hard on writing back then. Instead, I moved to other things.

I owned my own martial arts school. I was an infantryman in the Army, then a medic, then a nursing assistant, then finally a nurse. In the middle of that I also found time to run one of the world's most successful MMORPG guilds, play pro Magic: the Gathering, and produce art for various computer games. All of these careers helped inform and educate me, pushing the boundaries of my knowledge further. All of them inform my writing today.

I came back to writing in 2007 when a friend told me about NaNoWriMo: National Novel Writing Month. Over a million people from around the world all sit down every November and try to write a fifty thousand word novel in a month. I accomplished the task.

It was my first completed novel.

Oh, I'd had a few partials in the past, but I'd never seen one through. The feeling of accomplishment was a great high. I did NaNo again in 2008, again completing a book—but this time I was also hearing about the sea change happening in the writing community. I found Joe Konrath's blog and Dean Wesley Smith's. I learned that "Indie publishing" was exploding, and I saw the potential for this to be a career I could build myself, through effort rather than luck.

I published my first short story in 2011, followed immediately by that first novel. Neither were breakout successes right away, although the novel went on to hit the USA Today bestseller list many years later. Publishing was a slow thing for me in those days, because I was working sixty hours a week as a nurse and had small kids at home. Time was a precious commodity, but I kept struggling forward.

Every year I wrote more words than the year before. In fact, I've written more words than the year before every year since 2007. More words means more books. More books means more chances for readers to find me, and it also meant my skills as a storyteller improved. By 2017, I went full-time as an author, quitting my day job for good and moving to just telling stories for a living. I've been doing that ever since.

### Education

I'm not a big proponent of paid writing education. None of the creative writing classes I took in college moved the needle much for me at all, to be honest, and I haven't seen any college programs worth the expense. I'm sure there are a few, but I worry that, in most cases, the faculty lacks the experience to teach well. After all, if an author is an apprentice writer until they've had a million words published, most creative writing faculty are... apprentice writers.

If you can find a program that isn't run by apprentices, by all means, go for it!

For me, education was mostly in the details.

Being an early reader helped a ton. I read "The Hobbit" in kindergarten and "The Lord of the Rings" trilogy in first grade. I didn't slow down from there. My reading habits have always been fairly intense, and, even today, I read a book a week or more. Reading has helped inform my process enormously.

Of special note were a couple of boxes of my father's books which I read quietly because I wasn't entirely sure mom would approve. These were pulp and silver era fiction, and some of it was a bit risqué. But these stories taught me how to tell a tale people would want to read; the pulp era was famous for action-oriented adventure dramas, along the same lines as the films which are most popular today. In many ways, the Marvel Cinematic Universe is a direct descendant of certain pulp lines. Reading those books as a child helped me learn how to tell stories people want to read.

In terms of "regular" education, I need to make a special mention of Mrs. Carol Borland. She was my English teacher for both 8th and 9th grades, and, although her son was my best friend, she and I had a problematic relationship. She was determined to teach me grammar: conjugations, declensions, and even diagramming sentences! I was determined that these things were a waste of my time.

Hint: they were not, in fact, a waste of my time.

That foundation is what enabled me to learn to write such clean first drafts. These days, my first draft work is almost identical to my published manuscripts. That saves me enormous time; Heinlein's rules mention that one should only rewrite to editorial order, and he wasn't wrong. I wouldn't be able to tell nearly so many stories otherwise, and it's by writing that we grow in our craft—not by rewriting.

In college, I studied broadly. Again, this was instrumental for me later in life. I took classes in psychology, biology, physics, paleontology, astronomy, political science, teaching, communication, English, writing, and much more. The more things I learn, the more different dots I have which I can connect in new ways for new art.

The only other thing I'd add would be to never stop learning. Nobody ever has it all figured out. Nobody ever knows everything. By continuing to learn, we continue to grow as authors and as human beings. Strive to keep learning something new every day.

### Influences

I've already mentioned my mom above. Her influence on me was incredibly noteworthy. I fell asleep night after night listening to her typing away. That made me want to do the same, so she gave me her old manual typewriter, which I used for years. It's funny, but the things we want to do when we're young (and have yet to be told it's impossible) are often the best things for us to pursue as adults. The passion I had for writing at age seven never went away. It hid behind other things from time to time, but it was always there waiting.

The more recent influence I feel is most noteworthy has to be Dean Wesley Smith. I ran into him first in the comments on Joe Konrath's blog and went from there back to *his* blog. Dean has a wealth of material there for writers. It's… stunning just how much knowledge is available in that one place. Dean taught me how to unlearn most of the crap I thought I knew about writing—most of which was wrong. His essays on "killing the sacred cows of publishing" are treasures. His thoughts on "pulp speed" and Heinlein's Rules for Writers were some of the most important influences I've ever had. Basically, Dean feels like: writing should be fun, telling stories isn't hard, most of the problems around writing stem from our fears, trusting your voice is paramount, practice is vital, patience is necessary, and publishing yourself is the future. All of which I completely agree with.

### Path to Publication and/or Becoming a Publisher

I got back into writing at precisely the right time. November 2007 was right before the Kindle explosion changed publishing forever, and doing NaNoWriMo that month set me up for success. After "winning" NaNoWriMo again in 2008, I began casting about to see what was happening in the writing world and ran into the Indie writer revolution's earliest days.

The more I read about being an Indie author, the more I liked the idea. No longer would authors have to wait forever *hoping* their manuscripts might someday be published. Now, anything we wrote could be published, and we'd get to keep all the proceeds rather than sharing with a publishing house.

I'd gotten out of writing precisely because it seemed far more luck based than anything else back in the 90s. I wasn't into pouring a ton of work into something in the *hopes* that it would work out. But the Indie road seemed far more based on work ethic than anything else: the harder you work, the luckier you get, as Joe Konrath put it. He was right.

That doesn't mean it was *easy*.

I had little money, three small kids, and a sixty hour a week nursing job which I needed to keep to pay the bills. I couldn't afford to pour much money into the publishing end of things. Fortunately, I had a college professor friend who was willing to edit my earliest books for me. That saved me one large expense. I also did the unthinkable and made my own early covers. Thanks to the art training I had for computer game art, this was relatively easy to pick up. My first covers still weren't that good, but they weren't *awful*.

But I still made just about all the mistakes one could make along the way. I jumped from one genre to another, abandoned series to start something new and shiny, wrote whatever cool idea I had rather than thinking about what the market might want, and a bunch of other common novice mistakes. As a result it took me six years to go from my first Indie publication to becoming a full-time writer.

**The Hard Lessons You've Learned**

Working for yourself means you don't have a boss anymore—which can be good, but it also means *you're* the boss. You're the one responsible. If things don't get done, we literally don't have anyone to blame but ourselves. If we want to make things happen, there's nobody there pushing us onward except ourselves. That sort of self-reliance and responsibility is uncomfortable for many folks; but if you want to be a full-time writer, get used to it.

*Delighting* readers is key. Nothing else really matters. If you delight your readers, they will return for future books and tell all their friends about you. If you don't, then no amount of marketing will sell book two.

If you think it's possible, it probably is. If you think it isn't, it probably isn't. Mindset matters, and the lies we tell ourselves bind us and slow us down more than just about anything else.

Be kind to everyone you can. The person you give advice to and help today may be the bestseller helping you get back on your feet a decade from now.

It's a marathon, not a sprint, and most of the "runners" will fall out along the way. Of the thirteen SF&F authors I was with in a 2012 anthology, only three are still writing today. Most of the authors you see writing today will be gone in five years. Almost all of them will be gone in ten. The ones who stick? They're precious. Those are your peers, your compatriots on this road.

### Where are You Now?

I just passed my ten year anniversary of Indie publishing my first short stories and book. Somehow, that makes me one of the old hands in this business, which is fascinating. I've watched so many authors fade away over the years, blossoming into a brilliant career and then burning out again. It's given me some perspective on how it's important to not merely build a good career, but one which is sustainable for the long term.

Today, I've hit the USA Today bestseller list twice. I'm routinely one of the top selling authors in science fiction, fantasy, or both. I'm what we call a "hybrid" author, which means I've got twenty-seven titles out through a traditional (small) publishing—LMBPN—and over fifty that I've published myself. I honestly can't tell you which is better; both are good for different reasons.

I'm working on building stronger relationships with a variety of publishers. In addition to a contract for six more books with LMBPN, I've got a novella set for a different publisher, and an invite from a third publisher to work with them on a new universe that sounds very exciting. These opportunities boost my overall visibility in the genre and help improve my bottom line as well.

But I'm not ignoring my own work. Publishing books myself has been a mainstay of my income for most of my career, and although that income source has dipped some when I focus elsewhere, it re-mains a big chunk of my earnings. Finding a balance point between the work I do for others and the work I produce myself will be an ongoing challenge, but I feel like those paths compliment each other very well.

For me, productivity is key. It's pretty much my "writing super-power"—my core strength. So I'm working on improving my ability to capitalize on that strength. I founded a writing group on Facebook called the "March to Pulp Speed 6," which is all about writers striving to reach the next level in their own productivity, sharing tips and tricks to improve their efforts. My aim is to reach two million words completed in a single year, eventually.

### Where do You See Things Going?

We're seeing the digital book market hit maturity right now, in 2021... By that, I mean things are beginning to settle down a bit. There are a lot of known qualities about the business which was much more of a "wild west" just a few years ago. I believe that will largely continue for the next decade, at least.

For example, we're seeing a new breed of publisher arrive on the scene. The new publishers to go with aren't the ones run by Random Penguin or Simon & Shuster. Instead, they're Indie presses run by Indie writers who have decided to publish other authors as well. Michael Anderle's LMBPN has become the largest SF&F publisher in the world, by volume of titles produced per year. Shadow Alley, Mountaindale, CKP, Aethon, and others have all risen to prominence in the field—and all started with a single author publishing their own work.

There will always be a need for publishers to produce books; many readers prefer this sort of branding, and many writers prefer to have someone else do the marketing, which (unlike larger presses) these small presses do with great expertise. So we will see this trend continue and expand, while the older presses contract. Sooner or later, we'll see these presses gobble each other up, merging and becoming bigger in the same manner that the current crop of large publishers did in the past...!

We're also seeing certain specific paths to repeatable success appear. I don't think that will go away, either. At this point, I can sit down with someone and hand them a one page business plan which, if followed to the letter, will give them a nearly 100% chance of being a full-time writer within a year, two at most. We haven't seen that level of surety in this business since the first half of the twentieth century. I don't see that going away anytime soon; rather, the patterns of success will become more ingrained over time, because they're actually *hard* to do. Like, yes, they virtually guarantee success, but it's so much work that most people won't bother, so the paths will continue to work well for the foreseeable future.

### How do you define success?

Success is one of those things that everyone needs to define for themselves. We're each going to have our own goals and ideas of what we want from life, all based on our childhood and past experiences.

For me, I'd have to say that "happiness" is the key to success, and that in turn, happiness is caused by making sure that one's goals and one's actions are in alignment. That is: when we say we want something but don't do the things required to arrive at that destination, we tend to end up unhappy. The thing we say we want and the actions we take are out of synch, causing this unhappiness.

The answer is to either change the goals or the actions. It might be that the things we *think* are our goals aren't what we truly want from life. In that case, we need to shift our goals toward what we really do want. Or it could be that we have fears holding us back from doing what must be done to accomplish the things we want most—in which case, overcoming those fears is key.

For me? I love storytelling. I hope to continue doing that, in a variety of forms (books, maybe comics, maybe film, maybe other things!) for the rest of my life. For one thing, it's fun; I enjoy this work. I'm also fairly good at it, and that helps! This line of work allows me to travel freely, to see more of the world, and to live wherever I want—all huge pluses for me.

And I'd be lying if I didn't add that I'd like to move the needle in little ways. Science fiction stories can change the world; we all know that. We've seen cell phones, tablets, and plenty of other inventions arrive in the real world decades after they first appeared in science fiction stories. Shows like Star Trek inspired an entire generation to want to head into space. Even other, smaller stories have their impact. I'd like to continue being a part of that: to make the world a better place, one story at a time.

**Contact Info**

You can find my (oft neglected, but I do try) blog at www.kevins.studio.

Or you can check out my Patreon—and taste a few stories—at https://www.patreon.com/KevinMcLaughlin.

The Pulp Speed 6 group is here: https://www.facebook.com/groups/pulpspeed6.

And of course, my list of books is here! https://www.amazon.com/Kevin-McLaughlin/e/B004WYXIUO

# Chapter Twenty-Four:
# Nora Phoenix

Nora Phoenix is an outlier for this book, writing Gay Romance instead of SFFH, but Titans are not limited to one genre. The concentration here is for SFFH, but that is not exclusive, and the editors considered it important to point out that the revolution of publishing goes beyond only the genres of SFFH. Lessons are lessons, and those intended for the readers of this work transcend genres, and few writers are more transcendental than Nora Phoenix.

**Biography**

Born and raised in The Netherlands, I've always wanted to be a writer. I made my own magazines when I was ten and started writing stories when I was thirteen. I still have them, by the way, and they're adorable.

Sadly, writing was not deemed a possible career option, so instead, I studied history. It's given me a broad understanding of the world and current events, and I'm still grateful for that choice. I've held various jobs over the years, ranging from PR to unit manager in a large hospital and leading an efficiency project. Life intervened with my plans to write, and it wasn't until 2011 that I got serious about it, though I kept writing stories all those years.

By the end of 2016, I was at a crossroads situation. I needed to either jump in and start publishing and make a career out of writing or take a fulltime job and give up on my dream. I chose writing. My first book came out in October of 2017, and, within a year, I made enough to support myself.

**Education**

I studied history, and, while at first glance that may not seem relevant, it is for me. History is a subject where reading and writing are crucial, and where I learned to distill the essential information and boil it down to a few sentences. It's also taught me a lot about the world, about people, about how cause and effect work. All those skills come in handy now.

But, other than that, my main education has been reading. I'm a little different than most writers because English is not my first language. I didn't learn it until I was twelve and that was just in school. I had to teach myself the reading and writing level required to write in English, and I did that by reading thousands and thousands of books. One reason why romances are so easy for me to write is that I've read so many that the structure, the beats, are deeply ingrained by now.

Craft books have been crucial, too. They taught me the concept of scenes, of transitions, of cause and effect within my writing, and much more. I devoured them, making notes as I went along, and then reread those notes again and again. I took the time to hone my craft before I published, reading books on creative writing and getting feedback from developmental editors and other authors. That was confronting at times, but I learned a lot.

When it comes to marketing, the Internet was my best friend. I read all the blogs, was a member of countless writing and publishing communities, followed a whole bunch of upcoming authors on their journey, gained an understanding of traditional publishing versus Indie, and I made pages and pages of notes. When I was getting ready to publish, networking with other authors in my genre taught me a lot about the details, like the keywords on Amazon, categories, blurbs, and more.

Conferences have been crucial, too, especially the 20Booksto50k conference. What I learned in that Facebook group and at those conferences about Indie publishing and marketing has been crucial for me.

Another game changer for me was Becca Syme's Write Better Faster course. That gave me new insights into how I'm wired and how I can use that to my advantage. I'm embracing my strengths now and learning to lean into those. It's definitely improved my writing process, but it's also helped me to find a much better balance between my work and my personal life. I highly recommend it.

Technically, I'm self-taught, but the reality is that I owe a mountain of gratitude to those that came before me and shared their knowledge and experiences so graciously.

### Influences

Nora Roberts is my hero, both because of her amazing books and her business attitude. She was the first romance author whose books I fell in love with, and that's never faded. Her mantra of "butt in chair" when it comes to writing and treating it as a job, a business, has inspired me from the get go, and I've embraced that same attitude.

308 | WEBB & KENNEDY

Once I started pursuing writing as a career, I made sure to "feed" myself with can-do books, blogs, and more. I wanted to learn from people who had a get-shit-done-attitude (not just from writing, but entrepreneurs in general), and that made all the difference. I grew up with a scarcity mindset, and it wasn't until I managed to change that into one of abundance that I was ready to publish.

The list of people who influenced me is long, but it includes people like J.A. Konrath, Amanda Hocking, Jeff Goins, Michael Hyatt, Pat Flynn, Joanna Penn, and many, many more. This was back in 2011 in that time when Indie publishing was exploding. Craig Martelle, Michael Anderle, Dakota Krout, and Elana Johnson are more recent examples.

In terms of craft and learning how to write, I learned a lot from author blogs like Roni Loren, Jody Hedlund, and Janice Hardy, and more. Again, most of these date from ten or so years ago, but they were very influential in showing me how to hone my craft.

My single biggest eye opener was a book called Story Trumps Structure, which gave me the reassurance that pantsing was okay and that I didn't need to plot everything into the smallest detail. Once I allowed myself to write like that, focusing on character development and letting the story flow naturally from there, my writing became much better and faster.

### Path to Publication and/or Becoming a Publisher

I'm by nature a logical, linear thinker, and I used that to my advantage. In October of 2016, I decided that I would give myself a year to publish my first book, and, in that year, I did nothing else but write and do research into self-publishing. I read books, blog posts, read through entire Facebook groups, and whatever I found, I made notes of.

All those notes resulted in the release and marketing plan I made for my first four releases (a series), and it included all the steps I had to take. After that, I followed the plan, which was a long list of small steps like setting up a Facebook profile, starting a Facebook group, setting up my KDP profile and author bio, networking with authors in my genre, starting a newsletter, finding cover artists, etc. The list was long, but, because I'd broken it down into actionable steps, it was a matter of just executing.

Based on the advice I had found, I decided to start with a series and rapid release, planning the four books a month apart. That turned out to be a great strategy that worked well for me, and for a long time, I kept releasing each month.

Of course I ran into unexpected challenges, but nothing I couldn't solve with the help of new author friends. More than anything else, that proved to be key. Whenever I ran into a problem, I'd ask them, and they'd usually know the answer or knew where I could find it. The support of my fellow authors has proven to be crucial, and I'll always be grateful for that. Networking is hard for a lot of people, but I'd really recommend growing in this skill because it'll be so helpful for any problem you encounter, as well as for continuous support and encouragement (which works both ways, of course).

I think the biggest challenge was how much work it was, how many hours I had to put into this. I was lucky in the sense that I did it fulltime and didn't have to focus on a job as well, but even then, it was a lot of work. The first two years, I easily worked between sixty and eighty hours a week. It paid off, but it wasn't necessarily healthy. I had little to no downtime other than the time I spent with my son.

**The Hard Lessons You've Learned**

I learned a LOT of lessons over the years, so let me focus on the crucial ones. The first is that you need to focus on what you can influence and change. Being an Indie author comes with frustrations and problems and challenges, and not all of those are within your power to change. Amazon, for example, has delivered some unexpected challenges over the years, like canceling preorders, releasing books without a cover, books that were stuck in publishing, ranking not showing up for days, etc. Yes, that is beyond frustrating, but it doesn't help to focus all your energy on it. I've learned to roll with the punches and be flexible so I can adapt to changing circumstances.

Lesson two: keep reader space sacred. By that, I mean that you shouldn't bother readers with business problems that don't directly affect them. Too often, I see writers rant about Amazon, for example, or ACX or bad reviews or something else... and they do it in a place where readers read and see it as well. Don't do that. Being an Indie author means running a business, and that means you have to be professional at all times. Treat it like a business.

Another biggie for me is to treat it like a business in every way, which means making decisions that are in the best interest of your business. That's not always easy, especially when it collides with personal relationships, for example when you have to tell someone that a collaboration isn't working out. But, at the end of the day, you can be kind and still be a business, and that's how I try to do it. Also, this is not a hobby. I don't write for exposure, for the sake of art, or to express myself. Yes, all of that is amazing, especially the last one, but that doesn't pay the bills. It's okay to focus on making money. People will give you shit for it, but whatever.

Bank over rank. I cannot stress this one enough. Rank doesn't pay my bills. Bank does. I want to be a bestselling author as much as the next person, but rank is not what determines my decisions. Money does. I do what will end up making me the most money, provide me financial stability, and build a sustainable business that can withstand changes in the landscape. My ego would love to rank higher at times, but then I look at my bank account, and I'm just fiiiiiine with the decisions I made.

Protect your mental health. If reading bad reviews puts you in a headspace where you have trouble writing, for example, don't read them. If certain groups or people get too negative for you and affect how you feel, walk away. To me, this also falls under the "treat it like a business" category, because if I can't write, I can't make money. Anything that affects my ability to write is something I need to consider cutting out.

Last but not least, walk your own path. Everyone is different, and, as cliché as that sounds, it's very true. You can't copy-paste someone else and expect the same results. You're you, so embrace it. Just because something works for someone else, doesn't mean it will work for you. Take the big discussion on plotting versus pantsing. There is no right or wrong answer here other than that you'll have to experiment and find a way that works well for you. Anytime someone tells you there's only one right way to do it, be very, very critical. Always question that premise because almost always, it's BS. This is your journey, so take it all in, gather different opinions and strategies, learn from everyone, and then determine what will be best for you.

### Where are You Now?

At this point, I'm a USA Today bestselling author who is solely self-published. I'm beyond excited that I've grown my business exponentially every year since I started, and that I'm able to not only provide well for myself and my son, but also put money away for the future and do fun things now. I'm doing what I love most and living my best life. More than anything else, that's what brings me joy.

### Where do You See Things Going?

Oh, this is such a tough one to answer. First of all, I think that trad publishers still have a long way to go when it comes to embracing ebooks, especially when they face ever increasing competition from Indie publishers. I'm curious if they'll finally start dropping their prices.

The number of books that releases each year is still growing, so competition will only get bigger, which means standing out and building personal relationships with readers will become crucial. I think that's what differentiates us from many trad-pubbed authors, is that we have that direct relationship with our readers. That can inspire tremendous loyalty.

On the other hand, quality will also become ever more important. In the beginning of Indie publishing, readers would accept bad editing, for example, or self-made covers. Now, not so much, and I think that's a great development that will make the best of us rise to the top.

I'm encouraged to see book prices for self-published books go up. When I started, $2.99 was common and $3.99 was the max. That's now $4.99 with many making the jump to $5.99. To me, that's still a fair price, one that reflects the increased quality of books over the last few years, and it's one that will allow Indie authors to make a better living, especially those who aren't bestselling authors.

I don't see Amazon losing its monopoly anytime soon, but I'm curious what new developments will happen. Man, I would kill to have the Kindle Unlimited pay rate increased, but I don't see that happening to be honest. Amazon doesn't really have an incentive, now do they?

### How do you define success?

To me, success is a personal thing that looks different for everyone. To me, it started as being able to provide for myself and my son with my writing. Then it grew into doing that, plus being able to put away money for the future. Then I added being able to do fun things, like traveling, which I love. The next layer was finding a balance between my work and my personal life while doing all that, especially spending time with my son. I've accomplished all that, and, to be honest, my life is pretty much amazing.

But I'll always keep dreaming. My big dream is to be able to afford a beach house once my son is off to college. I have a vision book where I collect pictures of beach houses to inspire myself to work toward this goal. I have every confidence I'll achieve it.

### Contact Info

You can find me online at noraphoenix.com or through email, nora@noraphoenix.com

If you'd like to see how I run my Facebook group, feel free to join: https://www.facebook.com/groups/norasnook/

You can also stalk me on Twitter: @NoraFromBHR

On Instagram: https://www.instagram.com/nora.phoenix/

On Bookbub: https://www.bookbub.com/profile/nora-phoenix

Or on Patreon: https://www.patreon.com/noraphoenix

# Chapter Twenty-Five:
## Principles and Actionable Lessons

If any lesson should be obvious by this point, it is that Rising Titans are publishing professionals who are achieving at the highest level. Rarely, if ever, have so many agreed to share their insights for the betterment of all. Yet, while there is no one path to achieving their writing success, there *are* ways to increase the odds that a new writer might join their ranks. Below are the principles and actionable lessons that have been distilled from their collective contributions.

### 1.   <u>Generosity of Spirit</u>

The writers in this book are those who responded when asked to help create a guidepost for their fellow writers. Many others invitations to participate were sent out, but these are the writers who answered the call, sometimes on very short notice. That willingness to help others is the first trait that makes these wonderful people more than just writers; it makes them Titans.

None of these people needs to reach out to help others, and yet they do. Kevin J. Anderson was a founder of Superstars Writing Seminar that occurs each February in Colorado Springs, Colorado; Craig Martelle is the heartbeat of 20Booksto50k®, both the Facebook group and the conference in Las Vegas; both will catapult your writing career ahead by *years*. Every single person in this book wants

316 | WEBB & KENNEDY

to help other writers succeed; as mentioned before, you cannot be a Titan unless you have that generosity of spirit.

### Actionable Lesson

Help others who deserve help. Writing is not a zero-sum game; the success of others does not diminish your own success. If you think that it does, you are missing the point of this work.

## 2. Deserve the Help You are Offered

Titans, as defined by their generosity of spirit, want other writers to succeed, but do those other writers *deserve* success? The harsh truth is that many do not, because they are not willing to grind through the hard work and often painful lessons that the Titans did. Instead, they want a shortcut, a magic trick to jump their careers forward. Such writers want the success of a Titan, but without the effort.

Perhaps, once upon a time, a writer could simply write books and let others do the selling, but that is no longer true, if indeed it ever was. For example, on September 5, 2021, Kevin J. Anderson posted the following in the Superstars Writing Seminar Facebook group, and gave permission for it to be used here.

"For WordFire Press, I just had to reject a really decent novel sent to me by a major New York agent. The book itself is fun and well written, but when I did some digging, I found that the author had a twitter profile with 163 followers, NO Facebook page, a website and a blog that hasn't been updated since 2019, no previous publications, no con attendance, and basically no platform anywhere.

The Invisible Man can't sell books. I had to turn it down, because this author simply wouldn't be able to do his share of the heavy lifting."

Imagine having endured all the sweat and pain that giving birth to a novel entails, followed by the Byzantine machinations necessary to acquire an agent, who then uses their reputation to put that book into the hands of a Titan, only to have that work rejected because the author was not willing to meet the publisher halfway. But that is reality in the world of publishing in 2022 and beyond.

What does that mean for *you*, the readers and writers who hope to learn from these amazing people? It means that you have to be worthy of their generosity of spirit by NOT WASTING THEIR TIME. If that seems harsh, it is not, because all you have to do is take their advice. Find whatever nuggets you deem appropriate and apply them to your career. Maybe you will discover that one thing that changes everything, or maybe you recognize a nudge in the right direction, but listen to them and make your own decisions.

Lastly, do not expect a mentor or Titan to work harder for your own success than you do. Earn their attention by your determination to win.

### *Actionable Lesson*

If another writer has what you want, do what they do. Respect their time; if someone offers to help you, do *not* let them worker harder for your success than you do. If they tell you to do something, do it. If they have written a book or books on writing, read them, so you do not ask the same questions they have already answered; after all, if you value their input enough to ask for it—or accept it if offered—not reading what they have already written on the subject is insulting. If you attend a panel where they are speaking at a convention or seminar, know something about them before asking a question. Not doing at least minimal research shows disrespect for someone you hope will help your career. Excuses only satisfy those who make them.

### 3. <u>Know Your Why</u>

Joe Solari mentioned "Know Your Why" in his opening essay to this section, and it is critically important to understand.

Business is hard. Winning at business often requires everything you have to give and more than you knew you had. Knowing Your Why is the single most important foundation for *any* business, because it is the reason that will carry you through the most difficult parts, the moments when you want to quit.

#### *Actionable Lesson*

Your "Why" should make you cry. Spend time in self-examination to discover the core of your inner drive. The motivation behind your writing business must be so powerful that it drives you to finish your work regardless of circumstances, because *not* finishing is inconceivable. It is what lets you ignore Imposter Syndrome when it flares up and helps you push through fatigue or rejection, when all you really want to do is sit down and relax.

### 4. <u>Education</u>

The Titans in this book are all well educated, but that does not necessarily mean a formal study program, although many have a college degree. What it *does* mean is a never-ending effort to know more about their craft and the industry that supports it than they did the previous day.

"I love educating myself," R.J. Blain declared in her piece earlier in this work. Those might be the four most powerful words in this entire book. The universality of that remark applies to all of the Titans, because it is not expressed as the more passive "I love education" or "I love being educated," but rather is active and takes personal responsibility for continuing to learn.

Kevin J. Anderson would have been a Titan whether he earned his Master's Degree or not, yet he did so because it was necessary to accomplish the goal of teaching at the college level. That level of work and commitment is rarely seen in any profession, let alone in writing.

Craig Martelle left the Marines and then graduated from Law School. Dakota Krout graduated from college, served as an intern at JPL and his business-minded wife Danielle earned her PhD. Chris Kennedy has three Master's Degrees and a PhD. But lest this read like an advertisement for higher education, the point is not the diploma; it is the relentless search for betterment. Graduating from college is just one way of showing you have the necessary discipline. What matters most is the endless thirst for learning, in whatever way best fits the individual writer.

Toni Weisskopf has a college degree in Anthropology, but in practical terms that relate to publishing, her higher education began when she met Jim Baen. No school could ever replicate that experience. When William Alan Webb finished the books that became

320 | WEBB & KENNEDY

"Standing The Final Watch" and "Standing In The Storm" in 2015, the first thing he did was print out a copy to measure how much postage would be required for submissions, unaware that physical copies were no longer the industry norm. In the intervening years since he had last tried to sell fiction, the publishing industry had fundamentally shifted toward digital submissions, a fact of which Webb was unaware. Yet a publisher accepted his first book within two months, because he educated himself on the latest practices for selling a book.

Kevin Steverson sold "Salvage Title" to the first publisher he contacted, has never had a rejection, and blind luck is nowhere involved. Once Steverson wrote the book, he began researching which publisher was the best fit. Rather than trial and error, he educated himself. Once he determined that Theogony Books would be a good fit, Steverson read Chris Kennedy's book "Indie Publishing for Profit: How to Get Your Book Out of Your Head and Into the Stores." Kennedy owned Theogony Books, so Steverson followed every single step in the book. When he finally contacted Kennedy to submit the book, Steverson's chances of success were very high, and the Salvage Title series has been a bestseller ever since.

Titans never stop learning, but perhaps the most important secret they all share is the skill of *learning how to learn*. Since no two humans ever absorb information in precisely the same way, this is necessarily a trial and error process, but merely taking in the lessons available is not enough. Learning how to put them into action is the often-forgotten component.

For example, taking notes at a conference or seminar is well and good, if those notes are studied afterward with the intention of putting them into practice. Yet, all too often, the person taking the notes never gets around to working through them.

### *Actionable Lesson*

If you find a writer with the success you want, do what they do. If they offer advice, take it. If they have a Youtube channel, subscribe. If they have a paid platform behind which they share works-in-progress, pay the monthly fee. Use every opportunity to further your education in the profession and craft of writing. Between Kindle Unlimited, Patreon, Kobo, Youtube, Facebook, Google, MeWe, and good old-fashioned networking, the largest cost to continuing your writing education is the sweaty equity of actually doing it.

### 5. Relentless Work Ethic

There is one thing you cannot do, and that is to outwork a Titan. Titans understand that being a writer means far more than simply clacking a keyboard, dictating into a microphone, or scratching words on paper. That is the *Act of Writing*. Being a *Writer* is something much more encompassing, something for which the Act of Writing is only the beginning.

Being a Writer means running your own business. The days of an author simply writing and leaving everything else to a publisher are long gone, as we found out with Kevin J. Anderson's example of a very good book that he turned down because the author did not want to help sell his own product.

## *Actionable Lesson*

Simply put, to have what others don't, you must do what others won't.

Statistics tell us that the vast majority of those who want to be working writers cannot or will not achieve that goal. There is no guilt associated with what some might perceive as failure, because each writer defines success in a different way. However, if your aim is to become a Titan, you have a blueprint to follow. Whether you follow it or not is up to you.

## 6.   Define Success

When asked what they would like to accomplish as a writer, one of the most common answers is "to make a living from my writing." That's all well and good, but what does it mean?

Lydia Scherer makes a salient point by advising you not to pay attention to gross income, what matters is net income. If someone made a quarter million dollars last year, but spent 80% of that on marketing, they wound up with $50k to pay the mortgage, buy food, put gas in the car, and keep the lights on. In rural Tennessee, that would be a nice living; in Los Angeles not so much. Everything is relative.

Craig Martelle wants to lead other writers to have successful careers, but knows that unless he shows the way with sales of his own books, fewer people may listen to the lessons he wants to share.

## *Actionable Lesson*

Define your personal concept of success and do not stop working until you achieve your goal. Then set new goals and repeat.

## 7. <u>Run Your Career Like A Business</u>

Writers are business people, and their words are the products they sell. This is true regardless of *what* you write. Screenwriters, travel writers, resume design specialists, or novelists, the core of those professions remains the same: telling a story for a specific purpose, in a specific format. Think about a resume specialist, for example.

When looking for a job, many people pay someone to help them create and format a document to make their life, education, activities, and work history more appealing to a prospective employer. The resume thus created is no different from a query letter to an agent or publisher, an enticement for them to seek more information about that individual.

Learning how to write books that earn enough money to pay the bills mirrors that process, except in reverse, and requires that the new writers differentiate between reading for pleasure, and reading for business. Devouring the latest book in your favorite LitRPG series does not mean you can write LitRPG for a living or that you should try. Nor does it mean that you cannot and should not. That decision is a business one that differs from writer to writer, and, like any business, the right decision requires market research.

That research involves "interviewing" writers to follow, and the Titans' books are their resumes, which new writers may sift through to find a good match for their own interests and talents. Once they have found a good match on which to pattern their own career, the new writer should go out of their way to analyze the business decisions of the Titan(s) thus selected and incorporate the ones that are relevant to them.

What would such discovery look like? Study the composition of their books. How do they label their chapters, Chapter 1, Chapter One, Chap. 1, or perhaps with a simple 1? Do they have a Cast of Characters? If so, is that list in the front or back of the book? What social media platforms do they use? How often do they post? What organizations do they belong to? Do they provide a playlist of music for their books, and if so, is it hard rock, pop, country, hip-hop, or classical? What do they listen to while writing?

Do not worry about appearing derivative of the Titan, because no business can prosper in the long-term by simply copying another one. Over time you will be forced to develop your own identity, which likely will involve lessons and business practices incorporated from numerous sources. But as a starting point, it would be hard to find a better one than emulating a Titan.

### *Actionable Lesson*

Understand that the biggest difference between Titans and less financially successful authors lies in their business practices and expertise. Studying this book is a great way to begin learning those lessons, but it is only a beginning. Relentless application is the key.

## 8. Titans Do It Their Way

Words and stories are the products that writers sell. In their business environment, Titans are the head of everything, and that includes research and development. What will sell, and what will not? The difference with Titans is that they do not write to market, the market writes to them. In the case of Toni Weisskopf, the market comes to her because she is the accessible face of Baen Books, a traditional publisher whom authors know is one of them at heart.

Titans sell what they write, every single word. A careful reading of their entries in this book shows few mentions of query letters, agents, or submissions to publishers and publications that require months (and sometimes years) of waiting for a response. That was publishing as it used to be, the cloistered world of gatekeepers bargaining for the fruit of the labors of others, while dribbling crumbs to the authors with the vague promise of a future feast. That was, and is, corporate publishing, where authors are a necessary evil.

Even when they participate in that business model, Titans simultaneously reject allowing the gatekeepers of traditional publishing to hold them back. Sports analogies work well to illustrate this point.

Kareem Abdul-Jabbar stood well over seven feet tall, and, many years after his retirement, he remains an icon of the National Basketball Association. The combination of his immense size and superior athleticism made him virtually unstoppable when someone passed him the ball close to the basket. Even opposing players who stood well over six and a half feet tall were helpless to do more than try to distract him while he scored. They were the gatekeepers of traditional publishing, and he was a Titan.

But if Abdul-Jabbar brought the ball down to his waist, or tried to dribble, his advantage disappeared. Smaller players could easily steal the ball, thereby negating everything that made him a Titan. He would have voluntarily given power back to the gatekeepers.

Titans do not do that. Titans learn the rules, figure out which ones are to their advantage and which are not, and proceed to break the ones that do not benefit them. They know who to listen to and who to ignore. If a trusted developmental editor says there is a plot hole in their latest work, Titans listen and react. Whether or not they take the editor's advice is their choice, although successful business people know that when you hire a professional, you should listen to them. Otherwise, why hire them in the first place?

The flip side is in knowing who to ignore. When a gatekeeper holds up a hand to indicate "Stop," Titans wave as they drive past. That is not to say that Titans do not write for traditional publishers, because they do. Many of the Titans have books or stories currently available from the big corporate publishers and publications, to the mutual benefit of both.

To be clear, small press publishers such as Quillcraft Press, the imprint for this book, have gatekeepers. The editors are gatekeepers. But, and this is a critical point of difference, the rules for small press publishers are vastly different than from traditional publishers. Titans know this, and so should you. Those differences deserve an actionable lesson of their own.

### *Actionable Lesson*

You cannot break the rules until you first learn them. Study all aspects of your business, master your craft, make a list of best practices that works for you. Only then can you identify how to reinforce success and avoid failure.

### 9.  The Evolving Rules, or You Are Your Own Gatekeeper

The rules for publishing in 2022 are evolving faster than might once have been thought possible, and those changes are driven by the Titans in this book. A few others may equal or, in some cases even surpass, the sales for a Titan, but only the Titans had the generosity of spirit to respond when asked to help others through their participation in this book. The lesson is that sales alone do not define a Titan.

By definition therefore, it is pointless to try and list all of the rules here, since some will change nearly as soon as this book is released. What will *not* change are the broader rules, the ones which lead to actionable lessons. That is where a vast difference exists between Indies, small press publishers, and traditional publishers.

As noted earlier, the speed of reaction for Indies and small press publishers is their greatest advantage over traditional publishers. The top-heavy staff system of the big corporations, with layers of editorial, acquisitions, art, administrative, and sales departments, and possibly a truncated marketing department, combined with a ponderous, expensive and inherently inefficient supply chain system of distribution, are much like the S.S. Titanic once the lookouts spotted the faint outlines of an iceberg in the darkness. Regardless of how large and powerful the ship might have been, its own momentum made it impossible to turn fast enough to avoid disaster.

Small press publishers do not have the mountains of capital available to traditional publishers, but that is their inherent advantage. They are connected to their businesses directly, instead of being one rung in a long corporate ladder. Indies are essentially small press publishers too, except with one author in their stable of writers.

One example of how market conditions are shifting in favor of Indies and small press publishers is to look at the limits forced upon publishers in general by a tighter budget. The only things limiting a small press publisher from acquiring a book and releasing it is an available date in its schedule and the time for editing and production of a cover. In many cases, that can all be done very well in a matter of weeks, or at the most, a few months. Such a timeline is unheard of for traditional publishers, who are limited by their system of distribution as much as anything else.

To be clear on the rules, however, there *are* advantages to traditional publishing. Baen Books, for example, has a very loyal and well-defined audience, built over many years by the personal efforts of Toni Weisskopf. When a Titan publishes a book with such a traditional publisher there are obvious advantages for both.

During video calls with several Titans during the first week of 2022, William Alan Webb asked what their greatest need as a publisher was for 2022. The answer was immediate and definitive: more top-notch content. Although immensely successful, they are actively looking for new authors to bring into the fold, new series to promote, new products to sell. That would likely be true of every Titan-publisher in this book, but it does illustrate the point about authors having publication choices they have never had before.

To that end, most publishers, including traditional publishers, have some sort of open call for submissions. For writers wanting to access or work with the Titans, *pay attention to them.* That is, subscribe to their newsletters, follow them on social media, read their books, watch their videos. In short, do what they do.

Most small press publishers want to give new authors a chance. Certainly the Titans do, and one way they do that is through anthologies. By and large, and regardless of genre or sub-genre, there are three types of anthologies: General, Themed, and Shared Universe.

A General Universe is both the most and least attractive option for an open submission. In such a book, Titans are invited to be the headliners, while a certain number of spots are reserved for open submissions. The stories will be broadly connected by a theme such as magic swords or mechs, with no other subject requirements. This allows established writers like Titans to produce something without the homework of learning a new universe. In all likelihood, they will produce a story based in one of their own popular universes, which both helps sales of the book and gives new readers a look into their series.

A Themed anthology will feature a tighter relationship between the various stories. Depending on the theme, it might or might not require a great deal of time to learn the story parameters. For newer writers, though, Themed anthologies offer a better chance of publication. A Titan's most valuable asset is time, and the more time it takes for them to write a story, the less likely they are to be involved. Remember, Titans generally write nothing without a contract. They know to the penny how much a minute of their writing time is worth, so producing a story that takes twice as long to create as something else has to have added value somewhere else. Barring that, they will not be involved, because Titans are running a business, and the numbers do not justify their commitment of time.

Lastly, the best chance for new writers to leverage Titans and more established writers to find an audience is via a Shared Universe anthology. The catch is that the Intellectual Property owner of that universe will be very protective of their creation. So how does a new writer overcome such an obstacle, where the IP owner is the ultimate gatekeeper? By doing the necessary homework.

If a Titan announces an open call for one of their IPs, the rules will be made very clear about how and what to submit. A Universe Bible should also be available. These can range from a few pages to longer than a door-stopper fantasy novel.[65] There is no universal answer as to whether or not the author should write such a story on speculation, but if you decide to do so, *do not rely simply on the Bible to learn details of that particular universe. Read the books!*

Look at it this way: being accepted into an anthology is a business decision. Like most business decisions, the answer as to whether your story gets accepted or not hinges on a number of variables. That you must demonstrate a competent level of craftsmanship goes without saying, but it should also go without saying that an IP owner can tell whether your story is written strictly from what is in the Bible, or whether you understand the style and tone of the universe from having read the books.

Remember, as a new writer you do not yet have the following of a more established writer, especially a Titan. The publisher and/or IP

---

[65] When asked to contribute to an old and well-known science fiction universe, William Alan Webb discovered the Bible topped 139,000 words, while the top length of the requested story was 30,000. Inquiring about a plot point concerning lighting on a particular world, he received 47 pages of graphs and charts. Wading through so much material is a choice each author must make for himself or herself, with royalties usually being the least important factor. In Webb's case, he decided that the answer was "yes."

owner is taking a chance on you and your story. The more elements that match that universe, the better your chances they will like your story and include it.

Does that take a lot of time? Yes, likely even more than you may think. But ask yourself which is a better use of your time, writing more stories on speculation, or stories that may never find an audience, or focusing on the business agreement to spend a lot of time producing a story that fits well in a given universe, in return for access to the fans of that universe.

One last word about knowing the rules of a given universe; the better you know that of which you write, the more chance that you can find a way to surprise the IP owner. Let us say that you have read all of the *Viridian Gate Online* series from Shadow Alley Press, or "Sentenced to War" by J.N Chaney and Jonathan Brazee, and they hold an open submission for those top-selling universes. While reading through the books, you develop a great idea for something you would love to write, and, although it pushes up against the universe boundaries a little, you decide to write and submit anyway. Maybe they will take it and maybe they won't, but if you can cite the book and chapter that first inspired the idea, and demonstrate intimate knowledge of the books, and why your story doesn't break the rules, it would surely make them more likely to work with you than to simply reject it out of hand.

### *Actionable Lesson*

You are your own gatekeeper. You and you alone determine how much effort you are going to make on your own behalf, but while effort alone does not determine success, lack of effort virtually guarantees failure.

# Chapter Twenty-Six:
# Conclusion

Reading this book was the easy part; the hard part comes next when you begin to digest and implement the lessons given to you by the Titans. More so than any time in Human history, success or failure is up to you.

If "Titans Rising" teaches anything, however, it is the value of persistence and determination, combined with a refusal to quit. One thing that successful entrepreneurs in all business sectors have in common is a willingness to fail their way to success. The people in this book are relentless in pursuit of their goals, which might be the most important lesson of them all. If you don't have the work ethic to become a Titan, you never will.

# Chapter Twenty-Seven:
# Epilogue

If "Titans Rising" has shown nothing else, it is that not only has the world of publishing changed forever, but that the *speed* of publishing is evolving at a dizzying pace. The archaic distribution model associated with the historic traditional publishing model has no place in the world of Indies, as this book has repeatedly noted. But the revolution in publishing—and it is nothing less than a revolution—may threaten to bring down traditional publishing even faster than previously believed.

As this book was going to press, everything changed. *EVERYTHING.*

On March 1, 2022, international best-selling traditional author Brandon Sanderson posted a video that launched a crowd-funded series of four novels. The author wrote them during an involuntary hiatus from traveling during the COVID shutdown. By the next day, when this addendum was written, the total pledged was a staggering $16 million.

*Sixteen million dollars raised in* one *day!*

And, roughly halfway through the month it was open, the kickstarter had received $29 million in pledges. For context, that is roughly *70 percent* of the money Amazon allots for its monthly KENP fund *worldwide*. To compare that number to the revenue of

Tor Books, publisher of Sanderson's immensely popular *Mistborn* series, in 2017, Tor brought in $4.2 million. That's for all their authors, for an entire year. Sanderson quadrupled that number in one day, and you can bet that every author who has developed lines of communication with their own fanbase will be closely watching developments. Trad publishing will be, too, and Barnes & Noble, and Ingram, and every other link in the outmoded supply chain model. But now, even Amazon has to take note, because Sanderson is doing this direct to consumer, including bypassing Amazon, too.

Self-publishing is coming of age. Sanderson will keep 100 percent of his profits, without paying an agent, without having to settle for a miniscule royalty rate, or Amazon taking 30 percent off the top simply for supplying a platform, and then charging a delivery fee on top of that. Sanderson will have to absorb all production and mailing costs, but those are a pittance against a number that will likely exceed $40 or even $50 million by the time it's over. And not one dime of that will go to Amazon, a traditional publisher, or anyone in the supply chain.

If the CEO of a traditional publisher wasn't already scared for his or her long-term future, this gives them good reason to pause. Traditional publishers make their money from the Brandon Sandersons of the world, not the new writers they take a chance on or even writers with a bigger name and multiple award nominations. Leaked documents in early 2022 showed that some of the most famous writers for traditional publishers sell very few books, often measured in the hundreds of copies or less. A writer with multiple Nebula nominations tallied sales of less than one hundred copies.

Try as they might, the traditional publishers simply cannot force their audience to buy anything other than what that audience wants, and that audience currently wants Brandon Sanderson... and others like him. And it is the thought that others at Sanderson's level might decide to keep the money for themselves that should terrify those executives. Because savvy authors are no longer willing to hand over the bulk of their earnings to publishers who are so disengaged from their audience that they continue to promote writers who have failed in the marketplace.

For decades now, the imprints of the huge corporations that dominate publishing have treated authors as a necessary evil, paid them no more than the absolute minimum necessary to acquire their work, and abandoned them without a second thought once their work failed to sell. Confiscatory contracts gave them the power over the works they bought, in many cases forever. Those days may be ending, though—if not immediately, then soon. The Day of the Writer is coming. For Brandon Sanderson, it has already arrived.

# Chapter Twenty-Eight:
# Epilogue II

The fact of a second addendum being necessary to this book is the best indicator yet of how fast the publishing industry is changing. Writers in the 21st Century are trying to hit a moving target with managing a successful book career.

On Wednesday, March 9, 2022, Amazon announced they were closing all Amazon 4-Star Stores. As related earlier, those stores were seen as a threat to all other established bookstores, Barnes & Noble being only the most obvious target. And now they, too, are going away.

This addition to "Titans Rising" is being written in real time, that is, only minutes after the announcement was made, so there has been no time for in-depth analysis. However, on the surface, it seems to dovetail perfectly with previous conclusions regarding the supply-chain business model being obsolete. Gasoline prices in the United States are currently more than $4.00 per gallon in most places, a rise of 60-70 percent in less than a year. By itself, that would be enough to wipe out the already thin profit margins made by traditional publishers when supplying a third-party seller, because that extra fuel cost not only affects shipments to physical bookstores, but also when unsold books are returned to the publisher.

In the past, the publisher would resell those books for pennies on the dollar after taking a tax deduction. Because they were *repurchased* so cheaply by the same bookstores that had just returned them, it made economic sense to *reship* them for sale at a reduced price. Those are the bargain books a customer sees in Barnes & Noble, and most other retail bookstores. However, with fuel prices nearing all-time highs, that model is no longer so attractive. Add to that vastly increased labor costs and the labor shortage, the lingering effects of the COVID pandemic, and a critical paper shortage, and the reasons for Amazon shutting their stores becomes more readily apparent.

Nor does it seem likely that Brandon Sanderson's success with crowd-funding doesn't play into this decision in some way. If the top best-selling authors follow Sanderson's lead—and there is no reason to think they will not—then not only does that cut Barnes & Noble out of the equation, but Amazon, too, and Kobo, and ibooks, and all the others.

The question at hand, therefore, is how does this affect the average writer moving forward into 2022 and beyond? More than ever, the successful author must be a master of their own career. Anything and everything they can do to build their audience is critical to future success. Traditional publishers have already curtailed efforts to boost all but the biggest-selling authors in their stable, but what happens if those authors leave, as it increasingly looks like would be in their own best financial interest?

When Amazon first opened up their platform to self-published authors and let those authors keep the majority of royalties for novel-length books, it freed writers from the quasi-indentured servitude offered by traditional publishers. Aside from miniscule royalty rates and long times between paychecks, authors with no leverage had little control over their own products. Worse, they had to sign away all media rights, not because the traditional publisher wanted to sell them to TV or Hollywood, but because those rights were a corporate asset which added value to the corporation. Thus, even when a book has gone out of print and the publisher has no plans for it to be re-printed, the author who has signed with a traditional publisher has little realistic hope of getting those rights returned.

But now another brick and mortar outlet has closed. What effect it will have on the small press and Indie author cannot be foreseen with certainty. What *can* be seen is the path those authors should pursue, and it is laid out perfectly in the Actionable Lessons of the Rising Titans.

# Bibliography

**Electronic Sources**

AZ Quotes, *Carrie Nation Quotes*, (https://www.azquotes.com/author/24362-Carrie_Nation).

*Barnes & Noble 2007 Annual Report*, (https://www.annualreports.com/HostedData/AnnualReportArchiv e/b/NYSE_BKS_2007.pdf).

Bhattacharjee, Monojoy, *Publishers Still Rely on Traditional Revenue Streams, Research Shows*, What's New in Publishing, 2019, (https://whatsnewinpublishing.com/publishers-still-rely-on-traditional-revenue-streams-research-shows/).

Brainy Quotes, (https://www.brainyquote.com/quotes/kevin_oleary_424984).

E-Commerce Revenue Analytics, (https://ecommercedb.com/en/store/booksamillion.com).

Ferriera, Becky, *Mythical Beings May Be Earliest Imaginative Cave Art by Humans*, (https://www.nytimes.com/2019/12/11/science/cave-art-indonesia.html).

Friedman, Jane, *The New Holy Grail of Traditional Publishers: Direct-to-Reader Relationships*, May 7, 2021 (https://www.janefriedman.com/holy-grail-grail-of-trade-publishers-direct-to-reader-relationships/)

Government BookTalk, (https://govbooktalk.gpo.gov/2014/03/10/the-history-of-e-books-from-1930s-readies-to-todays-gpo-e-book-services/).

Grady, Constance, *The Great Book Shortage of 2021, explained*, Vox.com: October 6, 2021, (https://www.vox.com/culture/22687960/book-shortage-paper-ink-printing-labor-explained),

Ingham, Tim, *Every Music Company is Morphing into the Same Thing*, (Rolling Stone, 2020, as reproduced at https://getpocket.com/explore/item/every-music-company-is-morphing-into-the-same-thing?utm_source=pocket-newtab).

Levin, Michael, *Why Book Publishers Hate Authors*, (https://www.huffpost.com/entry/why-book-publishers-hate-_b_2122317).

Locus Publications, *Publishing News, November, 2020*, (https://locusmag.com/category/news/publishing) Accessed November 14, 2020.

Miller, Laura, *Is the Literary World Elitist?* (Salon.com, February 7, 2014, www.salon.com/2014/02/07/is_the_literary_world_elitist/).

Morris, Tee, *The Scifi Superiority Complex: Elitism in SF/F/H*, (http://strangehorizons.com/non-fiction/articles/the-scifi-superiority-complex-elitism-in-sffh/).

Schneider, Avie, *Amazon's Latest Retail Shift Means Closing 87 Kiosks*, (NPR.org: March 7, 2019, https://www.npr.org/2019/03/07/701044877/amazons-latest-retail-shift-means-closing-87-pop-up-kiosks).

Smith, Dean Wesley, *Why am I so Against Traditional Publishing?*, May 31, 2020, (https://www.deanwesleysmith.com/why-am-i-so-against-traditional-publishing/).

Petite, Steven, *Literary Fiction v. Genre Fiction*, (https://www.huffpost.com/entry/literary-fiction-vs-genre-fiction_b_4859609).

Sherman, Eric, *Here's How People Fake Being Best-Selling Authors*, Inc.com, Undated, (https://www.inc.com/erik-sherman/heres-how-people-fake-being-best-selling-authors.html).

Silverberg, Robert, *Science Fiction in the Fifties: The Golden Age*, (https://web.archive.org/web/20120825082507/http://www.loa.org/sciencefiction/why_silverberg.jsp).

Sturgeon, Jonathan, *How Much Money Are Authors Making?*, (https://www.flavorwire.com/579201/how-much-money-are-authors-making).

346 | WEBB & KENNEDY

Technavio, *E-Book Market size to increase by USD 6.93 Bn | Technavio's Research Insights Highlights Benefits & Reader Engagement of E-books as Key Driver*, November 10, 2021,

(https://www.prnewswire.com/news-releases/e-book-market-size-to-increase-by-usd-6-93-bn--technavios-research-insights-highlights-benefits--reader-engagement-of-e-books-as-key-driver-301420115.html).

The Pulp Magazine Project,
(https://www.pulpmags.org/contexts/graphs/pulp-circulations.html).

Trachenberg, Jeffrey, *Barnes & Noble's New Boss Tries to Save the Chain—and Traditional Bookselling*, December 5, 2021,
(https://www.wsj.com/articles/barnes-nobles-new-boss-tries-to-save-the-chainand-traditional-bookselling-11607144485).

United States Government,
(https://www.census.gov/newsroom/cspan/1940census/CSPAN_1 940slides.pdf).

Washburn, Michael, *Robert E. Howard, Literary Artist or Pulp Hack?*
(https://bookandfilmglobe.com/creators/robert-e-howard-literary-artist-or-pulp-hack/).

Weller, Sam (February 4, 2019), *"Ray Bradbury, The Art of Fiction No. 203"*, (https://www.theparisreview.org/interviews/6012/the-art-of-fiction-no-203-ray-bradbury).

West, Edwin, *The Spread of Education before Compulsion: Britain and America in the Nineteenth Century*, (https://fee.org/articles/the-spread-of-education-before-compulsion-britain-and-america-in-the-nineteenth-century/).

**Printed Matter**

Asimov, Isaac, *Nightfall and other Stories*, (New York: Doubleday, 1969)

Etherington, Norman A., *Rider Haggard, Imperialism and the Layered Personality*, (Victorian Studies Vol. 22, No. 1, Autumn, 1978).

Friedman, Walter A., *"Selling US Grant's Memoirs, The Art of the Canvasser," Birth of Salesman, The Transformation of Selling in America*, (Cambridge: Harvard University Press, 2004).

Golsan, Richard J., *Perversion and Pulp: Reading Edgar Rice Burroughs and Figuring America in "Les Bienveillantes,"* (Yale French Studies No. 121, Literature and History: Around "Suite Française" and "Les Bienveillantes," 2012).

Haining, Peter, *The Fantastic Pulps: Twenty-One Tales of Fantasy, Horror, Mystery and Science Fiction from Famous Pulp Magazines of Yesteryear*, (New York: Vintage Books, 1976).

Ruber, Peter; Richardson, Darrell C. & Berch, Victor A. King of the Pulps: The Life and Writings of H. Bedford-Jones, (The Battered Silicon Dispatch Box, 2003).

Tymn, Marshal B., *Science Fiction: a Brief History and Review of Criticism*, (American Studies International, Volume XXIII, No. 1, April, 1985).

# About William Alan Webb

Telling stories has been the main obsession of Bill's life since first grade. During summer camp in his early teens, he entertained fellow campers with tales around the campfire or at night after "lights out." In one memorable summer, he told the tale of "The Lord of the Rings," surrounded by dark forest where the nights' only light came from stars, flickering flames, and fireflies.

Somewhere along the way, he developed an intense desire to help other writers succeed. To that end, he developed and presented a free novel-writing course at the local library, took over organizing the largest writing group in West Tennessee for two years, and has met dozens of writers in person to answer questions and help any way that he can.

After majoring in English and History, with an emphasis on Creative Writing, at the University of Memphis, Bill realized that it's impossible to teach people *what* to write, and very difficult to teach them *how*. Studying the rules of writing, story structure, etc. are part of the continual learning process writers must embrace, but ultimately Heinlein's Rule #1 is the best way to improve: "You must write."

So as he (not so gracefully) ages in a modest home east of Memphis, TN, the desire to write books and tell stories remains as strong as it was 60 years ago. The big difference now is how much better the coffee tastes.

Follow Bill on social media:
Twitter: @jointhebrigade1
Facebook:
https://www.facebook.com/keepyouupallnightbooks/

# About Chris Kennedy

A Webster Award winner and three-time Dragon Award finalist, Chris Kennedy is a Science Fiction/Fantasy author, speaker, and small-press publisher who has written over 30 books and published more than 200 others. Get his free book, "Shattered Crucible," at his website, https://chriskennedypublishing.com.

Called "fantastic" and "a great speaker," he has coached hundreds of beginning authors and budding novelists on how to self-publish their stories at a variety of conferences, conventions, and writing guild presentations. He is the author of the award-winning #1 bestseller, "Self-Publishing for Profit: How to Get Your Book Out of Your Head and Into the Stores."

Chris lives in Coinjock, North Carolina, with his wife, and is the holder of a doctorate in educational leadership and master's degrees in both business and public administration. Follow Chris on Facebook at https://www.facebook.com/ckpublishing/.

Get the free Four Horsemen prelude story "Shattered Crucible"

and discover other titles by Quillcraft Press at:

http://chriskennedypublishing.com/

\* \* \* \* \*

Meet the author and other CKP authors on the Factory Floor:

https://www.facebook.com/groups/461794864654198

\* \* \* \* \*

Did you like this book?

Please write a review!

\* \* \* \* \*

The following is an

**Excerpt from Volume One of the Author Fundamentals series:**

# Have Keyboard, Will Type:
# Hard Lessons Learned Hard

---

## William Alan Webb

Now Available from Quillcraft Press

eBook and Paperback

**Excerpt from "Have Keyboard, Will Type:"**

### Determination

First and foremost, quit giving a damn whether other people will like your book. Write something you'd like to read, not what other people say you should be writing. Of all the lessons I've learned, this might be the most important, because it gave me the determination to endure.

Once I really focused on writing *Standing The Final Watch,* nothing else mattered. I don't even remember writing it now because I became so absorbed in the process. Once I'd made the critical decision to write the book for me and not for anybody else—just for me—I finally got out of my own way. If everybody else hated it, I didn't care. I had a determination to finish that drove me like no project ever had before, and I believe the lesson is that all writers need that same fire.

I mean the kind of determination that drives everybody around you nuts. You *know*, without any doubt, you were born to write the book you're working on. It's ordained by God that you do so, and you're not shy about telling that to anybody who asks...or doesn't ask. You have a messianic fervor so deep that when the checkout clerk at your grocery store asks, "How are you today," your response isn't the standard, "fine," but instead it's something like, "oh my god, I wrote the *best* page of fiction on my book yesterday!" If you scare the clerk into calling the manager because they're afraid you might have rabies, you've got the necessary determination to succeed at this.

\* \* \* \* \*

Get "Have Keyboard, Will Type" now at:
https://www.amazon.com/dp/B08HX2MZRJ

Find out more about William Alan Webb and "Have Keyboard, Will Type" at: https://chriskennedypublishing.com/

\* \* \* \* \*

The following is an
**Excerpt from Volume Two of the Author Fundamentals series:**

# Indie Publishing for Profit:

## How to Get Your Book Out of Your Head and Into the Stores

---

# Chris Kennedy

Now Available from Quillcraft Press

eBook and Paperback

**Excerpt from "Indie Publishing for Profit:"**

**Chapter 41 – The Power of Writing More**

One of the most important things you, as an author, can do to increase your sales is to write more books. Why is that? Four reasons. First, you are seen as more of a professional if you have more books. You look like you are in the business of writing, so your work is probably going to be edited and worth reading. As such, readers will see it as a "safe" option to spend their money on. It's the "trust" part of the whole "know, like, and trust" equation.

Second, readers like to fall in love with authors and read all their books. If an author only has a single book for sale, readers won't want to invest in the author because they don't pass the "what next?" test. The reader will subconsciously worry about the fact that, if I like this author, he/she doesn't have anything else for me to read when I finish this book. Maybe it's just not worth getting hooked on the author to start with. Remember, marketing is all about relationships.

Third, having more books increases your chances of being found. Despite your best intentions (and marketing efforts), Amazon and all the other ebook retailers are crowded stores, and it's possible some readers missed your first offering. By putting a second book on the site, you double your chances of being found. When you are found, readers will usually go back and start at the beginning of the series. For example, the month my fourth book came out, the first three books all had their second best sales months ever as readers went back to start at the beginning of the series.

The fourth reason is related to the third; once readers get hooked on a series, they are probably going to stay with you to the end. With a series, readers become attached to a central character or characters, and the subsequent books sell themselves. The momentum carries over from book to book, as readers want to know what happens next. In most cases, you don't even have to market the sequel to "sell" it to your fans; they will buy the book because they are already invested. All you need to do is send them an email to let them know when it is going to be out (you captured their email addresses way back in Chapter 10, right?).

\* \* \* \* \*

Get "Indie Publishing for Profit" now at:
https://www.amazon.com/dp/B08LR3G1FD

Find out more about Chris Kennedy and "Indie Publishing for Profit" at: https://chriskennedypublishing.com/

\* \* \* \* \*

The following is an

**Excerpt from Book One of Hit World:**

# The Trashman

_____

# William Alan Webb

Available from Hit World Press

eBook and Paperback

**Excerpt from "The Trashman:"**

"Your time is up. Come or not, live or die?"

"What are you?" I said, knowing that if somebody had gone to this much trouble to kidnap me, their muscle wouldn't kill me that fast. "You smell like a fish."

He didn't rise to the bait. "Is that a yes or a no?"

"What about Dawn, was she in on this?"

"She's a useful idiot. This is your last chance, or I'll assume your answer is 'no.'"

I was stalling. As I spoke, I pushed and strained against whatever bonds held me in check, all the while knowing my life was probably measured in seconds, and then…something gave way, just a little bit, but I felt it like a crack in a sheet of ice. First my right hand moved, then my left, and suddenly I was free of whatever was holding me in place.

He didn't hesitate. Quantrill snarled as he lunged at me. He was deadly fast, much faster than I had been a month ago. But all that clean living saved my life now, paring down my reaction time to milliseconds. Point first, the blade slid past my abdomen, missing by an inch. Momentum left his neck within my reach. I was still holding the knife and fork, so I spread my arms wide and jammed the metal utensils into the sides of his neck so hard that the knife slipped out of my hand from the force. They had no effect, and then a backhand hit me in the stomach and I reeled against the wall. It was like getting run over by a moderately speeding Audi. My back hit the bricks and I fell to my knees, gagging.

\* \* \* \* \*

Get "The Trashman" at
https://www.amazon.com/dp/B08SVZF2HF/

Find out more about William Alan Webb and "The Trashman" at:
https://chriskennedypublishing.com

\* \* \* \* \*

The following is an

**Excerpt from Book One of the Lunar Free State:**

# The Moon and Beyond

------------------------

# John E. Siers

Available from Theogony Books

eBook and Paperback

**Excerpt from "The Moon and Beyond:"**

"So, what have we got?" The chief had no patience for inter-agency squabbles.

The FBI man turned to him with a scowl. "We've got some abandoned buildings, a lot of abandoned stuff—none of which has anything to do with spaceships—and about a hundred and sixty scientists, maintenance people, and dependents left behind, all of whom claim they knew nothing at all about what was really going on until today. Oh, yeah, and we have some stripped computer hardware with all memory and processor sections removed. I mean physically taken out, not a chip left, nothing for the techies to work with. And not a scrap of paper around that will give us any more information…at least, not that we've found so far. My people are still looking."

"What about that underground complex on the other side of the hill?"

"That place is wiped out. It looks like somebody set off a *nuke* in there. The concrete walls are partly fused! The floor is still too hot to walk on. Our people say they aren't sure how you could even *do* something like that. They're working on it, but I doubt they're going to find anything."

"What about our man inside, the guy who set up the computer tap?"

"Not a trace, chief," one of the NSA men said. "Either he managed to keep his cover and stayed with them, or they're holding him prisoner, or else…" The agent shrugged.

"You think they terminated him?" The chief lifted an eyebrow. "A bunch of rocket scientists?"

"Wouldn't put it past them. Look at what Homeland Security ran into. Those motion-sensing chain guns are *nasty*, and the area between the inner and outer perimeter fence is mined! Of course, they posted warning signs, even marked the fire zones for the guns. Nobody would have gotten hurt if the troops had taken the signs seriously."

The Homeland Security colonel favored the NSA man with an icy look. "That's bullshit. How did we know they weren't bluffing? You'd feel pretty stupid if we'd played it safe and then found out there were no defenses, just a bunch of signs!"

"Forget it!" snarled the chief. "Their whole purpose was to delay us, and it worked. What about the Air Force?"

"It might as well have been a UFO sighting as far as they're concerned. Two of their F-25s went after that spaceship, or whatever it was we saw leaving. The damned thing went straight up, over eighty thousand meters per minute, they say. That's nearly Mach Two, in a *vertical climb*. No aircraft in *anybody's* arsenal can sustain a climb like that. Thirty seconds after they picked it up, it was well above their service ceiling and still accelerating. Ordinary ground radar couldn't find it, but NORAD *thinks* they might have caught a short glimpse with one of their satellite-watch systems, a hundred miles up and still going."

"So where did they go?"

"Well, chief, if we believe what those leftover scientists are telling us, I guess they went to the Moon."

\* \* \* \* \*

Get "The Moon and Beyond" here:
https://www.amazon.com/dp/B097QMN7PJ.

Find out more about John E. Siers at:
https://chriskennedypublishing.com.

\* \* \* \* \*